India's Approach to Development Cooperation

India is emerging as a key player in the development cooperation arena, not only because of the increasing volume and reach of its South-South cooperation but more so because of its leadership and advocacy for the development of a distinctly southern development discourse and knowledge generation.

This book traces and analyses the evolution of Indian development cooperation. It highlights its significance both to global development and as an effective tool of Indian foreign policy. Focusing on how India has played an important role in supporting development efforts of partner countries in South Asia and beyond through its various initiatives in the realm of development cooperation, the book tracks the evolution, genesis, and the challenges India faces in the current international context. The contributions provide a rich mix of academic and government, policy and practice, Indian and external perspectives. Theory is complemented with empirical research, and case studies on countries and sectors, as well as comparisons with other aid-providing countries, are presented.

The book is of interest to researchers and policymakers in the field of development cooperation, the role of emerging powers from the South, international development, foreign policy and global political economy.

Sachin Chaturvedi is the Director General at the Research and Information System for Developing Countries (RIS), New Delhi, India. His research focuses on issues related to development cooperation policies and South-South cooperation.

Anthea Mulakala is Director, International Development Cooperation at The Asia Foundation where she leads the Foundation's work on Asian Approaches to Development Cooperation. She has written and published on the changing development and aid landscape, conflict dynamics in Asia, and on the Malaysian political economy.

Routledge Contemporary South Asia Series

1 **Pakistan**
Social and cultural transformations
in a Muslim nation
Mohammad A. Qadeer

2 **Labor, Democratization and
Development in India and
Pakistan**
Christopher Candland

3 **China–India Relations**
Contemporary dynamics
Amardeep Athwal

4 **Madrasas in South Asia**
Teaching terror?
Jamal Malik

5 **Labor, Globalization and the
State**
Workers, women and migrants
confront neoliberalism
*Edited by Debdas Banerjee and
Michael Goldfield*

6 **Indian Literature and Popular
Cinema**
Recasting classics
Edited by Heidi R. M. Pauwels

7 **Islamist Militancy in Bangladesh**
A complex web
Ali Riaz

8 **Regionalism in South Asia**
Negotiating cooperation,
institutional structures
Kishore C. Dash

9 **Federalism, Nationalism and
Development**
India and the Punjab
economy
Pritam Singh

10 **Human Development and
Social Power**
Perspectives from South Asia
Ananya Mukherjee Reed

11 **The South Asian Diaspora**
Transnational networks and
changing identities
*Edited by Rajesh Rai and
Peter Reeves*

12 **Pakistan–Japan Relations**
Continuity and change in
economic relations and security
interests
Ahmad Rashid Malik

13 **Himalayan Frontiers of
India**
Historical, geo-political and
strategic perspectives
K. Warikoo

14 **India's Open-Economy Policy**
Globalism, rivalry, continuity
Jalal Alamgir

15 **The Separatist Conflict in Sri Lanka**
Terrorism, ethnicity, political economy
Asoka Bandarage

16 **India's Energy Security**
Edited by Ligia Noronha and Anant Sudarshan

17 **Globalization and the Middle Classes in India**
The social and cultural impact of neoliberal reforms
Ruchira Ganguly-Scrase and Timothy J. Scrase

18 **Water Policy Processes in India**
Discourses of power and resistance
Vandana Asthana

19 **Minority Governments in India**
The puzzle of elusive majorities
Csaba Nikolenyi

20 **The Maoist Insurgency in Nepal**
Revolution in the twenty-first century
Edited by Mahendra Lawoti and Anup K. Pahari

21 **Global Capital and Peripheral Labour**
The history and political economy of plantation workers in India
K. Ravi Raman

22 **Maoism in India**
Reincarnation of ultra-left wing extremism in the twenty-first century
Bidyut Chakrabarty and Rajat Kujur

23 **Economic and Human Development in Contemporary India**
Cronyism and fragility
Debdas Banerjee

24 **Culture and the Environment in the Himalaya**
Arjun Guneratne

25 **The Rise of Ethnic Politics in Nepal**
Democracy in the margins
Susan I. Hangen

26 **The Multiplex in India**
A cultural economy of urban leisure
Adrian Athique and Douglas Hill

27 **Tsunami Recovery in Sri Lanka**
Ethnic and regional dimensions
Dennis B. McGilvray and Michele R. Gamburd

28 **Development, Democracy and the State**
Critiquing the Kerala model of development
K. Ravi Raman

29 **Mohajir Militancy in Pakistan**
Violence and transformation in the Karachi conflict
Nichola Khan

30 **Nationbuilding, Gender and War Crimes in South Asia**
Bina D'Costa

31 **The State in India after Liberalization**
Interdisciplinary perspectives
Edited by Akhil Gupta and K. Sivaramakrishnan

32 **National Identities in Pakistan**
The 1971 war in contemporary Pakistani fiction
Cara Cilano

33 **Political Islam and Governance in Bangladesh**
Edited by Ali Riaz and C. Christine Fair

34 **Bengali Cinema**
'An other nation'
Sharmistha Gooptu

35 **NGOs in India**
The challenges of women's empowerment and accountability
Patrick Kilby

36 **The Labour Movement in the Global South**
Trade unions in Sri Lanka
S. Janaka Biyanwila

37 **Building Bangalore**
Architecture and urban transformation in India's Silicon Valley
John C. Stallmeyer

38 **Conflict and Peacebuilding in Sri Lanka**
Caught in the peace trap?
Edited by Jonathan Goodhand, Jonathan Spencer and Benedict Korf

39 **Microcredit and Women's Empowerment**
A case study of Bangladesh
Amunui Faraizi, Jim McAllister and Taskinur Rahman

40 **South Asia in the New World Order**
The role of regional cooperation
Shahid Javed Burki

41 **Explaining Pakistan's Foreign Policy**
Escaping India
Aparna Pande

42 **Development-induced Displacement, Rehabilitation and Resettlement in India**
Current issues and challenges
Edited by Sakarama Somayaji and Smrithi Talwar

43 **The Politics of Belonging in India**
Becoming Adivasi
Edited by Daniel J. Rycroft and Sangeeta Dasgupta

44 **Re-Orientalism and South Asian Identity Politics**
The oriental Other within
Edited by Lisa Lau and Ana Cristina Mendes

45 **Islamic Revival in Nepal**
Religion and a new nation
Megan Adamson Sijapati

46 **Education and Inequality in India**
A classroom view
Manabi Majumdar and Jos Mooij

47 **The Culturalization of Caste in India**
Identity and inequality in a multicultural age
Balmurli Natrajan

48 **Corporate Social Responsibility in India**
Bidyut Chakrabarty

49 **Pakistan's Stability Paradox**
Domestic, regional and
international dimensions
*Edited by Ashutosh Misra and
Michael E. Clarke*

50 **Transforming Urban Water
Supplies in India**
The role of reform and
partnerships in globalization
Govind Gopakumar

51 **South Asian Security**
Twenty-first century discourse
Sagarika Dutt and Alok Bansal

52 **Non-discrimination and Equality
in India**
Contesting boundaries of social
justice
Vidhu Verma

53 **Being Middle-class in India**
A way of life
Henrike Donner

54 **Kashmir's Right to Secede**
A critical examination
of contemporary theories of
secession
Matthew J. Webb

55 **Bollywood Travels**
Culture, diaspora and border
crossings in popular Hindi cinema
Rajinder Dudrah

56 **Nation, Territory, and
Globalization in Pakistan**
Traversing the margins
Chad Haines

57 **The Politics of Ethnicity in
Pakistan**
The Baloch, Sindhi and Mohajir
ethnic movements
Farhan Hanif Siddiqi

58 **Nationalism and Ethnic
Conflict**
Identities and mobilization after
1990
*Edited by Mahendra Lawoti and
Susan Hangen*

59 **Islam and Higher Education**
Concepts, challenges and
opportunities
Marodsilton Muborakshoeva

60 **Religious Freedom in India**
Sovereignty and (anti) conversion
Goldie Osuri

61 **Everyday Ethnicity in
Sri Lanka**
Up-country Tamil identity politics
Daniel Bass

62 **Ritual and Recovery in Post-
Conflict Sri Lanka**
Eloquent bodies
Jane Derges

63 **Bollywood and Globalisation**
The global power of popular Hindi
cinema
*Edited by David J. Schaefer and
Kavita Karan*

64 **Regional Economic Integration
in South Asia**
Trapped in conflict?
Amita Batra

65 **Architecture and Nationalism in
Sri Lanka**
The trouser under the cloth
Anoma Pieris

66 **Civil Society and
Democratization in India**
Institutions, ideologies and
interests
Sarbeswar Sahoo

67 **Contemporary Pakistani Fiction in English**
Idea, nation, state
Cara N. Cilano

68 **Transitional Justice in South Asia**
A study of Afghanistan and Nepal
Tazreena Sajjad

69 **Displacement and Resettlement in India**
The human cost of development
Hari Mohan Mathur

70 **Water, Democracy and Neoliberalism in India**
The power to reform
Vicky Walters

71 **Capitalist Development in India's Informal Economy**
Elisabetta Basile

72 **Nation, Constitutionalism and Buddhism in Sri Lanka**
Roshan de Silva Wijeyeratne

73 **Counterinsurgency, Democracy, and the Politics of Identity in India**
From warfare to welfare?
Mona Bhan

74 **Enterprise Culture in Neoliberal India**
Studies in youth, class, work and media
Edited by Nandini Gooptu

75 **The Politics of Economic Restructuring in India**
Economic governance and state spatial rescaling
Loraine Kennedy

76 **The Other in South Asian Religion, Literature and Film**
Perspectives on Otherism and Otherness
Edited by Diana Dimitrova

77 **Being Bengali**
At home and in the world
Edited by Mridula Nath Chakraborty

78 **The Political Economy of Ethnic Conflict in Sri Lanka**
Nikolaos Biziouras

79 **Indian Arranged Marriages**
A social psychological perspective
Tulika Jaiswal

80 **Writing the City in British Asian Diasporas**
Edited by Seán McLoughlin, William Gould, Ananya Jahanara Kabir and Emma Tomalin

81 **Post-9/11 Espionage Fiction in the US and Pakistan**
Spies and 'terrorists'
Cara Cilano

82 **Left Radicalism in India**
Bidyut Chakrabarty

83 **"Nation-State" and Minority Rights in India**
Comparative perspectives on Muslim and Sikh identities
Tanweer Fazal

84 **Pakistan's Nuclear Policy**
A minimum credible deterrence
Zafar Khan

85 **Imagining Muslims in South Asia and the Diaspora**
Secularism, religion, representations
Claire Chambers and Caroline Herbert

86 **Indian Foreign Policy in Transition**
Relations with South Asia
Arijit Mazumdar

87 **Corporate Social Responsibility and Development in Pakistan**
Nadeem Malik

88 **Indian Capitalism in Development**
Barbara Harriss-White and Judith Heyer

89 **Bangladesh Cinema and National Identity**
In search of the modern?
Zakir Hossain Raju

90 **Suicide in Sri Lanka**
The anthropology of an epidemic
Tom Widger

91 **Epigraphy and Islamic Culture**
Inscriptions of the Early Muslim Rulers of Bengal (1205–1494)
Mohammad Yusuf Siddiq

92 **Reshaping City Governance**
London, Mumbai, Kolkata, Hyderabad
Nirmala Rao

93 **The Indian Partition in Literature and Films**
History, politics, and aesthetics
Rini Bhattacharya Mehta and Debali Mookerjea-Leonard

94 **Development, Poverty and Power in Pakistan**
The impact of state and donor interventions on farmers
Syed Mohammad Ali

95 **Ethnic Subnationalist Insurgencies in South Asia**
Identities, interests and challenges to state authority
Edited by Jugdep S. Chima

96 **International Migration and Development in South Asia**
Edited by Md Mizanur Rahman and Tan Tai Yong

97 **Twenty-First Century Bollywood**
Ajay Gehlawat

98 **Political Economy of Development in India**
Indigeneity in transition in the state of Kerala
Darley Kjosavik and Nadarajah Shanmugaratnam

99 **State and Nation-Building in Pakistan**
Beyond Islam and security
Edited by Roger D. Long, Gurharpal Singh, Yunas Samad, and Ian Talbot

100 **Subaltern Movements in India**
Gendered geographies of struggle against neoliberal development
Manisha Desai

101 **Islamic Banking in Pakistan**
Shariah-compliant finance and the quest to make Pakistan more Islamic
Feisal Khan

102 **The Bengal Diaspora**
Rethinking Muslim migration
*Claire Alexander, Joya Chatterji,
and Annu Jalais*

103 **Mobilizing Religion and
Gender in India**
The role of activism
Nandini Deo

104 **Social Movements and
the Indian Diaspora**
Movindri Reddy

105 **Religion and Modernity in
the Himalaya**
*Edited by Megan Adamson
Sijapati and Jessica Vantine
Birkenholtz*

106 **Devotional Islam in
Contemporary South Asia**
Shrines, journeys and
wanderers
*Edited by Michel Boivin and
Rémy Delage*

107 **Women and Resistance in
Contemporary Bengali
Cinema**
A freedom incomplete
Srimati Mukherjee

108 **Islamic NGOs in Bangladesh**
Development, piety and
neoliberal governmentality
Mohammad Musfequs Salehin

109 **Ethics in Governance in India**
Bidyut Chakrabarty

110 **Popular Hindi Cinema**
Aesthetic formations of the seen
and unseen
Ronie Parciack

111 **Activist Documentary Film in
Pakistan**
The emergence of a cinema of
accountability
Rahat Imran

112 **Culture, Health and
Development in South Asia**
Arsenic poisoning in Bangladesh
M. Saiful Islam

113 **India's Approach to
Development Cooperation**
*Edited by Sachin Chaturvedi and
Anthea Mulakala*

114 **Education and Society in Bhutan**
Tradition and modernisation
Chelsea M. Robles

India's Approach to Development Cooperation

Edited by Sachin Chaturvedi and Anthea Mulakala

Routledge
Taylor & Francis Group

LONDON AND NEW YORK

First published 2016
by Routledge

2 Park Square, Milton Park, Abingdon, Oxfordshire OX14 4RN
52 Vanderbilt Avenue, New York, NY 10017

Routledge is an imprint of the Taylor & Francis Group, an informa business

First issued in paperback 2019

British Library Cataloguing in Publication Data
A catalogue record for this book is available from the British Library

Library of Congress Cataloging-in-Publication Data
Names: Chaturvedi, Sachin, editor. | Mulakala, Anthea, 1964– editor.
Title: India's approach to development cooperation / edited by Sachin
    Chaturvedi and Anthea Mulakala.
Description: 1st Edition. | New York : Routledge, 2016. | Series: Routledge
    contemporary South Asia series ; 113 | Includes bibliographical references
    and index.
Identifiers: LCCN 2015044491 | ISBN 9781138947733 (hardback) |
    ISBN 9781315669915 (ebook)
Subjects: LCSH: Economic development—India. | Cooperation—South Asia. |
    India—Foreign economic relations—South Asia. | South Asia—Foreign
    economic relations—India.
Classification: LCC HC435.3 .I62433 2016 | DDC 338.91/54—dc23
LC record available at http://lccn.loc.gov/2015044491

ISBN: 978-1-138-94773-3 (hbk)
ISBN: 978-0-367-87417-9 (pbk)

Typeset in Times New Roman
by Apex CoVantage, LLC

Contents

List of figures   xiii
List of tables   xv
List of boxes   xvi
Notes on contributors   xvii
Foreword   xxiii
Acknowledgements   xxiv
List of abbreviations   xxvi
Introduction   xxxi

1 **Shaping Indian development cooperation: India's mission approach in a theoretical framework**   1
SAROJ KUMAR MOHANTY

2 **The role of aid in India's economic development cooperation: finance, capacity building, and policy advice**   14
MANMOHAN AGARWAL

3 **India's development cooperation through capacity building**   29
KUMAR TUHIN

4 **Towards health diplomacy: emerging trends in India's South-South health cooperation**   45
SACHIN CHATURVEDI

5 **India's credit lines: instrument of economic diplomacy**   60
PRABODH SAXENA

6 **Civil society organisations and Indian development assistance: emerging roles for commentators, collaborators, and critics**   79
EMMA MAWDSLEY AND SUPRIYA ROYCHOUDHURY

7 **Prosper thy neighbour: India's cooperation with Nepal** 94
BISHWAMBHER PYAKURYAL AND SACHIN CHATURVEDI

8 **The India–Afghanistan development partnership** 110
GULSHAN SACHDEVA

9 **India's evolving blueprint for cooperation with Africa** 125
RUCHITA BERI

10 **Chinese perspectives on India's development cooperation** 141
XIAOYUN LI AND TAIDONG ZHOU

11 **Australian and Indian development cooperation: some
similarities, more contrasts** 157
STEPHEN HOWES AND JONATHAN PRYKE

12 **Conclusion** 178
ANTHEA MULAKALA AND SACHIN CHATURVEDI

Index 183

Figures

1.1	India's increasing commitments to development cooperation, 1990–2015	6
1.2.	Value of India's development assistance to South Asia, 1990–2015	7
1.3	Value of India's assistance through the ITEC Programme, 1990–2015	10
3.1	Growth in budget allocation for ITEC, fiscal 2008–2013	34
3.2	Growth in number of participants under ITEC/SCAAP/TCS, fiscal 2008–2012	36
4.1	Co-authored papers from India, 1996–2009	49
4.2	India's South-South health and biotech collaborations, 1996–2009	50
5.1	India: lines of credit – the growing portfolio	63
5.2	Distribution of LOCs by sector as of 31 March 2009 and 31 March 2014	64
5.3	LOC approvals: numbers and volumes	64
11.1	Australian and Indian aid in local currency, 1999–2000 to 2014–2015	158
11.2	Australian and Indian aid in USD at constant prices, 1999–2000 to 2014–2015	158
11.3	Australian and Indian aid in USD for PPP, 1999–2000 to 2014–2015	159
11.4	Australian and Indian aid as a proportion of GNI, 1999–2013	160
11.5	Government aid as a proportion of total government expenditure in Australia and India, 1999–2013	160
11.6a	Top ten Indian aid recipient nations and regions, 2014–2015	162
11.6b	Top ten Australian aid recipient nations and regions, 2013–2014	162
11.7a	Top nine Indian aid recipient nations and regions, 1999–2000	163
11.7b	Top ten Australian aid recipient nations and regions, 1999–2000	163
11.8a	Australian per capita GDP compared to top ten Australian aid recipients, 2012	164
11.8b	Indian per capita GDP compared to its main aid recipients, 2012	164

11.9a	Australia and its aid recipients: levels of permitted waste, 1999–2014	165
11.9b	India and its aid recipients: levels of permitted waste, 1999–2014	165
11.10a	Australia's government effectiveness percentile rating, compared to major aid recipients, 2012	166
11.10b	India's government effectiveness rating percentile rating compared to major aid recipients, 2012	166
11.11	Indian development assistance by loans and grants, 1999–2015	168
11.12	Australian aid expenditure by mode of delivery, 2005–2006	170
11.13	The relative importance of Australian aid objectives: responses from the 2013 Australian aid stakeholder survey	171

Tables

2.1	India aid inflows, gross fixed capital formation, foreign direct investment, and external debt on goods and services, First through Eleventh Plans, 1951–2011	18
2.2	India aid inflows: multilateral and bilateral grants and loans, 1962–2011	19
3.1	Monetary allocations for LOCs versus ITEC, SCAAP, and TCS, fiscal 2008–2013	35
3.2	Types of courses covered under ITEC, fiscal 2008–2013	36
3.3	Partner countries under ITEC/SCAAP/TCS, 2013	37
3.4	Regional distribution of ITEC programme participants, 2013	37
3.5	Top ten partner countries for ITEC/SCAAP civilian training slots, fiscal 2008–2012	37
4.1	India's contribution to global health funds	48
5.1	Annual phasing of IDEAS LOCs	62
5.2	Indian credit line terms and conditions	62
5.3	Regional distribution of LOCs: numbers and credits in FY 2014–2015	63
5.4	Africa's share of all Indian LOCs	66
5.5	India LOC-financed African projects: a representative sample	66
5.6	Sample relaxations under GOI-supported LOCs, March 2014	68
7.1	Nepal trade volumes with India, 2003–2013	97
7.2	India and other countries' FDI to Nepal, 2003–2013	101
8.1	India–Afghanistan trade values, 2001–2002 to 2013–2014	114
10.1	Comparison of Indian and Chinese development cooperation	150

Boxes

3.1   Capacity building through ITEC: a statistical profile   34
7.1   Indian assistance: a quest for confidence-building   104
7.2   South-South cooperation: technology transfer for converting
      waste agricultural biomass into energy   105
9.1   Ethiopia: a case study in Indian cooperation   131

Notes on contributors

Manmohan Agarwal, a native of Kolkata, is currently Reserve Bank of India Chair at the Centre for Development Studies, in Trivandrum, India. He is also a visiting fellow at Research and Information Systems (RIS) in New Delhi. Previously, he was Senior Visiting Fellow at the Centre for International Governance Innovation (CIGI) in Waterloo, Canada. Before joining CIGI, he taught for almost three decades at the Centre for International Trade and Development in the School of International Studies at Jawaharlal Nehru University (JNU) in India. He has also worked as an economist for the World Bank and as senior economist with the International Monetary Fund. When he joined CIGI, he focused his research on the growth of emerging economies and their role in the global economy and international development. In 2009, he edited *India's Economic Future: Technology, Energy and Environment*; he has also co-edited two books with John Whalley in the series Asia and the World Economy and contributed numerous papers, policy briefs, and commentaries to other publications. His current work focuses on India's interactions with the world economy. Agarwal holds a bachelor of arts (BA) in Economics from Calcutta University, a master of arts (MA) in Economics from the Delhi School of Economics, and a doctorate (PhD) from the Massachusetts Institute of Technology (MIT).

Ruchita Beri is a Senior Research Associate and Coordinator for Africa, Latin America, Caribbean and the United Nations Centre at the Institute for Defence Studies and Analyses (IDSA) in New Delhi, specialising in sub-Saharan African political and security issues. Her current research focuses on India–Africa relations. She is currently Vice President of the African Studies Association of India, a member of the Africa Committee of the Confederation of Indian Industry (CII), and an alumna of Women in International Security (WIIS). Beri has participated in many international conferences and lectured at several institutions in India, such as the National Defence College and College of Naval Warfare and the Foreign Service Institute. She is the editor of *Africa Trends* and *Indian Ocean Watch* (published by the IDSA) and serves on the Editorial Board of *Austral: Brazilian Journal of Strategy & International Relations*. She has also contributed to numerous publication and edited books such as *India and Africa: Enhancing Mutual Engagement* (2014).

Sachin Chaturvedi is Director General at Research and Information System for Developing Countries (RIS), an autonomous think tank in New Delhi. He is also a Global Justice Fellow at the MacMillan Center for International Affairs at Yale University. Chaturvedi works on development cooperation policies and South-South cooperation, as well as trade and innovation linkages, with a special focus on the World Trade Organisation. He has served as Visiting Professor at the Jawaharlal Nehru University in New Delhi. He has authored and edited several research articles and books, most recently a volume titled *Logic of Sharing: Indian Approach on South-South Cooperation* (2015).

Stephen Howes is the Director of the Australian National University's (ANU) Development Policy Centre in Canberra, Australia. Prior to joining ANU in 2009, Professor Howes was Chief Economist at the Australian Agency for International Development. He worked from 1994 to 2005 at the World Bank, first in Washington, D.C. and then in New Delhi, where he was Lead Economist for India. In 2008, he worked on the Garnaut Review on Climate Change, where he managed the review's international work stream. Howes serves as a Board Member for CARE Australia, and is Chair of Femili PNG, an NGO that supports survivors of family and sexual violence in Papua New Guinea. He has previously served on the Board of the Pacific Institute of Public Policy and on the Advisory Council of the Asian Development Bank Institute. The author of numerous publications and papers, he recently co-edited a book-length study with M. Govinda Rao, *Federal Fiscal Reform Strategies: Lessons from Asia and Australia* (2013).

Xiaoyun Li is an internationally renowned development studies scholar, one of the most influential in setting China's development agenda. Professor Li is the former Dean of the College of Humanities and Development Studies at China Agricultural University (Beijing), and currently serves as chair of China International Development Research Network. He also serves as Senior Advisor to the International Poverty Reduction Centre in China, as Director of the OECD/China-DAC Study Group, and as Chair of the China International Development Research network. In 1987, he received a doctorate in Agricultural Sciences from Beijing Agricultural University (now China Agricultural University). Li holds advisory posts at many institutions, acting as Standing Trustee of Chinese Agriculture Economics Society, Deputy General Secretary of the China Women's Studies Society, and Trustee of the China Foundation for Poverty Alleviation. He is also an advisory committee member of the Economic and Social Research Council and the Rising Power Initiative Institute of Development Studies, both associated with the Department for International Development (DFID) in the United Kingdom. Li's research covers development issues, including intervention, gender, poverty reduction, climate change, international and Chinese foreign aid, China and Africa relations, and Africa's agricultural development. He has been a senior expert for multi- and bilateral organisations such as the World Bank, Asian Development Bank, and United Nations, as well as NGOs in China, Africa, Asia, and Latin America.

Emma Mawdsley is a Reader in the Department of Geography at the University of Cambridge, and a Fellow of Newnham College. Her earlier work centred on regional and environmental politics in India, and she has published extensively on the Uttarakhand separate-state movement and on issues of class, religion, and environment. Mawdsley has collaborated with colleagues from the United Kingdom, Ghana, India, and Mexico in examining power within transnational nongovernmental organisation (NGO) networks and changing NGO–state relations. She is the author of *From Recipients to Donors: The Emerging Powers and the Changing Development Landscape* (2012). Mawdsley's current work addresses Indian South-South cooperation, particularly 'traditional' donor responses to current opportunities and challenges, focusing on the United Kingdom's Department for International Development (DFID). She has been awarded a Leverhulme Research Fellowship (2016–2017) to examine DFID's growing focus on private-sector–led development strategies. Mawdsley is a Council Member of both the Royal Geographical Society and the United Kingdom's Development Studies Association.

Saroj Kumar Mohanty is a professor at Research and Information System for Developing Countries (RIS) in New Delhi. His research covers regional trading arrangements, bilateral trade engagement with China, manufacturing trade with Southern economies, regional integration in Asia, computer general equilibrium (CGE) modelling, and multilateral trading issues. Previously, he taught at Jawaharlal Nehru University, New Delhi. Mohanty has directed and coordinated several international studies on bilateral and regional free-trade agreements, the regional value chain in South Asia, and food-processing industries in Asia. He is currently working on the 'Blue Economy', mega–free-trade agreements, Africa–India trade engagement, development cooperation, and the formation of an Indian Ocean regional economic community.

Anthea Mulakala is The Asia Foundation's Director of International Development Cooperation. From 2007 to 2014, she served as Country Representative in Malaysia. Since 2010, she has also led the foundation's engagement on development effectiveness and aid policy. Between 1991 and 2006, Mulakala worked for several multilateral, bilateral, and nongovernmental organisations in Asia, including the World Bank (in support of Indonesian decentralisation), South Asia Partnership (in support of NGO capacity building in Sri Lanka and regional gender issues), and the United Kingdom's Department for International Development (DFID), where she led a large health project consortium in Bangladesh and served as DFID's Reconciliation and Development advisor in Sri Lanka. Mulakala holds a bachelor of arts (BA Hons) in Political Science and English from the University of Western Ontario and a masters of arts (MA) in International Affairs from the Norman Paterson School of International Affairs at Carleton University in Ottawa, Canada. She has published works on conflict dynamics in Asia, the changing development-aid landscape, and various issues in the Malaysian political economy.

Jonathan Pryke is a research fellow in the Myer Foundation Melanesia Program at the Lowy Institute for International Policy in Sydney, Australia. Prior to joining the institute, he was a Research Officer at the Development Policy Centre at the Australian National University (ANU), where he also edited the Development Policy blog and served as a co-convener of the Australasian Aid Conference. Pryke's research addresses economic development in the Pacific Islands region, Australia's relationship with Melanesia, the role of aid and the private sector in Pacific Islands development, and Pacific labour mobility. He holds a bachelor of commerce from The University of Sydney, a master of public policy in Development Policy, a master of diplomacy, and a graduate diploma in International and Development Economics from ANU.

Bishwambher Pyakuryal, a freelance consultant, was a Professor of Economics at Tribhuvan University (TU) in Nepal for 29 years. He received his master of arts (MA) and doctoral degrees (PhD) in Economics from TU. He also has a master of international affairs with a major in development studies from Ohio University, and completed post-doctorate research in Economics at the University of Maryland at College Park, both in the United States. He has held residencies and fellowships at numerous policy institutes around the world, including the East-West Center in Hawaii, the Rockefeller Foundation in Italy, the International Food Policy Research Institute (IFPRI) in Washington, D.C., and the South Asian Network of Development and Environmental Economics (SANDEE). Pyakuryal has also served on the governing body for the Nepal Rastra Bank, and has acted as Chair of the High-Level Public Expenditure Commission (Government of Nepal) and as Commissioner of the Independent South Asian Commission on Poverty Alleviation (SAARC). Pyakuryal has worked as a consultant and resource for many international organisations; publishes numerous research and feature articles; and co-authored and edited several books on conflict, aid, development, and environmental economics, including *Macro Economics: A Radical Rethinking in Growth, Inequality and Inclusiveness* (2015).

Supriya Roychoudhury is an independent expert working on South-South development cooperation. Previously, she led Oxfam India's Global Engagement Program, which focused on strengthening the role of emerging economies in international development cooperation processes and multilateral policy. She coordinated several advocacy initiatives, both at the national and international level, to influence outcomes at G20 and Brazil, Russia, India, China, South Africa (BRICS) summit meetings. Roychoudhury has conducted research and authored papers on India's growing role as a provider of international aid. Prior to Oxfam, she worked with think tanks and political consultancies in New Delhi and London. She has received fellowships from the United States Department of State and the European Commission. She holds a bachelor of arts (BA Hons) in English Literature from the University of Delhi, as well as a master of arts (MA) in International Relations from the University of Warwick.

Gulshan Sachdeva is Chairperson of the Centre for European Studies and Director of the Energy Studies Programme at the School of International Studies at Jawaharlal Nehru University (JNU) in New Delhi. From 2006–2010, he headed Asian Development Bank and Asia Foundation projects on regional cooperation at the Afghanistan Ministry of Foreign Affairs in Kabul. He has served as the Indian Council for the Cultural Relations Chair for the study of Contemporary India at the University of Leuven, and as Visiting Professor at the University of Trento, the University of Antwerp, Corvinus University of Budapest, and Mykolas Romers University in Vilnius. He also teaches on International Development Policy at the Corvinus University of Budapest, and serves on the steering committee of the Forum for Indian Development Cooperation (FIDC). Sachdeva has authored numerous research papers in academic journals and edited books; recent publications include *Emerging Dynamics of Indian Development Cooperation* (2014). He is a regular contributor to national print and broadcast media on both economic and security issues. He holds a doctorate in Economics from the Hungarian Academy of Sciences.

Prabodh Saxena, a career civil servant from the Indian Administrative Service, is currently Senior Advisor to the Director for Afghanistan, Bangladesh, Bhutan, India, Lao PDR, Tajikistan, and Turkmenistan at the Asian Development Bank. Previously, he served for two years as Joint Secretary in the Bilateral Cooperation Division of the Department of Economic Affairs in the Ministry of Finance, working on bilateral relations and dialogues with India's major partners, including issues of economic diplomacy. He has also acted as Joint Secretary to the Multilateral Division, India's interface with institutions such as The World Bank Group, the International Monetary Fund (IMF), the Asian Development Bank (ADB), and the African Development Bank (AfDB). This résumé has given him a rare first-hand exposure to both the bilateral and multilateral aspects of Indian engagement. Saxena's previous positions include Secretary of Home and Vigilance/Director of Vigilance to the Government of Himachal Pradesh, Chief Executive Officer of Himachal Energy Development Agency (HIMURJA), and Deputy Commissioner of Kangra and Mandi. When in India, he regularly teaches at national institutes such as the Lal Bahadur Shastri National Academy of Administration. Saxena has published extensively on diverse topics in academic journals; recent examples include 'Pathological Pace of Dispute Settlement in India: Implications of International Arbitration' (*Jindal Journal of Public Policy* 2012). Saxena obtained his bachelor of laws (LL.B) from Delhi University and his master of laws (LL.M) from the London School of Economics and Political Science (LSE).

Kumar Tuhin is currently India's High Commissioner to Namibia. He previously acted as Joint Secretary of the Development Partnership Administration (DPA) at the Indian Ministry of External Affairs in charge of capacity-building programmes, including the Indian Technical and Economic Cooperation Programme (ITEC), Special Commonwealth African Assistance Programme

(SCAAP), and the Technical Cooperation Scheme of the Colombo Plan. High Commissioner Tuhin has also overseen aid for disaster relief and grant projects in Asia and Latin America. A career diplomat, he has served as Deputy Consul General at the Consulate of India in San Francisco, Counsellor at the Embassy of India in Hanoi, and both Director for East Asia and Deputy Secretary for China at the Indian Ministry of External Affairs in New Delhi. Tuhin has also served at the Permanent Mission of India to the United Nations in Geneva, at the Embassy of India in Beijing, and at the Commission of India in Hong Kong.

Taidong Zhou currently serves as Manager for the China-UK Partnership Programme on Knowledge for Development at the Development Research Centre (DRC) of the State Council, a policy research, strategic review, and consulting agency focused on the economic and social development of China. Previously, Zhou worked as a Program Officer for Law and Regional Cooperation at the Asia Foundation's office in China, where he oversaw projects related to good governance, open policymaking, and regional cooperation initiatives. Before that, he served as Deputy Division Director, Project Implementation Division of the China Aid Program for General Goods at China's Ministry of Commerce. Earlier, as a Program Officer for the Programming and Planning division for the same ministry, he assisted in developing the Country Program Framework for United Nations Development Programme (UNDP) assistance in China and designed governance and rule-of-law projects. Zhou is pursuing a doctorate on China and international development at the China Agricultural University. He holds a master of arts (MA) in Public Policy from the Australian National University, and a master of laws (LLM) from the School of International Law at the China University of Political Science and Law. He has written extensively and has co-authored a Chinese-language book, *A Comparative Study on Regulatory Systems of Foreign Aid* (2015).

Foreword

India's development cooperation has a long history, intimately linked to a sense of solidarity with the oppressed of other colonial countries who, like the people of India, had undergone bitter struggles for political independence and freedom. After gaining its own independence in 1947, India continued to play a leading role in the process of decolonisation. Under the inspiration of its first generation of leaders – and despite its own modest resources – India extended economic assistance and a helping hand to newly emerging countries across the world.

Although successful in achieving political independence, India was conscious that it could not hope to become the arbiter of its own destiny without economic development, which in turn required educating its people, building their skills and capacities, and mastering modern science and technology. It is precisely in these areas that India began its development cooperation programmes as part and parcel of its foreign policy. Capacity building, upgrading of skills, and sharing development experiences constitute the continuing themes of these programmes, both in philosophy and practice. They are most evident in the long history of India–Africa development partnership.

The present volume, edited by Sachin Chaturvedi, Director General of Research and Information Systems, and Anthea Mulakala of The Asia Foundation, makes a valuable contribution to the literature on India's development cooperation, tracing its evolution over the decades and assessing its successes as well as its shortcomings. This volume will serve as a most useful and timely reference work for both scholars and practitioners alike. Dr. Chaturvedi and Ms. Mulakala deserve accolades for their fine effort.

Ambassador Shyam Saran

Acknowledgements

With the sharp rise in their budgets for development cooperation, the emerging economies have attracted major academic attention in the past decade. The analytical lens, however, has focused more on China than on any other emerging aid provider. This Chinese focus proves misleading in light of the growing global demand for expanded South-South cooperation. In this context, India's development cooperation offers several fascinating dimensions that deserve greater analysis and detailed substantiation. The present volume is the product of this realisation.

A long-standing partnership between The Asia Foundation (TAF) and Research and Information System for Development Countries (RIS) in the 'Asian Approaches to Development Cooperation' (AADC) Programme provided an opportunity to develop this idea. AADC has provided a forum for development cooperation practitioners, analysts, and government officials from Asian providers (including India, China, Thailand, and Korea) to share their views on the evolving objectives and modalities of development cooperation.

TAF and RIS are honoured to collaborate with prominent experts from India and beyond to produce and disseminate knowledge and experience on India's growing role in international development cooperation. We hope this seminal volume will support increased understanding and collaboration between India and the wider development cooperation community.

We would like to thank the following individuals whose contributions and support made this book possible: Ambassador Shyam Saran, Chairman of Research and Information System for Developing Countries (RIS), and Ms. Sujata Mehta, Secretary of Multilateral and Economic Relations for the Indian Ministry of External Affairs, for their many years of commitment to advancing India's South-South cooperation efforts; Dr. Gordon Hein, Senior Vice President of TAF, for championing the Asian Approaches to Development Cooperation Programme; and our authors for sharing their opinions and experiences on India's development cooperation path. We also wish to thank the Australian Department of Foreign Affairs and Trade (DFAT), for its generous support for the production of this volume. In addition, we thank individuals working at RIS and TAF who provided invaluable assistance: Dr. Sabysachi Saha, Associate Fellow; Mr. Pratyush, Research Assistant; Mr. Tish Malhotra, Publication Officer; Dr. Sagar Prasai, Country Representative;

Mr. Thakar D. Aggarwal, Director of Programme and Administrative Services; Ms. Mandakini Surie, Senior Programme Officer; Ms. Sunita Anandarajah, Programme Officer; and Ms. Ritu Parnami, Ms. Mariko Rabbetts, and Ms. Amanda Yeoh for their support in coordinating, researching, editing, and providing logistical support to the authors and editors. Finally, we thank Ms. Suzan Nolan and Ms. Leila Whittemore from BlueSky International for their patient and meticulous editorial work, and Routledge for recognising this volume's contribution to the literature on Indian development cooperation.

The knowledge developed prior to, but used in the creation of this publication, was obtained through the financial support of the Australian government to The Asia Foundation, and the views expressed in the publication are those of the authors and not necessarily those of the Commonwealth of Australia. The Commonwealth of Australia accepts no responsibility for and loss, damage or injury, resulting from the reliance on any of the information or views contained in this publication.

Sachin Chaturvedi and Anthea Mulakala

Abbreviations

AARDO	Afro-Asian Rural Development Organisation
AARRO	Afro-Asian Rural Reconstruction Organisation
ACD	Asia Cooperation Dialogue
ACMECS	Ayeyawady-Chao Phraya-Mekong Economic Cooperation Strategy
ADB	Asian Development Bank
AfDB	African Development Bank
AFN	Afghanis, the currency of Afghanistan
AIIB	Asia Infrastructure Investment Bank
APTTA	Afghan-Pakistan Transit Trade Agreement
ARV	Antiretroviral
ASEAN	Association of Southeast Asian Nations
AusAID	Australian Agency for International Development
BCIM	Bangladesh-China-India-Myanmar
BICS	Brazil, India, China, South Africa
BIMSTEC	Bay of Bengal Initiative for Multi-Sectoral Technical and Economic Cooperation
BIPPA	Bilateral Investment Promotion and Protection Agreement
BMTPC	Building Materials and Technology Promotion Council
BOP	Balance of payments
BRICS	Brazil, Russia, India, China, South Africa
BWI	Bretton Woods Institution
CAADP	Comprehensive Africa Agriculture Development Programme
CAD	Current account deficit
CAREC	Central Asia Regional Economic Cooperation
CARICOM	Caribbean Community
CAU	China Agricultural University
CCEA	Cabinet Committee on Economic Affairs
CEPA	Comprehensive Economic Partnership Agreement
CIDRN	China International Development Research Network
CII	Confederation of Indian Industry
CIS	Commonwealth of Independent States
CLMV	Cambodia, Lao PDR, Myanmar, and Vietnam

Colombo Plan	Colombo Plan for Economic Development and Cooperation in South and South East Asia
COMESA	Common Market for Eastern and Southern Africa
CPLP	Community of Portuguese-Speaking Countries
CSO	Civil society organisation
DAC	Development Assistance Committee
DEA	Department of Economic Affairs
DFAT	Department of Foreign Affairs and Trade
DFID	Department for International Development
DPA	Development Partnership Administration
DPR	Detailed project report
DRC	Democratic Republic of the Congo
EAC	East African Community
EBRD	European Bank for Reconstruction and Development
ECCAS	Economic Community of Central African States
ECOWAS	Economic Community of West African States
EdCIL	Educational Consultants India, Ltd.
EDGS	External debt on goods and services
EDI	Entrepreneurship Development Institute
Exim	Export-Import
FCRA	Foreign Contribution Regulation Act
FDI	Foreign direct investment
FICCI	Federation of Indian Chambers of Commerce and Industry
FIDC	Forum on Indian Development Cooperation
FNCCI	Federation of Nepalese Chambers Of Commerce and Industries
FY	Fiscal year
G7	Group of 7 industrialised nations
G77	Group of 77
Gavi	Global Alliance for Vaccines and Immunization
GDP	Gross domestic product
GFCF	Gross fixed capital formation
GHD	Global health diplomacy
GIS	Geographic information systems
GNI	Gross national income
GOI	Government of India
GPFA	Gas Pipeline Framework Agreement
GRAIN	Genetic Resources Action International
HIPC	Heavily Indebted Poor Countries
HIV/AIDS	Human immunodeficiency virus infection and acquired immune deficiency syndrome
IAI	Initiative for ASEAN Integration
IAIEPA	India-Africa Institute of Education, Planning and Administration
IAIFT	India-Africa Institute of Foreign Trade
IBRD	International Bank for Reconstruction and Development

IBSA	India, Brazil, South Africa
ICD	Inland container depots
ICGEB	International Centre for Genetic Engineering and Biotechnology
ICM	Indian Cooperation Mission
ICSID	International Center for the Settlement of Investment Disputes
ICSO	International civil society organisation
ICT	Information and communications technology
IDA	International Development Association
IDB	Inter-American Development Bank
IDEAS	Indian Development and Economic Assistance Scheme
IDI	Indian Diamond Institute
IES	Interest equalisation support
IFC	International Finance Corporation
IGA	Inter-Governmental Agreement
IGAD	Inter-Governmental Authority on Development
IGICH	Indira Gandhi Institute of Child Health
IIDCA	India International Development Cooperation Agency
IIDEM	International Institute of Democracy and Election Management
IIFT	Indian Institute for Foreign Trade
IIM	Indian Institutes of Management
IIT	Indian Institutes of Technology
IMF	International Monetary Fund
INR	Indian rupees
INSAF	Indian Social Action Forum
INSTC	International North-South Corridor
IOR-ARC	Indian Ocean Rim-Association for Regional Cooperation
IPEA	Instituto de Pesquisa Econômica Aplicada
IPR	Intellectual Property Rights
IT	Information technology
ITEC	Indian Technical and Economic Cooperation Programme
JC	Joint commission
JICA	Japan International Cooperation Agency
JNU	Jawaharlal Nehru University
LAC	Latin America and the Caribbean
LDC	Least-developed countries
LIBOR	London Interbank Offered Rate
LIC	Low-income countries
LIEDC	Laos-India Entrepreneurship Development Centre
LOC	Line of credit
MDG	Millennium Development Goal
MEA	Ministry of External Affairs
MFN	Most favoured nation
MGC	Mekong-Ganga Cooperation
MIC	Middle-income countries

MIGA	Multilateral Investment Guarantee Agency
MMSME	Ministry of Micro, Small and Medium Enterprises
MNC	Multinational corporations
MOF	Ministry of Finance
MOFCOM	Ministry of Finance and Commerce
MOU	Memorandum of understanding
MRI	Magnetic resonance imaging
MTCP	Malaysian Technical Cooperation Programme
MW	Megawatts
NAM	Non-Aligned Movement
NAPM	National Alliance of People's Movements
NATO	North Atlantic Treaty Organisation
NDN	Northern Distribution Network
NEPAD	New Partnerships for African Development
NEsT	Network of Southern Think Tanks
NGO	Nongovernmental organisation
NIAR/NCGG	National Institute of Administrative Research/National Centre for Good Governance
NNJS	Nepal Netra Jyoti Sangh
NRP	Nepalese rupees
NSIC	National Small Industries Corporation
ODA	Official development assistance
OEAM	Office of the External Affairs Minister
OECD	Organisation for Economic Co-operation and Development
ONGC	Oil and Natural Gas Corporation
PAeN	Pan African e-Network
PM	Prime Minister
PMC	Project management consultant
PPP	Purchasing power parity
PRIA	Participatory Research Institute of Asia
PTA	Power Trade Agreement
PV	Present value
R&D	Research and development
REC	Regional Economic Communities
RECCA	Regional Economic Cooperation Conference on Afghanistan
RIS	Research and Information System for Developing Countries
SAARC	South Asian Association for Regional Cooperation
SADC	Southern African Development Community
SAFTA	South Asian Free Trade Area
SAIIA	South African Institute on International Affairs
SAIL	Steel Authority of India
SAP	Structural adjustment programme
SCAAP	Special Commonwealth Assistance for Africa Programme
SCO	Shanghai Cooperation Organisation
SENAI	Serviço Nacional de Aprendizagem Industrial

SEWA	Self-Employed Women's Association
SME	Small and medium-sized enterprise
SPLT	Substantive Patent Law Treaty
SSC	South-South cooperation
TA	Technical assistance
TAPI	Turkmenistan–Afghanistan–Pakistan–India Pipeline
TCI-CBM	Trade Commerce and Investment Opportunities Confidence Building Measure
TC	Technical cooperation
TCS	Technical Cooperation Scheme
TEAM	Techno-Economic Approach for the India-Africa Movement
TICA	Thailand International Cooperation Agency
TOR	Terms of reference
TRIP	Trade-Related Aspects of Intellectual Property Rights
UN	United Nations
UNASUL	Union of South American Nations
UNDP	United Nations Development Programme
UNEP	United Nations Environmental Programme
UNFPA	United Nations Population Fund
UNICEF	United Nations Children's Fund
UNIDO	United Nations Industrial Development Organization
US	United States (of America)
USAID	United States Agency for International Development
USD	United States dollars
VANTI	Voluntary Action Network of India
WHO	World Health Organization
WIPO	World Intellectual Property Organisation
WNTA	Wada Na Todo Abhiyan
WSG	Wits School of Governance
WTO	World Trade Organization

Introduction

Although contemporary literature on international aid architecture refers to India, China, and others as 'emerging donors', this distorts both historical realities and the accepted classification of donor countries. India's engagements with fellow developing countries evolved during its own freedom struggle, a period that also gave rise to its vision of industrial and economic reconstruction.

India soon realised that social and economic development would not prove feasible in the absence of adequate skills. Even during their struggle for independence, Indian leaders found time to confer with social reformers, scientists, and academicians in an effort to create a road map for future cooperation. During the colonial period, they had already focused on science, technology, and innovation and envisioned building institutions of technical excellence. The 1909 creation of the Indian Institute of Science (IISc) in Bangalore already demonstrated the importance that India attached to up-to-date skill development, many decades before independence.[1] This focus would form the basis for many early cooperation efforts.

Provenance and evolution

Development cooperation with a skill development focus assumed an early role in Indian foreign policy as well. Even before independence, and to this day, India has provided training and knowledge exchange in response to requests from partner countries in Africa and elsewhere (GOI 1927; 1946; 1949a; 1949b). In 1946, Jawahar Lal Nehru, prime minister of the interim government, asked Education Minister Shafaat Ahmed Khan to invite agricultural scientists from China and Indonesia for training in India, against the wishes of British Viceroy Viscount Wavell (Gopal 1984). This engagement deepened when India joined the Commonwealth in 1950 and thence the Colombo Plan: India not only sent its personnel abroad for training, but also invited a number of candidates to Indian institutions (Oakman 2010: 179; Chaturvedi 2015: 61–62). As a result, capacity building assumed foundational importance in Indian development cooperation architecture.

In its early stages, development cooperation followed various trajectories of engagement; in this volume, we have referred to these collectively as the 'development compact'. Many of the first efforts focused on India's neighbours. In

1948, India gave a major loan to Burma out of its sterling account and supplied economic and social development aid to Nepal after the 1951 collapse of Rana rule. The Nepal portfolio grew to cover development projects ranging from the health sector, to building dams for flood prevention, to construction of an airstrip for Kathmandu's airport. The number of projects multiplied so quickly that in 1954 India launched the India Aid Mission (IAM; later ICM)[2] in Kathmandu, charged with coordinating and monitoring India-funded projects – soon to become a cornerstone of Indian-Nepali friendship. In its later incarnation as the ICM, the mission also undertook studies and reviews of projects, particularly focusing on their socioeconomic impact.[3]

When the emperor of Afghanistan approached India for a similar arrangement in the late 1960s, India agreed to a joint commission (JC) at the ministerial level. Assistance volumes and initiatives assumed a scale similar to Nepal's; they not only included development projects, but also focused on identifying resources and capabilities that would foster projects of mutual interest and expanded trade, including trade transit arrangements. India concluded the Afghan agreement in 1969; within the next few years, it extended JC arrangements to a few other countries such as Ethiopia and Tanzania. Even now, JCs remain India's preferred instrument for bilateral engagement.

However, we observe that historically, the spirit of joint-assessment transparency and unequivocal commitment gradually disappeared from the Indian scene. It re-emerged only in 2003 with the announcement of a new cooperation policy and effectively waited for implementation until the 2012 creation of the Development Partnership Administration (DPA). As various chapters in this volume demonstrate, India has yet to consolidate its approach to affect assessment and data collection in partnership with relevant stakeholders.

Evaluation and assessment take on considerable urgency with the shift of focus towards mutual benefit (within the framework of South-South cooperation). This principle emerged relatively late in India's cooperation policy. Initially, as per Gandhi's vision, that policy had articulated the idea of 'one world', a notion that Prime Minister Nehru stressed in his address to the Constituent Assembly on 15 August 1947: 'Peace has been said to be indivisible; so is freedom, so is prosperity now, and so also is disaster in this one world that can no longer be split into isolated fragments'. India's pressing challenge at present lies in ensuring appropriate priorities and institutional frameworks aimed at effective sectoral governance and service delivery. Even within the analytical framework of South-South cooperation, India must build consistency and scope for evaluation.

This may prove all the more challenging as India strives to maintain resource allocation while expanding budget lines. The global economy has entered a new phase: In 2015, China faced a manufacturing squeeze, and South Korea's exports declined by more than 14 per cent from September 2014 to September 2015 (Economist 2015a; 2015b). Brazil's economy, which had expanded at 7.6 per cent in 2010, will probably shrink by at least 2 per cent in 2015. A 2010 Brazilian trade surplus of USD 20 billion has dropped to USD 14 billion in 2015 (Trading

Economics 2015). Against this backdrop, India's development cooperation policy faces its own challenges – but also sees many more opportunities.

In this volume

In the literature on emerging donors, analyses of China dominate, with India often overlooked or lumped together with other nontraditional actors. This volume is unique in addressing this void in development scholarship. No other available publication provides so comprehensive an overview of Indian development cooperation from such diverse voices: Indian academics, government officials, and nongovernmental organisation (NGO) leaders, as well as Chinese and Western perspectives.

The volume is organized in four parts. The first discusses the fundamentals of Indian development cooperation. In Chapter 1, S. K. Mohanty raises the classic debate between monetarist and structuralist approaches, and argues that India's current 'mission approach' has emerged from the structuralist camp. He explains India's engagement at five levels within the development compact framework. M. Agarwal similarly grounds contemporary Indian South-South cooperation in its experience as an aid recipient. In Chapter 2, he describes how India strategically used its incoming foreign aid not only to expand its investible resources, but also to address technical and capacity gaps, both at the national and human resources level. As India transitioned to provider status (starting as early as the 1950s), this experience in skilled human resource development laid the foundation for India's flagship cooperation programme, Indian Technical and Economic Cooperation (ITEC). In Chapter 3, K. Tuhin, India's former Joint Secretary in the Development Partnership Administration, details the evolution and impact of ITEC since its inception in 1964, when India was still a recipient country.

The second set of chapters focus on distinctive contemporary features of Indian development cooperation. In his discussion of India's engagement in the health sector (Chapter 4), S. Chaturvedi illustrates how India's traditional bilateral health focus – supporting medical infrastructure, human resource development, and medicine and vaccine supply – has diversified in the last decade to include multilateral engagement through vertical funds and collaborative research. P. Saxena of India's Administrative Service, formerly in charge of lines of credit (LOCs) in the Ministry of External Affairs, demystifies India's fastest-growing cooperation instrument in Chapter 5. With Indian LOCs soon expected to exceed USD 40.108 billion PPP and active in over sixty-six countries, Saxena's insider's perspective provides a timely assessment of the impacts and challenges that LOCs offer. In December 2015, the Department of Economic Affairs produced a new set of LOC guidelines which respond to many of the issues raised by Saxena. In Chapter 6, E. Mawdsley and S. Roychoudhury focus on India's vibrant and vocal civil society, which provides critical and constructive input on a range of domestic policy issues. The authors discuss how complex state–civil society organisation (CSO) relations within India may shape the future evolution of CSO roles in external development cooperation.

The third section takes a geographical focus, examining India's cooperation with Nepal, Afghanistan, and Africa. B. Pyakuryal and S. Chaturvedi provide both Indian and Nepali perspectives on one of India's oldest and most important bilateral relationships in Chapter 7. The analysis contrasts relatively successful development cooperation efforts with the countries' more politically incompatible trade and investment relations. Chapter 8 notes that India is the now the fifth-largest provider of development cooperation in Afghanistan. G. Sachdeva presents India's commitment to Afghanistan as primarily developmental, trade related, and long term, contrasting it with Western interventions that tend to the strategic and time bound. R. Beri's study of India's engagement in Africa (Chapter 9) illustrates the range of instruments and strategies characterizing India's South-South cooperation (SSC). Although this African assistance has rested on human resource development and capacity building, LOCs have grown at an exponential pace, with African countries comprising six of the top ten recipients of Indian credit lines as of 2014.

The final section presents external perspectives on Indian development cooperation. X. Li and T. Zhou (Chapter 10) fill an important gap in the development literature, drawing an extended comparison between the two largest SSC providers – China and India. The authors also reflect on China's experience in SSC, offering lessons and challenges for India as it expands the scope and scale of its cooperation. Finally, they discuss prospects for collaboration between the two countries. S. Howes and J. Pryke (Chapter 11) provide a similar comparison between India and Australia. They note that as of 2014–2015, India's aid volumes exceed Australia's in purchasing power parity terms, and will continue to grow relative to the Indian economy. They also conclude that although the Organisation for Economic Co-operation and Development's Development Assistance Committee (DAC) and non-DAC assistance show areas of possible convergence, their differences in philosophy and approach will probably persist into the future.

In brief, the present volume explores the evolution and impact of Indian development cooperation on the global dynamics of aid. India has emerged as a key player in the development cooperation arena because of the increasing volume and reach of its South-South cooperation – but even more because of its leadership and advocacy for the development of a distinctly Southern development discourse.

Notes

1 On a voyage from Japan to Chicago in 1893, Jamshedji N. Tata and Swami Vivekananda envisaged a science and leadership role for India. Later, H. E. Sri Krishnaraja Wadiyar, Maharaja of Mysore, would donate 371 acres of land in Bangalore; Tata supplied the funds for buildings and other infrastructure. Sir C. V. Raman became the first director of IISc at its opening. This marks the beginning of Bangalore's pre-eminence in Indian technology.
2 Later renamed the Indian Cooperation Mission after Prime Minister Indira Gandhi's 1966 visit, this was an important watershed in India–Nepali relations (see Pyarkuryal and Chaturvedi in this volume).
3 This extended competence reflected commitments made by Foreign Minister Swaran Singh in 1964.

Works cited

Chaturvedi, S. (2015). *Logic of sharing: Indian approach to South-South cooperation.* New Delhi: Cambridge University Press.

Economist (2015a). A tightening grip. *The Economist*, 14 March. Available at www. economist.com/news/briefing/21646180-rising-chinese-wages-will-only-strengthen-asias-hold-manufacturing-tightening-grip.

Economist (2015b). Why a big slump in South Korea's exports matters. *The Economist*, 1 September. Available at www.economist.com/news/business-and-finance/21662952-steepest-year-drop-trade-2009-mark-sagging-global-demand-why-big-slump.

Gopal, S. (1984). *Selected works of Jawaharlal Nehru: second series,* vol. 1. New Delhi: Oxford University Press.

Government of India (GOI) (1927). Supply of information regarding land and agricultural banks in India to Uganda Government (Agriculture Proceedings, August 1927, Nos. 154–155, B). In S.A.I. Trimizi (ed.), *Indian sources for African history,* vol. 1. New Delhi: International Writers Emporium, p. 372. Available at http://unesdoc.unesco.org/images/0019/001925/192536eo.pdf.

GOI (1946). Invitation from Dean of Faculty of Science, Foud I University, Cairo to Prof J.N. Mukherjee of the Imperial Agricultural Research Institute, New Delhi, as a Visiting Professor, 186 Indian Sources for African History during 1946–47 (Middle East, File No. 8(14)-ME/1946). In S.A.I. Trimizi (ed.), *Indian sources for African history,* vol. 1. New Delhi: International Writers Emporium, p. 185. Available at http://unesdoc.unesco.org/images/0019/001925/192536eo.pdf.

GOI (1949a). Invitation to Indian talent and capital for the economic development of Ethiopian agriculture, commerce and industry (Africa, File No. 42(10)-FR-I/1949-Secret). In S.A.I. Trimizi (ed.), *Indian sources for African history,* vol. 1. New Delhi: International Writers Emporium, p. 207. Available at http://unesdoc.unesco.org/images/0019/001925/192536eo.pdf.

GOI (1949b). Recruitment of Indian teachers, doctors, nurses, engineers etc. for service in Ethiopia; report of the goodwill mission to Ethiopia (Africa, File No. 41(15>AFR-I/, 1949). In S.A.I. Trimizi (ed.), *Indian sources for African history,* vol. 1. New Delhi: International Writers Emporium, p. 207. Available at http://unesdoc.unesco.org/images/0019/001925/192536eo.pdf.

Oakman, D. (2010). *Facing Asia: A history of the Colombo Plan*, second edition. Canberra: Australia National University E Press. Available at www.oapen.org/download?type=document&docid=459231.

Trading Economics (2015). *Brazil balance of trade* [webpage]. Available at www.tradingeconomics.com/brazil/balance-of-trade. [Accessed 12 October 2015].

1 Shaping Indian development cooperation

India's mission approach in a theoretical framework

Saroj Kumar Mohanty

Introduction

India has a long history of supporting fellow developing countries through different forms of assistance; these efforts have occupied the centre stage of India's public policy since the pre-independence days. Over the years, the nature and content of Indian development assistance have undergone radical transformation, reflecting changing global situations and India's own varied experience as both an assistance recipient and provider. This has encouraged the development of a distinctively Indian cooperation strategy and a set of current concerns on improving aid efficacy.

India has a notable legacy of supporting those who have fought against colonial powers. It has championed the cause of anticolonialism across the globe and worked to unite like-minded countries in remaining nonaligned, independent of the super-powers. During the decolonisation period, India's mission aimed to empower and industrialise the newly independent countries, responding to their demands in diverse sectors, including trade, investment, technology, and capacity building, among others. Such a philosophy, informed by recipient experience and focused on the needs of friendly countries in the developing world, has largely shaped the economic foundation of Indian foreign policy. India's engagement with these countries has ranged across diverse sectors, even though support has remained limited and commensurate with the ability to deliver. However, in the absence of an established conceptual framework to guide long-term policies and actions – one evolved through academic research with firm theoretical foundations – India arguably has achieved limited success in crafting an effective, result-oriented development cooperation approach.

The present chapter has a two-fold objective: (1) to outline a suitable development cooperation approach that conforms to India's long-standing norms of foreign policy and (2) to situate this Indian strategy within a formal framework of South-South cooperation (SSC). The chapter begins with an overview of the economic theories most often applied to development assistance and argues that a strategy with theoretical underpinnings would presumably make India's cooperation initiatives more efficient, effective, and predictable. The succeeding section discusses the influence of development theories on development assistance approaches; it focuses on the theoretical foundations of the structuralist approach and their impact on cooperation. The third section will address salient features of India's development financing strategy, sometimes referred to as the 'mission approach'; this section also elaborates the 'development compact' underpinning this strategy. The conclusion will summarise our key findings and highlight the distinctive features of the Indian model.

Economics theory and development assistance: the Indian dilemma

The experiences of development assistance providers suggest that no individual country should require an independent and exclusive theory for aid and financial assistance. Yet conventional approaches generally reflect dominant perspectives on international development and their roots in macroeconomic theory. The world economy has witnessed two competing theories in the post-war period: monetarist and structuralist approaches to economic development and, by extension, development cooperation (Yanagihara 2006; Lim 2011; Mohanty 2015a). The Organisation for Economic Co-operation and Development Development Assistance Committee (OECD-DAC) approach rests on monetarist principles, supported by the Bretton Woods Institution (BWI)[1] and critically referred to as the Washington consensus (Mohanty 2011). The DAC approach has pursued the BWI policies in making aid disbursement decisions, focusing on macroeconomic targets, conditionality, budgetary support, and so forth.

India has vigorously pursued a sturdy development approach over the last decade, allying itself effectively with development assistance programmes in Southern countries. Yet Indian policy reflects a lack of comfort with the prevalent DAC narrative. India has consistently sought a prudent, well-defined development cooperation strategy, one consonant with the long-pursued strategy of promoting partnership, solidarity, and mutual respect in international relations – but rarely identified with the theories underpinning DAC aid. Although this approach thus reflects Indian foreign policy principles, it has not to date assumed the status of an alternative economic strategy and rarely undergoes scrutiny from that perspective.

Nonetheless, the emergence of Southern development assistance providers, along with their changing perceptions about economic assistance, has generated new debate on diverse, multifaceted approaches to development cooperation. Most of these Southern providers began their journey under the banner of SSC. The aid policies of emerging donors have become attractive for Southern recipients and contribute significantly to their growth efforts (Chaturvedi 2012; Chaturvedi, Fues and Sidiropoulos 2012). For a long time, India has searched for a credible development cooperation approach that would better utilise taxpayer resources with a greater degree of aid effectiveness, but without deviating from the main framework of SSC. The OECD-DAC has often criticised emerging-country approaches to development assistance for their lack of a sound theoretical basis and robust implementation policies; but India has yet to evolve an alternative model to justify, shape, and assess its practices. This chapter will give an overview of what such a model might look like. We will argue that emerging-country development assistance programmes share features that align them with the structuralist approach to growth. We will then evaluate how, by adapting to this tradition, India may improve the efficacy of its own strategy.

Divergent approaches to development cooperation

The monetarist and structuralist schools in economics

Conventional wisdom holds that the macroeconomic conditions determine the economic growth of nations (Mohanty 1996). Regarding linkages between economic growth and macroeconomic stability, monetarist and structuralist schools differ widely in their underlying principles and policies.[2]

Their fundamental disagreement centres on macroeconomic stability. According to the monetarists, macroeconomic stability is necessary to have growth, but structuralists consider that growth is possible with a certain level of macroeconomic instability. Macroeconomic stability refers to several variables, representing various facets of the macroeconomic situation. The barometer of macroeconomic stability has been inflation. Therefore, monetarists believe that inflation poses the main obstacle to economic growth because it reduces real income and thus aggregate demand in the economy. Structuralists believe inflation naturally accompanies growth and stems from structural inelasticity in economic systems (Valenzuela Silva 2008: 68–69). For example, the monetary approach to balance of payments (BOP) suggests that excess money supply causes disequilibrium in exchange rates and BOPs. In short, macroeconomic disequilibrium is a monetary phenomenon, manifested in rising prices, and can only be addressed effectively with monetary policies (that is, controlling inflation by influencing money supply in the economy through the adjustment of interest and exchange rates) (Mohanty 1996).

On the other hand, the structuralist approach defines macroeconomic disequilibrium in terms of supply constraints and underemployment (two forms of inelasticity). Hence, policy corrections focus on easing supply bottlenecks and creating demand, thus preserving macroeconomic stability and promoting economic growth. Structuralists argue that the convergence between aggregate demand and aggregate supply achieved through monetary policy interventions may not lead to price stabilisation if underlying sectoral imbalances persist (Bilquee 1988; Lim 2006; Valenzuela Silva 2008).

On the question of macroeconomic conditions conducive for economic growth, the schools once again differ. Whereas the monetarists argue that growth requires economically stable conditions, structuralists emphasise that it can occur even in situations of macroeconomic instability; many developing countries operate in a situation resembling 'underemployment equilibrium'[3] (Mohanty 1996), although inflation and other macroeconomic imbalances are bound to persist. Therefore, growth with instability could prove a reality for developing countries. Unsolicited intervention in arresting moderate levels of inflation could have a negative impact on growth prospects. Structuralists oppose policies such as conditionality, budgetary interventions, macroeconomic targeting, and so forth because these policies impede growth but cannot influence moderate levels of inflation (Chenery 1975; Mohanty 1996).

Many orthodox stabilisation programmes (embodying monetarist principles) have been implemented in developing countries, including Chile (1956–1958 and 1973–1978), Argentina (1959–1962 and 1976–1978), Brazil (1964–1973 and 1982–1983), Bolivia (1956 and 1985), Peru (1959 and 1975–1978), and Venezuela (1988), among others. In most cases, the programmes have failed to deliver either stability or growth (see e.g. Mann and Pastor 1989). Moreover, there is little theoretical justification for conditionality/stabilisation policies in crisis-ridden economies – which may be aid recipients at the same time (Kay 1990; Boianovsky 2012). Therefore, many critics do not see monetarist development cooperation approaches as likely to ensure speedy economic recovery (Meller 1994; Oxfam 2006; Boianovsky 2012; Mohanty 2015b).

On the other hand, the structuralist framework has evolved its own heterodox[4] stabilisation policies, implemented in several Latin American countries, including Argentina (Austral Plan), Brazil (Cruzado Plan), Peru (Inti Plan), and so on.[5] These policies have had mixed results in achieving macroeconomic targets (Ambler and Cardia 1992). However, some programme countries report encouraging outcomes from blending orthodox and heterodox stabilisation policies – notably Israel and Mexico. Upon completion, the programmes in these countries reached several of their goals, particularly in three areas: achieving macroeconomic targets, demonstrating their governments' intention of taking ownership of the programmes, and protecting the social sector to mitigate the adverse impact of SAPs.

Have development theories influenced cooperation approaches?

After reviewing seventy-five years of debate between monetarists and structuralists, we can see that the monetarist approach to BOP has deeply influenced DAC policies. Meanwhile, policies consistent with structuralist principles appear to have shaped development cooperation in emerging countries, although this link has yet to receive a coherent analysis. The DAC approach to development cooperation rests on the 2005 Paris Declaration, which draws its theoretical support from the Washington consensus (Williamson 1990). The lending principles of the IMF and the World Bank mostly reflect the overarching approach of the monetarists. A certain degree of policy coherence therefore exists between the BWIs and the DAC approach towards development assistance.

The DAC seeks to make aid programmes effective through policies of conditionality, budgetary support, macrotargeting, and other monetarist principles. This approach has often drawn criticism because of the complex nature of its financial procedures and the risks involved in adhering to conditionality (Oxfam 2006).

Moreover, several developing countries have failed in the past to comply with stringent conditionality because of domestic compulsions, despite sincere efforts. Severe natural disasters and other unforeseen situations have often prevented national governments from maintaining previously agreed macroeconomic targets, leading to programme failures – at an enormous cost to the programme countries. One might cite, for example, the emergency that arose when Bangladesh could not maintain its quarterly credit-flow limit because certain donors failed to abide by their commitments; the country faced acute problems in the 1980s following the withdrawal of IMF support in the midst of the structural adjustment programme (Matin 1986; Rahman 1992).

By contrast, emerging countries argue that their small-scale development cooperation efforts could support recipients in specific sectors, linking projects directly with people who may benefit from them. Although small in size, such projects operate in social and production sectors such as health, infrastructure, services, pharmaceuticals, agriculture, and manufacturing, among others, without linking the aid programme to the recipient countries' macroeconomic performances. The funding principles of emerging countries assert that improved supply conditions in needy sectors may support the potential for sustained growth. Such assertions, however, have not to date invoked the support of any theoretical principles. Therefore, traditional donors often criticise such project-based development cooperation on the grounds of its (often) partisan approach, nontransparency, and as suggested earlier, lack of sound theoretical basis (Smith, Fordelone and Zimmermann 2010; EIAS 2013).

Many emerging countries note that although the scale of cooperation resources they can offer lags behind that of more developed countries, the demand for such resources has surged.[6] This may reflect the fact that emerging countries often engage in sectors where 'traditional donors' have minimal or no presence. The growing dependence on cooperation from emerging countries may also indicate efficient delivery systems (Chaturvedi, Kumar and Mendiratta 2013). Such projects may prove highly effective precisely because their financing does not depend on the recipient's overall macroeconomic performance or on conditionality.

This has simplified the disbursement procedures for partner-country resources because they do not require the complex procedures of macrotargeting. Despite their lack of clear connection with a 'credible' theoretical foundation, the present funding principles of emerging countries could still be refined further in the service of greater efficacy. In this connection, what linkages might we find between existing theories of economic development and the *effectiveness* of emerging-country development assistance? It may well prove that the conditionality-linked DAC approach does not guarantee sustained growth potential in the partner country.

The development cooperation approach of emerging countries does, however, share views consistent with the structuralist approach. Because the OECD countries dominated development assistance in the postwar period, the structuralist approach did not receive the attention that might have established its relevance in cooperation strategies. The next section considers what aspects of the structuralist position have, or might, influence Indian policy.

India's theoretical framework for development cooperation

Structuralist foundations

India has engaged with development cooperation since the 1960s, and its policies towards specific sectors have evolved significantly over the last six decades. India has a clear vision of South-South cooperation and the potential for mutual gain in sharing prosperity with fellow developing countries. Towards this end, it seems appropriate to link India's development cooperation approach with existing paradigms of economic thought to improve its robustness, continuity, and consistency, on the one hand, and make it more appealing, acceptable, and relevant for its partners on the other.

India shares the structuralist view that macroeconomic management should address supply constraints. In developing countries, such constraints persist in agriculture, manufacturing, services, infrastructure, and several social sectors. Individual countries have sector-specific requirements, and therefore sector-specific, demand-driven needs that India must address according to its support capacity. Much current literature has consequently focused on assistance volumes (see e.g. Chaturvedi 2012; Fuchs and Vadlamannati 2013).

With the 'emergence' of the Indian economy in the 2000s, its support for development assistance went up significantly (Figure 1.1). The quantity of assistance in Indian rupees (INR) registered a five-fold rise during the period 1990–2010 and then quadrupled over the next five years, 2010–2015. Such assistance covers several activities (including a capacity-building programme, lines of credit, loans, and aid for trade) and ranges across several developing countries. Although India has often collaborated in agricultural and manufacturing activities, it has increasingly focused on services sectors such as telecommunication and health. Other emerging countries have also adopted similar sector-specific practices – for example, Brazil in energy and health, and China in infrastructure and manufacturing

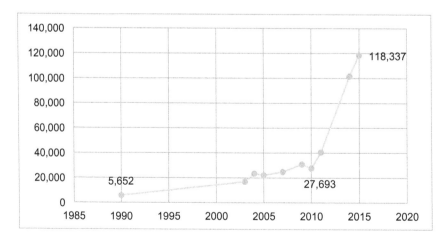

Figure 1.1 India's increasing commitments to development cooperation, 1990–2015
Source: Chaturvedi et al. (2012)

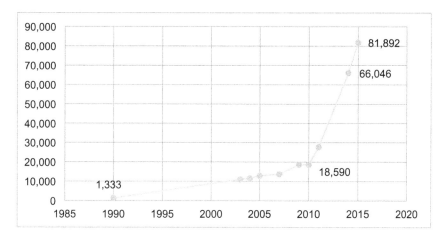

Figure 1.2 Value of India's development assistance to South Asia, 1990–2015
Source: Chaturvedi et al. (2012)

(Hong 2012; Saravia 2012). One may therefore argue that deeper, project-based engagement with developing countries to support their industrialisation and agricultural development has yielded positive results.

India has prioritised assistance for neighbouring countries in South Asia, where we see a steady growth in volumes since 1990, with a more than four-fold rise between 2010 and 2015 (Figure 1.2). India has experimented with several types of cooperation modules in these countries to improve efficacy and to make its programmes more 'people-centric' in nature.

Furthermore, India's external economic engagements and integration strategies provide an important backdrop for analysing its development cooperation. India has adopted a multiprong strategy, connecting with these recipient countries through trade and investment as well as cooperation policies. In order to enhance mutual gains, India seeks to bolster trade activities with improved bilateral cooperation, and furthers engagement with partner countries through free-trade agreements. Other trade engagement enhancements include improved trade financing, lines of credit, and easier terms for bilateral cooperation (Chaturvedi 2012). The engagement with trade cooperation differs from one emerging country to another, and further demonstrates assumptions closer to the structuralist position than the monetarist one. For example, China finances infrastructure projects in recipient countries, but uses trade goods in settling loans with these countries. Instead of recovering loan elements in monetary terms, China prefers to accept equivalent-receipt amounts in goods such as minerals (AFRODAD 2010).

The structuralist approach emphasises income redistribution in the recipient economy as an important condition for growth. India's cooperation has aimed to create income in specific locales through small projects that may generate local employment. Employing 'appropriate technology' in these projects leads to gainful jobs for local populations. Many of these projects occur in the social sector and other productive sectors, such as agriculture, industrialisation, and services.

From the structuralist perspective, imposing conditionality does little to influence the growth prospects of a programme country. According to structuralists, a certain level of inflation is a natural phenomenon in developing countries, which tend to experience long-term supply bottlenecks. Because the structuralist framework sees convergence between inflation and development as a long-term policy objective, it imposes no strict adherence to conditionality. Although this approach is too simplified to address short-term imbalances in the economy, it has long-term implications for allowing macroeconomic stability to go hand-in-hand with economic growth. Therefore, India's current practice – development cooperation programmes without conditionality – is very much consistent with the structuralist approach.

India's development assistance programme has the twin objectives of (1) mitigating poverty and (2) revitalising economic growth in recipient countries. This is unlike the heavily indebted poor countries (HIPC) initiatives of the BWIs and industrialised countries, which have focused on debt relief to poor countries. This type of programme aims to terminate their debt burden and alleviate poverty, but may not prove effective enough to boost economic development (Chaturvedi 2015a). India's development cooperation, we would argue, should therefore prioritise the resumption and sustainability of Southern growth.

Despite these aims, India has a long way to go toward confirming a self-contained policy framework for development cooperation. India's programme requires further restructuring as it enters a new proactive phase of dialogue with developing countries. This is evident from India's increased engagement with partner countries, backed by the aim of playing a larger global role in promoting Southern development. Unlike many industrialized countries that possess a separate Ministry for Development Cooperation, India has evolved a consolidated department, the Development Partnership Administration (DPA), within the Ministry of External Affairs (MEA) to oversee its cooperation initiatives in a coordinated manner. As resources and coverage of programmes have risen rapidly in recent years, the DPA has also consolidated its efforts to sharpen policies in several areas: aid effectiveness, choice of sectors for assistance, setting modalities for accountability, and so on.[7] To make suitable changes in these areas, India should collaborate with and learn from other donor countries; at the same time, the Indian core mission remains unchanged – empowering developing countries under the SSC umbrella, continuing to play the role of a 'partner' as opposed to a 'donor' in development assistance initiatives.

Mission approach and development compact

India's mission centres on campaigning against colonialism and helping empower developing countries. It has therefore aimed to sustain present levels of engagement with developing countries, further supporting them in efforts to come out of deprivation and engage in long-term, sustained development. This long-term development cooperation strategy has often been referred to as the mission approach (Mohanty 2015b). Conceptually, the mission approach aims to identify a set of growth drivers that support partner development efforts, setting them on a high-growth path. Technically, an understanding of economic conditions (based on macroeconomic paradigms) in partner countries could help identify these economic drivers and key growth sectors. This might also help in devising a 'road map' for providing consistent and predictable resources to selected areas, without conditionality and in the spirit of the 'partnership' principle.

Some of the salient features of the 'Mission Approach' draw from various past Indian initiatives to support developing countries in securing independence, in their postindependence reconstruction efforts, and their specific attempts to resume steady progress during Plan periods (Chaturvedi 2015a; Mohanty 2015b). For example, India has been engaged with Bhutan since 1955 and began extending yearly financial support to that country in 1960. In 1972, India also supported the establishment of two industrial estates, namely Nepalganj and Dharan, in Nepal and provided financial support to promote Nepalese cottage industries between 1968 and 1973. As a follow-up action, India also agreed to fully support these countries' national five-year plans (Chaturvedi 2015a). In contrast to the DAC approach on HIPC, India looks beyond debt issues and focuses on long-term development. The mission undoubtedly faces challenges in constantly rising resource flows – a pressing issue for Indian development cooperation in its present form.

In this context, we should address the prevalent understanding of other dominant approaches to development cooperation. Japanese economist T. Yanagihara (2006) has evolved a comparative analysis to distinguish different cooperation modes. He identifies two broad types of engagement: the 'framework' approach and the 'ingredient' approach. According to his definition, the framework approach represents the 'rules of the game': economic agents make decisions and take action in a given economy, itself conceived in terms of the functions of institutions and mechanisms. By contrast, the ingredient approach refers to tangible organisational units such as enterprises, official bureaus, and industrial projects, along with their aggregations in industries, sectors, and regions. Wonhyuk Lim (2011) ascribed the framework approach to North-South engagements and the ingredient approach to South-South ones.

India's mission approach differs distinctly from the framework approach, but it has some elements similar to those of the ingredient approach. It favours defining development cooperation as demand driven, impelled by aid-recipient requests and needs. In this view, development cooperation should adopt sectoral-support programmes, based on specific projects, rather than providing broader budgetary support. These projects may not be highly capital-intensive in nature, but should cover several desired sectors, depending upon the request of the partner country. These projects should also aim at improving supply conditions in these countries; the mission approach emphasises sectors such as agriculture and manufacturing, which create large forward and backward linkages in the partner country (Mohanty 2015b).

With the detailing of delivery modalities at the practical level, the broad goals of the mission approach dovetail with what Chaturvedi (2012) terms the development

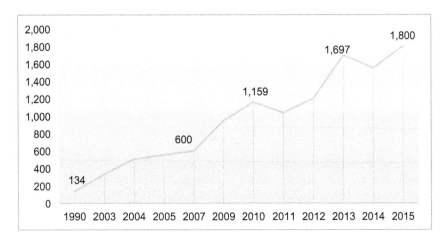

Figure 1.3 Value of India's assistance through the ITEC Programme, 1990–2015
Source: Chaturvedi et al. (2012)

compact. As described elsewhere in this volume, this compact rests on five action pillars: capacity building and skills transfer, concessional finance (further divided into grants and lines of credit), preferential trade, investment, and technical cooperation. It implicitly depends on the principle of equitable access to trade, investment, and technology in SSC initiatives.[8] According to Chaturvedi (2015b), India and other emerging BRICS donors have a larger concept of aid, wherein the contributors do not simply give hand-outs, but also bring and generate economic activities in the recipient country, and this compact for South-South cooperation rests solidly on the concept of mutual gain.

In short, we can see the mission approach as articulating the broad theoretical basis of Indian development cooperation, whereas the development compact represents the broad strategies flowing from that approach. Among these strategies, India has assigned a high priority to the capacity-building programme known as Indian Technical and Economic Cooperation (ITEC) Programme.[9] Indian funding for capacity building has grown rapidly over the years, most notably during the period of the post-2008 recession, as ITEC's 2007–2008 funding tripled by 2014–2015 (Figure 1.3).

Conclusion

Development assistance is passing through a phase of global concern: financing flows from industrialised countries have declined for the past two years, whereas recipient countries show a weakened preference for assistance with stringent conditionality. The presence of both traditional and new emerging partners in the arena of development financing has caused uneasiness and friction between the two. As noted earlier, the DAC follows monetarist principles in basing assistance on conditionality, macroeconomic targeting, budgetary support, and so on; the assumption remains that macroeconomic stability is essential for sustained growth in developing countries, requiring conditionality for aid effectiveness. The structuralist approach contradicts this view, arguing that persistent supply bottlenecks rather than macro-economic instability do the most to hinder growth in developing economies.

In examining the approaches and policies of monetarist and structuralist providers, we found that orthodox and heterodox stabilisation programmes have failed in most of the programme countries during the last five decades. Stringent conditionality associated with an orthodox stabilisation programme could not produce better results than structuralist heterodox stabilisation programmes. Therefore, the efficacy of development cooperation policies related to conditionality should come under close scrutiny.

We have argued that the development cooperation approach of emerging countries, particularly India, accords closely with the philosophy of structuralists. India's development strategy, which we term the mission approach, has considerable similarities to Yanagihara's ingredient approach. This insight helps us recognise the real (and legitimising) macroeconomic tenets of India assistance. India should adopt an evidence-based method in determining the sectors and volumes of assistance to specific developing countries, according to the strategies defined in the development compact. Empowered with the mission approach in terms of securing broad directions for specific sectoral funding, the development compact can steer India's development cooperation programme in the future.

Notes

1 The 1944 Bretton Woods Agreement established the International Monetary Fund (IMF) and the International Bank for Reconstruction and Development (IBRD), which today is part of the World Bank Group. Present-day members include these three institutions together with the International Finance Corporation (IFC), Multilateral Investment Guarantee Agency (MIGA), International Center for the Settlement of Investment Disputes (ICSID), World Trade Organization (WTO), African Development Bank (AfDB), Asian Development Bank (ADB), European Bank for Reconstruction and Development (EBRD), and the Inter-American Development Bank (IDB).

2 For background, see some of the major proponents of the structuralist approach: Celso Furtado, Michal Kalecki, E.V.K. FitzGerald, Karl Brunner, Allen Meltzer, David Laidler, and Lance Taylor; the main proponents of the monetarist approach include Clark Warburton, Milton Friedman, Anna Schwartz, Robert J. Barro, Stanley Fischer, and John Williamson.

3 On 'underemployment equilibrium' as a reality in developing countries, see Mohanty (1996).

4 Heterodox economics seeks 'reality-based' explanations for the economic aspect of human behaviour within social contexts, whereas orthodox (mainstream) economics rests on assumptions primarily drawn from nineteenth-century classical economic theories concerning rational choice and expectations and representative agency. Heterodox (outside the mainstream) schools include socialist, Marxian, institutional, Austrian, post-Keynesian, and others.

5 Monetarist policies meant to bring a fragile country back to normalcy under a structural adjustment programme (SAP) are orthodox policies. Similar structural policy packages are known as heterodox policies. Whereas heterodox policies are extensively implemented in Latin American countries, orthodox policies are widely implemented by Bretton Woods Institutions. For further discussion on orthodox versus heterodox policies, refer to Ambler and Cardia (1992).

6 On increased demand as reflected in increased assistance and line-of-credit volumes, see the chapters by Li and Zhou, Howes and Pryke, Beri, Agarwal, and Saxena in this volume.
7 For further discussion of the DPA and its role in the evolution of Indian aid, see the chapter by Agarwal in this volume.
8 See the chapter by Chaturvedi in this volume.
9 See also the chapter by Tuhin in this volume.

Works cited

African Forum and Network on Debt and Development (AFRODAD) (2010). *Assessing the growing role and developmental impact of China in Africa: An African perspective* [webpage]. Available at www.realityofaid.org/wp-content/uploads/2013/02/ROA-SSDC-Special-Report3.pdf.

Ambler, S., and Cardia, E. (1992). Optimal anti-inflation programs in semi-industrialized economies: Orthodox versus heterodox policies. *Journal of Development Economics,* 38(1): 41–61.

Bilquee, F. (1988). Inflation in Pakistan: Empirical evidence on the monetarist and structuralist hypotheses. *The Pakistan Development Review,* 27(2): 109–129.

Boianovsky, M. (2012). Furtado and the structuralist-monetarist debate on economic stabilization in Latin America. *History of Political Economy,* 44(2): 277–330.

Chaturvedi, S. (2012). India and development cooperation: Expressing southern solidarity. In S. Chaturvedi, T. Fues and E. Sidiropoulos (eds.), *Development cooperation and emerging powers: New partners or old patterns?* London: Zed Books, pp. 169–189.

Chaturvedi, S. (2015a). *Logic of sharing: Indian approach to south-south cooperation.* New Delhi: RIS and Cambridge University Press.

Chaturvedi, S. (2015b). The emerging institutional architecture of India's development cooperation. In E. Sidiropoulos, J.A. Perez Pineda, S. Chaturvedi and T. Fues (eds.), *Institutional architecture and development: Responses from emerging powers.* Midrand, ZA: South African Institute of International Affairs, pp. 138–154.

Chaturvedi, S., Sushil, K., and Mendiratta, S. (2013). Balancing state and community participation in development partnership projects: Emerging evidence from Indian SDPs in Nepal. *RIS Discussion Paper,* 183. Research and Information System, New Delhi.

Chaturvedi, S., Fues, T., Sidiropoulos, E., and Mawsdley, E. (eds.) (2012). *Development cooperation and emerging powers: New partners or old patterns?* London: Zed Books.

Chenery, H.B. (1975). The structuralist approach to development policy. *The American Review,* 65(2): 310–316.

European Institute for Asian Studies (EIAS) (2013). Japan and the EU: Development aid partners: A new line of donor cooperation. *EIAS Briefing Seminar,* 28 May. JICA and European Institute for Asian Studies, Brussels, Belgium.

Fuchs, A., and Vadlamannati, K.C. (2013). The needy donor: An empirical analysis of India's aid motives. *World Development,* 44: 110–128.

Hong, Z. (2012). China's evolving aid landscape: Crossing the river by feeling the stones. In S. Chaturvedi, T. Fues and E. Sidiropoulos (eds.), *Development cooperation and emerging powers: New partners or old patterns?* London: Zed Books, pp. 134–168.

Kay, C. (1990). The Latin American contribution to development theory. *ISS Working Paper,* 82. Institute of Social Sciences, The Hague. Available at http://repub.eur.nl/pub/18931/wp82.pdf.

Lim, J. (2006). Philippine monetary policy: A critical assessment and search for alternatives, *PERI Working Paper*. Political Economy Research Institute, University of Massachusetts.

Lim, W. (2011). Critical reviews of approaches to development cooperation. Paper presented at the *Emerging Asian Approaches to Development Cooperation Conference*, Seoul, 29 September. Korea Development Institute and the Asia Foundation, Seoul.

Mann, A.J., and Pastor Jr., M. (1989). Orthodox and heterodox stabilization policies in Bolivia and Peru: 1985–1988. *Journal of Interamerican Studies and World Affairs*, 31(4): 163–192.

Matin, K.M. (1986). *Bangladesh and the IMF: An exploratory study*. Dhaka: Bangladesh Institute of Development Study.

Meller, P. (1994). Latin American adjustment and economic reforms: Issues and recent experience. In A. Solimano, O. Sunken and M.I. Blejer (eds.), *Rebuilding capitalism: Alternative roads after socialism and dirigisme*. Ann Arbor, MI: University of Michigan Press, pp. 241–278.

Mohanty, S.K. (1996). Macroeconomic linkages between inflation, growth and employment: Experience of countries in the Indian Ocean Basin, *RIS Digest*, 13(2–4): 91–114.

Mohanty, S.K. (2011). Is the economic cooperation of emerging countries with Africa win-win situation? *Trade Negotiations Insights*, 10(3). Available at www.acp-eu-trade.org/tni.

Mohanty, S.K. (2015a). Theoretical framework for a southern development cooperation approach: Some methodological issues. Paper presented at the *Regional Consultations on Development Cooperation Conference*, 24 March, Kolkata. Research and Information System for Development Countries and Institute of Foreign Policy Studies (IFPS) at the University of Kolkata.

Mohanty, S.K. (2015b). Why development cooperation approaches differ: A perspective on India's mission approach. In E. Sidiropoulos, J.A. Perez Pineda, S. Chaturvedi and T. Fues (eds.), *Institutional architecture & development*: *Responses from emerging powers*. Midrand, ZA: South African Institute of International Affairs, pp. 1–23.

Oxfam (2006). Kicking the habit: How the World Bank and the IMF are still addicted to attaching economic policy conditions to aid. *Oxfam Briefing Paper*, 96. Oxfam International, London. Available at www.regjeringen.no/upload/kilde/ud/rap/2006/0164/ddd/pdfv/300505–9kicking_the_habit.pdf.

Rahman, S.H. (1992). Structural adjustment and macroeconomic performance in Bangladesh in the 1980s. *The Bangladesh Development Studies*, 20(2–3): 89–125.

Saravia, E. (2012). Brazil: Towards innovation in development cooperation. In S. Chaturvedi, T. Fues and E. Sidiropoulos (eds.), *Development cooperation and emerging powers: New partners or old patterns*? London: Zed Books. pp. 115–133.

Smith, K., Fordelone, T.Y., and Zimmermann, F. (2010). Beyond the DAC: The welcome role of other providers of development co-operation. *OECD Issues Brief*. OECD Development Co-operation Directorate, Paris. Available at www.oecd.org/dac/45361474.pdf.

Valenzuela Silva, L.A. (2008). A monetarist-structuralist debate on inflation. *Revita Chilena De Economia y Sociedad*, 2(1): 65–69. Available at http://rches.blogutem.cl/files/2012/06/rev_fae03_05.pdf.

Williamson, J. (1990). What Washington means by policy reform. In J. Williamson (ed.), *Latin American adjustment: How much has happened?* Washington, DC: Institute for International Economics, pp. 7–40.

Yanagihara, T. (2006). Development and dynamic efficiency: Framework approach versus ingredient approach. In O. Kenichi and I. Ohno (eds.), *Japanese views on economic development: Diverse paths to the market*. London: Routledge, pp. 70–76.

2 The role of aid in India's economic development cooperation

Finance, capacity building, and policy advice

Manmohan Agarwal[1]

Introduction

India has had a great deal of experience as a recipient of aid from both multi-lateral and bilateral sources, including food aid, financial assistance, technical assistance, and capacity building. This chapter discusses how India's experi-ence as a recipient has influenced its own development cooperation policies. Development economists towards the end of the Second World War (and later) stressed the role of aid in augmenting domestic savings (Rosenstein-Rodan 1943; Nurkse 1953). Aid also served to pay for the imports of capital goods needed to raise investment (Prebisch 1950). Indian policymakers initially per-ceived the lack of technical capacity as the key constraint to development, rather than financial resources – given the substantial foreign exchange reserves accu-mulated during the Second World War. They sought access for Indians in the universities and training institutes of developed countries, along with assistance to build domestic training capacity. Governmental officials insisted that tech-nology imports include agreements to train Indians and to transfer the relevant technology (GOI 1952: 44, 550; 1956: 164, 402, 403). The financial dimension of aid would assume importance later, after the 1957–1958 balance of payments (BOP) crisis when the government sought to implement its investment plan (Agarwal, 1997).

Even in these early phases, regardless of the internal priorities that aid served, India often found that it came with more or less invisible strings attached. As we shall see, Indian policymakers have found that dialogue works better than aid conditionality, creating consensus that provides a firmer basis for sustained action. However, bilateral aid to India often brought pressures for India to change its foreign policy, usually with disastrous consequences, as we show later. This, too, has shaped India's own approach to bilateral assistance and to multilateral solidarity.

We analyse the Indian aid experience through five interlinked topics. We first present a brief history of the evolution of aid rationales and policies at the interna-tional level. We then discuss the economic impact of aid on savings, investment, and growth in recipient countries. The third section addresses India's development strategy in the postwar period and its expectations for the role of aid; we then look at its actual (and sometimes contrasting) experience as a recipient. Finally, we examine how that experience has influenced India's emerging cooperation policies.

The objectives of aid

Growth, poverty alleviation, and welfare

The objectives of aid have varied over the years, in tandem with variations in development goals, the constraints stifling economic growth, and resources available to developing countries. When aid became significant in the mid-1950s, it first sought to augment low national savings and, by extension, the level of investment intended to go largely to infrastructure (Rosenstein–Rodan 1943; Nurkse 1953). Analysts expected that better infrastructure would also encourage investment in manufacturing, aided by policies that encouraged import substitution usually undertaken by the private sector (Prebisch 1950; Nurkse 1953).

Policymakers often applied the Harrod–Domar growth model to calculate the required aid – for instance, in India's First Five-Year Plan (1951–1955): subtracting domestic savings from the desired investment (obtained by multiplying the desired increase in output by the amount of capital required to produce one unit of output) gave the requisite amount of aid (Harrod 1939; Domar 1946). However, developing countries often experienced large current-account deficits; investment required import of machinery, and exports (mainly of primary products) could not grow rapidly enough. This prompted development of two gap models to determine the required aid. One gap was the domestic one (the difference between the required investment and national savings), and the other the foreign gap (the difference between exports and required imports). Aid would then fill the larger of the two gaps (Chenery and Bruno 1962; Chenery and Strout 1966). These models seemed to govern donor policies from the mid-1960s to the 1970s.

After its BOP crisis in 1957–1958, India became the first major recipient to have aid organised through a consortium, which allowed donors to coordinate their aid efforts; consortia were later adopted for other countries. At these meetings, the recipient government would state its requirements based on a plan (however imperfectly detailed), and then the donors would assess the country's needs and pledge their aid. India's plans provided detailed requirements (see e.g. GOI 1961).

From the mid-1950s until the end of the 1970s, developing countries successfully raised their growth and national savings rates, meeting an expected decline of aid dependence. Concerns persisted, however, that increases in job creation remained inadequate, and that this in part had prevented substantial reductions in poverty levels. The Indian government, concerned by the limited impact of its economic plans on poverty, set up a committee to examine this issue; among other efforts, this committee calculated the world's first national poverty line (Pant 1962; Dandekar and Rath 1971; Singh 1989).

Later global efforts refined the objectives of aid: Robert McNamara, as president of the World Bank, shepherded a shift in aid allocation criteria, with greater stress on reducing poverty (McNamara 1973a). Integrated rural development and nutrition projects became integral components of a poverty reduction strategy (McNamara 1973b; Bottrall 1974). In the late 1970s, the World Bank also developed its 'basic needs' approach, seeking to provide bundled goods and services considered essential for a decent standard of living (Streeten et al. 1981), a precursor to the later concept of the Millennium Development Goals (MDGs).

The debt crises of the 1980s, however, effectively derailed this strategy. Donors now more frequently granted aid for broad BOP support and not specific projects. Aid for growth also took a back seat, although some argued that bringing macro and BOP stability would lay the basis for sustainable growth (Williamson 1990). They contended that serious weaknesses stemming from excessive government interference prevented a supply response in export sectors (Williamson 1990). Therefore, the BOP aid became tied to broad reforms designed to reduce government controls and increase reliance on the market – reforms now known as 'structural adjustment' or the Washington consensus.[2] These reforms would provide the basis for growth. India came under severe criticism for an apparent lack of market-oriented reforms (Bhagwati 1993).[3]

Structural adjustment lending proved very controversial. Some (e.g. Cornia, Jolly and Stewart 1987) criticised these loans for their harmful social effects. Others challenged their premises (Bruton 1998) or their effectiveness (Toye 1987; Moseley, Hartigan and Toye 1995). These criticisms and other developments resulted in a reorientation of aid in the early 1990s. Activists, appalled at the social cost of structural adjustment, took a prominent part in United Nations' conferences on women, children, and other social objectives throughout the 1990s; meanwhile, aid ministers and bureaucracies, aiming to wrest control from treasuries and development economists, brought about a shift in aid targets (Hulme 2009; Agarwal 2013). These targets now focused on newer areas such as the environment, improved governance, and strengthening civil society to improve delivery of government services, particularly for the poor.

Institution building and capacity creation

Several early aid programmes rested on the belief that developing countries needed technology, and skilled people to operate it, more than they needed financial assistance. Attempts to improve the technological capacity in developing countries preceded large financial transfers. In January 1949, President Truman announced his Four-Point Programme (Truman 1949), making US technical know-how and training available to developing countries. Meanwhile, former members of the British Empire established the Colombo Plan in 1949 to promote technical cooperation and assist in the sharing and transfer of technology among members. Originally projected as a six-year commitment, the Colombo Plan saw several extensions before becoming permanent in 1980. Its membership grew from the original seven members to twenty-seven, and has included both Commonwealth and non-Commonwealth members (Colombo Plan n.d.).

The effectiveness of aid

The debate on aid effectiveness historically has identified two concerns: first, whether aid substituted for domestic savings or resulted in increasing total investment; second, whether growth could even occur above a minimal level if the recipient country lacked the capacity to implement projects and programmes effectively (Mosley 1986; Burnside and Dollar 2000).

Aid and savings

Initial analysis using panel regression equations found a negative effect of aid on savings (Weisskopf 1972). This generated considerable controversy, along with further work that has clarified the issues. A broad consensus prevails, exemplified by a 2007 study (Shields 2007) which found that savings declined in only 9 of 119 countries (the increase in consumption proving greater than the incremental resources made available). In eight countries, the increase in savings was greater than the aid provided; here, aid had a 'crowding-in' effect. In the other countries, the levels of savings and investment proved higher than they would be in the absence of aid. Other estimates suggest that a 10 per cent increase in aid results in a 6.5 per cent increase in savings (Balde 2011); the marginal propensity to save from aid is 0.65, much higher than the marginal propensity to save from income.

Aid and growth

Meta-analysis (Tseday and Tarp 2011) showed that the average effect of aid on growth after the Second World War was a positive and statistically significant 0.16. Given the previous estimate of the effect on savings, this would imply an incremental capital output ratio of about 4, supported by other evidence (Agarwal 2008). In other words, aid generally increases the growth rate because of its positive effect on savings and investment.

The growth effect depends on the quality of institutions and policy design (Burnside and Dollar 2000; Hansen and Tarp 2000). But no agreement has arisen on the institutions necessary to produce positive aid outcomes. The literature often stresses institutions that exist only in developed countries and not in developing ones (Chang 2002). But in analysing European patterns of growth, Gerschenkron (1962) has found that the art of policymaking may substitute for institutional lacks, with success depending on *appropriate* substitution (see also Chang 2002). Attempts to follow Western institutions blindly have little likelihood of success.

India's development strategy: the role of external factors

Aid to India has come in many forms. We have already mentioned the financial resources and foreign help in providing technology and developing capacity. But a continuous interaction has also evolved between Indian policymakers and foreign economists in particular. Whether they favoured economic planning or not, many foreign economists did engage in the policy debates shaping Indian economic development policies after independence. This dialogue about appropriate development policies continues based on the experience of different countries.

At the beginning of planning in 1951, Indian policymakers sought a development strategy that would take into account the major structural constraints of the economy, the low level of savings, the very limited scope of the industrial sector, and the low level of agricultural output (Bhagwati and Chakravarty 1969). Because of limited import capacity, a high rate of growth required that the necessary capital goods be produced domestically (Mahalanobis 1953; 1955).

Financial aid

In the postindependence period, Indian policymakers believed that financing the current account deficit (CAD) – a product of efforts to raise the investment rate and thereby raise the rate of gross domestic product (GDP) growth – would not prove difficult, given their large accumulation of foreign exchange reserves.

However, the drawdown of the foreign balances proved much more rapid than anticipated, leading to a BOP crisis in 1958.[4] India then followed a pattern of behaviour repeated in later BOP crises. The government tightened import controls, cut back on investment (thereby reducing capital goods imports), and sought new sources of financing (Agarwal 1997). It approached the World Bank for assistance and received a favourable response echoed in the United States.[5]

Aid helped to raise investment considerably, from about 10 per cent to about 15 per cent. Aid accounted for about a sixth of gross fixed capital formation in the Second and Third Five Year Plans (1957–1967; Table 2.1). Going by the aforementioned calculations, aid therefore added almost 100 basis points to the growth

Table 2.1 India aid inflows, gross fixed capital formation, foreign direct investment, and external debt on goods and services, First through Eleventh Plans, 1951–2011 (GDP %)

Plan	Net Official Development Aid	Net Aid(% of GFCF)	GFCF	FDI Net Inflow	EDGS
First Plan (1951–1955)	0.4	4.2	9.5		−0.2
Second Plan (1956–1960)	2.3	17.7	13.0		2.8
Third Plan (1961–1966)	1.9	13.1	14.3		1.8
Fourth Plan (1969–1973)	1.2	8.4	14.3		0.2
Fifth Plan (1974–1978)	1.2	7.0	16.6		0.5
Sixth Plan (1980–1984)	0.9	4.5	19.0		2.2
Seventh Plan (1985–1989)	0.7	2.8	21.7	.1	1.6
Eighth Plan (1992–1996)	0.6	2.6	22.7	.4	0.7
Ninth Plan (1997–2001)	0.3	1.4	23.8	.8	1.4
Tenth Plan (2001–2006)	0.2	0.6	27.7	1.1	1.9
Eleventh Plan (2007–2011)	0.2	0.4	31.9	2.4	5.1

Source: Reserve Bank of India (2012)

rate. The stoppage of aid in the mid-1960s resulted in a collapse of this strategy and the adoption of a new approach (Agarwal 1997).

The effect of aid also appears in the reduction in the growth rate after the aid withdrawal in the mid-1960s. Growth of GDP plummeted from about 4.5 per cent a year to about 2 per cent, although not all of this is attributable to the stoppage. Although large in absolute amounts, Indian aid had less significance relative to GDP or investment than in many other countries (Bhagwati 1970). When aid resumed in the early 1970s, it never became quantitatively as important as previously. Although the average share of gross fixed capital formation (GFCF) in GDP increased in successive Plans, the importance of aid decreased. Even so, during the Fifth and Sixth Plans (1975–1984) aid comprised almost 5 per cent of GFCF, implying a growth rate increase of about one percentage point. Meanwhile, the importance of foreign direct investment (FDI) inflows increased, and these have proven significant since the Ninth Plan (1997–2001).

Aid played a critical role in the government's development strategy. In the Second (1956–1960) and Third (1961–1965) Plans, this strategy depended on government reinvestment of the capital goods produced by public-sector units. Aid financed almost a third of government investment. The cutback in US and World Bank aid in the mid-1960s, therefore, had serious consequences. The US and World Bank assistance, pledged through the Aid India Consortium, was slashed from USD 545 million and USD 320 million, respectively, in 1961–1962 to only USD 8.7 million and USD 15 million, respectively, in 1968–1969 (Lele and Bumb 1994). Overall, this led to a cutback in external assistance loans from about USD 1 billion in 1961–1962 to USD 318 million in 1968–1969. The resumption of aid in the early 1970s was mostly multilateral and mainly from the World Bank – particularly its 'soft' arm, the International Development Association (IDA)[6] (Table 2.2).

Table 2.2 India aid inflows: multilateral and bilateral grants and loans, 1962–2011

Plan	Multilateral Loans (%)	Grants (%) Total	
	Total	Multilateral	Bilateral
Third Plan (1961–1966)	7.8	8.8	50.1
Fourth Plan (1969–1973)	18.3	21.0	23.2
Fifth Plan (1974–1978)	36.4	21.9	44.1
Sixth Plan (1980–1984)	54.7	16.6	56.7
Seventh Plan (1985–1989)	45.3	21.4	50.0
Eighth Plan (1992–1996)	39.2	18.5	44.9
Ninth Plan (1997–2001)	41.6	15.4	42.5
Tenth Plan (2001–2006)	43.9	19.0	55.7
Eleventh plan (2007–2011)	36.2	24.2	37.3

Source: OECD (2015)

Multilateral institutions provided almost 50 per cent of the total aid to India up to the Eleventh Plan (2007–2011), when India began to graduate from recipient status. The World Bank Group's share rose from a mere 11.3 per cent in the Third Five-Year Plan (1961–1965) to over a half for the Sixth Plan (GOI 1961; 1976). Forty per cent of IDA funding was allocated to India, apparently with the tacit approval of the United States, its majority shareholder. Furthermore, grants comprised a significant share of bilateral aid, but much less of multilateral aid, most of which came at very soft terms from IDA. Overall, India was the largest recipient of aid from the World Bank, receiving an accumulated net amount over USD 20 billion in historical-year dollars (much less than if measured in current dollars) from 1951 through 1989 (Kamath 1992).

The economy barely grew during 1967–1973 because of the aid cut-off and other shocks. It had grown at 4 per cent during 1956–1964, an acceleration from the 3.6 per cent rate achieved during the First Plan – itself a sharp contrast with the stagnation of the 50 years before independence (Blynn 1966). Public-sector GFCF declined from 8.4 per cent of GDP during the Third Plan, 1961–1965, to 7 per cent during the Fourth Plan 1969–1973, because of the aid cutback. The economy had to depend more on domestic savings, both public and private, which increased from 14.3 per cent in the Third Plan to 17 per cent in the Fourth Plan.

Aid and creation of technological capacity

Ever since independence in 1947, the government of India has stressed the importance of aid in overcoming the technical inadequacies in the economy and the shortage of skilled personnel. This capacity building would arrive in a number of forms (Parthasarathi 2015; Ray 2015).

Efforts to overcome the skills shortage predate the beginning of planning; in fact, they started before independence. Sir Ardeshir Dalal, a member of the Viceroy's Executive Council, foresaw that India's future prosperity would depend on technology; in 1946 he proposed the creation of the Council of Scientific and Industrial Research. To staff these laboratories, he persuaded the US government to offer hundreds of doctoral fellowships under the Technology Cooperation Mission programme. By the early 1960s, India had signed agreements with almost all developed countries to provide scholarships and fellowships to Indians. Furthermore, Dalal realised the necessity of training personnel domestically and envisioned institutes to accomplish this – the origin, apparently, of the Indian Institutes of Technology (IITs). The Indian government set up five IITs in the 1950s and 1960s, often with cooperation from foreign institutions. For instance, a consortium of nine US universities provided inputs for the new Kanpur IIT and supported teacher exchanges over several years; the Bombay IIT received Soviet assistance, and the Madras IIT got help from Germany (Bassett 2009).

Aid also diversified India's industrial structure with establishment of capital goods industries. This allowed higher levels of investment without strain on the current account. Creating capacities for this sector required foreign technical assistance. For instance, three steel plants were initially set up with financial and technical assistance from the United Kingdom, Germany, and the Soviet Union. The Indian government insisted in each case that the aid donors transfer the technology and train Indians in order to develop domestic capacity, efforts that eventually succeeded (Parthasarathi 2015); Indians undertook all subsequent plant expansions. In general, the Soviet Union proved the most willing and effective aid partner, both in transferring technology and training Indian personnel.

Foreign expertise had other uses. US food aid played an important role in meeting the Indian food production shortfall. To tackle the problems of the agricultural sector, the Indian government set up committees to analyse it and to strategize means of overcoming the gap. Experts from the United States, usually supplied by the Ford and Rockefeller foundations, served on many of these committees (Lele and Agarwal 1991).

India's aid experience: the international and political dimension

Initially, prior to the BOP crisis of 1958, aid consisted mainly of technical and food assistance; the latter helped bridge the growing gap between supply and demand and freed resources for investment, including the use of under- and unemployed rural labour, as per the balanced growth approach (Rosenstein-Rodan 1943; Nurkse 1953). From 1958 to the mid-1960s, India received significant amounts of both food aid and bilateral aid, mainly from the United States, with the latter helping to build up industrial capacity. When aid resumed in the early 1970s after the mid-1960s cut-off, it primarily took the form of soft multilateral aid from IDA. From about the mid-1980s to the present, the importance of aid has dwindled, and India has even sought to limit bilateral aid to only a few significant lenders. This phase will likely continue (particularly when India graduates from IDA within a few years); since the mid-1990s, inflows of private capital, chiefly FDI and remittances, have grown significantly.

Dependence on bilateral aid

Most of the aid during the 1950s bridged the growing supply–demand gap for food grains, and came primarily from the United States under Public Law 480 governing commodity aid (U.S. Senate 1976). This aid eased the pressure on the current account, as well as on prices. Establishment of heavy industries during the Second Five-Year Plan, 1956–1960, required foreign financial and technical assistance (GOI 1956). Furthermore, a BOP crisis erupted in 1958, requiring the Indian government to approach the World Bank for financial relief. As noted earlier, this came largely from the World Bank and the United States, with the latter also mobilising resources from other developed countries (see Table 2.2 for the importance of bilateral aid). Meanwhile, food aid from the United States continued to grow, especially during the droughts and poor harvests in the mid-1960s.

This dependence, however, had political ramifications. For instance, after the poor 1950 harvest, the Indian government requested food aid from the US government. However, when India voted against the US-sponsored United Nations resolution branding China the aggressor in the Korean War, the US Senate decided to postpone consideration of India's request, pending a re-examination of Indo-US relations (Eldridge 1969). The United States, and only the United States, suspended its aid in the mid-1960s, ostensibly because of differences regarding agricultural policies (Bowles 1971). Indian requirements, particularly of food aid, had grown large enough to alarm the US administration and raise questions about its capacity to meet them. However, the agriculture ministers in the Indian and US governments had already reached agreement over agricultural policies. Many analysts believe that the main reason for the aid suspension was India's refusal to support US policies in Vietnam (Bowles 1971). When it became clear in 1963 that the US Congress, under pressure from domestic corporations, would not approve aid for the proposed fourth steel plant, the Indian government, at the request of President Kennedy, withdrew the request, and the Soviet Union stepped in to provide the assistance (Desai 1972).

As part of the agreement on agriculture in 1965, the United States provided considerable technological assistance and helped establish the institutions neces-sary to raise agricultural productivity – the so-called Green Revolution. But here again, President Johnson advised the Indian government to approach the founda-tions for help, because the US government would not be able to provide it (Lele and Goldsmith 1990).

India also reformed its trade and industrial policies in 1966, including a devalu-ation of the rupee and reform of the licensing system (Bhagwati and Desai 1970; Bhagwati and Srinivasan 1975). However, the government either could not or did not sustain these reforms. The donors delayed in providing the aid required to support this liberalisation, and when finally made available, it proved less than adequate. As Krueger (1978) has noted, in the short term liberalisation usually requires increased aid. Furthermore, because much of the bilateral aid came double-tied – both by the source and by required commodities imports – its full utilisation required licensing (Bhagwati 1970).

India's experience since the 1970s: the shift to multilateral aid

As noted earlier, when aid resumed in the 1970s, it came principally from mul-tilateral sources, mainly IDA (Table 2.2). This aid, less tied to foreign policy and political issues, proved more assured and less open to disruption. It also came with a continuous policy dialogue. The World Bank, however, has made no apparent attempt to impose its policy preferences on the Indian government. It has encouraged the Indian government to liberalise its trade and industrial poli-cies and to cut back on subsidies. However, because the change came after the 1991 BOP crisis, the role of this policy dialogue remains unclear; after all, some analysts – including Bhagwati, India's foremost trade economist – have advo-cated such reforms since the mid-1960s. In any event, subsidies reform has yet to take place, with analysts offering varying definitions (direct welfare vs. corpo-rate subsidy) according to their policy preferences.

India's multilateral aid experience also faces changes, as its share in the total has started to decline (Table 2.2) and will fall rapidly when India graduates from

IDA by June 2017. Although India could borrow from the World Bank, these loans are considerably more expensive – only slightly cheaper than market loans. As mentioned earlier, FDI, portfolio flows, and remittances have become much more significant. Indian policymakers will have to decide on their preferred structure of capital inflows.

Lessons for India's development cooperation programme

The changing character of Indian aid inflows over the period we have discussed has several implications for its own model of cooperation. In particular, India's experience with financial, technical, and training aid has shaped its own strategies. India has often faced aid conditionalities based on different economic models of development. It has also had to deal with pressures arising from its foreign policy choices. Its cooperation policies reflect a strong turn away from such limitations.

Importance of financial aid

The Indian experience shows the importance of financial aid in relaxing the savings, investment, and foreign exchange gaps, particularly in the early stages of development.

India also demonstrates the importance of aid reliability as sudden cut-offs prove costly. Aid may also act as insurance for new policies with uncertain outcomes[7] (Mellor 1979).

Capacity building

Aid to India has included two important forms of capacity building. First, India received aid to set up many heavy industry plants, with transfer of technology and training of Indian personnel as part of the aid package. When Western sources could not supply such aid, India had to depend on the Soviet Union. Second, India pursued capacity building through agreements with foreign governments that provided for scholarships and fellowships for Indians.

We believe that the IITs and Indian Institutes of Management (IIMs) created during this phase have played an important role in the upgrading of technology in Indian companies, in innovation, and in diffusing technologies developed elsewhere. We suspect that graduates of the IIMs have helped introduce improved management practices in companies. We now observe signs that suggest that IIT and IIM graduates have begun to create new ventures utilising modern technologies, even technologies that they have developed themselves.

Aid and policy design and implementation

Foreign experts played a role in the two major shifts in Indian policies, one in the mid-1960s and the other beginning in 1992.

Agricultural and trade policies changed substantially in the mid-1960s. The first grew out of long analysis with considerable foreign participation and took the form of a US–India agreement. It required a long-term commitment to develop the appropriate infrastructure, which came chiefly from US foundations (Lele and Goldsmith 1990). The second entailed a substantial rupee devaluation and reduction in tariffs and subsidies. But it proved short-lived, as no domestic political consensus on the reforms emerged (nor did studies that might have supported one), and it held an element of coercion by foreign donors. Furthermore, the trade reforms did not receive sufficient financial support (Bhagwati and Srinivasan 1975).

By contrast, the reforms in trade and industrial licensing begun in 1991 had a solid research foundation (Bhagwati and Desai 1970; Little, Scitovsky and Scott 1970; Bhagwati and Srinivasan 1975) that created a political consensus on policy change. The key lesson is that reform cannot be forced, but must grow from study and internal policy dialogue; foreigners may credibly participate in the former but not dictate the latter.

The Indian aid experience and the framework of development cooperation

India's experience as an aid recipient has influenced the evolution of international aid architecture, as well as its own development cooperation programme. Donors have set up other aid consortia similar to India's and have encouraged other governments to prepare detailed investment plans as a basis for aid.

India has also made important contributions to international thinking on aid-related issues, including the concept of program lending, the role of aid consortia, the development of project appraisal techniques, local cost financing, and the use of preferential treatment for local contracting industries to establish indigenous capacity (Mason and Asher 1973). India has also pioneered attempts to marry growth with social justice concerns, exploring the links between growth and poverty reduction; as noted earlier, India was the first nation to develop an official poverty line.

The impact of these cumulative experiences appears in a number of Indian cooperation policies and practices:

1   **Respect for the other country's sovereignty**. This is reflected in a lack of conditions in granting assistance. Reforms have to be constructed through research and dialogue.
2   **Avoidance of judgment about partner projects**. This also avoids disputes. India offers assistance in response to partner requests; it takes for granted the partner's ability to develop a coherent plan.
3   **Development cooperation to provide mutual benefits.** A substantial portion of the assistance comes through letters of credit spent on purchase of Indian goods. Mutual benefit should obviate the appearance of aid fatigue.
4   **Develop technological capabilities**. Having paid so much attention to its own capacity building, India now allocates significant resources to providing

scholarships at Indian institutions. In addition, India runs many domestic training programmes open to or dedicated to foreigners.

5 **Fewer aid restrictions**. Despite India's pioneering efforts in untying aid, its cooperation assistance continues to require purchase of Indian imports. However, aid is not double-tied, a factor that hampered India's reform efforts in the 1960s.

As India graduates to full donor status in the coming years, we should expect further developments in its cooperation programmes. In many ways, India serves as a paradigmatic emerging donor, one experienced in both the shocks and benefits of the older aid models, and capable of transmitting the best of its experience to its new partners. At the same time, it continues to recognise the key values of political dialogue and consensus building, both internally and internationally.

Notes

1 This chapter is part of research undertaken under an Ontario Research Fund project at the University of Western Ontario, Canada. I would like to thank Susmita Mitra and Sushil Kumar for assistance in writing this chapter. I would also like to thank the participants of the author's workshop for helpful comments. The views expressed, however, are those of the author, as are any mistakes.
2 The term derives from policy enforcement by the twin Bretton Woods Institutions, the International Monetary Fund (IMF) and the World Bank, both situated in Washington, DC (Williamson 1990).
3 The World Bank and the IMF in their reports on the Indian economy were a major source of this criticism.
4 Indian importers, anticipating a crisis as reserves fell, imported more goods than current consumption required, and this in itself contributed to the BOP crisis. As has become accepted theory in exchange rate crises models (Krugman 1979), at some stage when reserves run low but have not reached zero, such speculative attacks occur in anticipation of reserve depletion.
5 The US Senate adopted a resolution, sponsored by Senators Cooper and Kennedy, that India's economic development served US strategic interests.
6 The International Development Association, a member of the World Bank Group, provides concessional loans and grants.
7 Dr. Manmohan Singh, an important member of the Indian government's economic team in the 1970s and 1980s, stressed the importance of McNamara's assurance of further US aid when needed (McNamara 1973a); this assurance played a valuable role in prompting Indian policymakers to undertake policy changes. He said this in his comments on an earlier version of the paper by Lele and Agarwal (1991) when it was presented at a conference on aid and development at Talloires, France, in September 1987.

Works cited

Agarwal, M. (1997). Liberalization of the Indian economy. In P. Desai (ed.), *Going global: Transition from plan to market in the world economy*. Cambridge, MA: M.I.T Press, pp. 473–498.

Agarwal, M. (2008). The BRICSAM countries and changing economic power: Scenarios to 2050. *CIGI Working Paper*, 39. Centre for International Governance Innovation, Waterloo, Canada.

Agarwal, M. (2013). Reshaping international institutions for achieving MDGs. In H. Besada and S. Kindornay (eds.), *Multilateral development cooperation in a changing global order*. London: Macmillan Palgrave, pp. 36–62.

Balde, Y. (2011). The impact of remittances and foreign aid on savings/investment in sub-Saharan Africa (SSA). *African Development Review*, 23(2): 247–262.

Bassett, R. (2009). Aligning India's interests in the Cold War era. *Technology and Culture*, 50(4): 783–810.

Bhagwati, J. (1970). Amount and sharing of aid. Washington, DC: Overseas Development Council.

Bhagwati, J. (1993). *India in transition: Freeing the economy*. Oxford: Clarendon Press.

Bhagwati, J., and Chakravarty, S. (1969). Contributions to Indian economic analysis: A survey. *American Economic Review*, 59(4): 1–73.

Bhagwati, J., and Desai, P. (1970). *Planning for industrialization*. Oxford: Oxford University Press.

Bhagwati, J., and Srinivasan, T.N. (1975). *India: Anatomy and consequences of exchange control regimes*. New York: Columbia University Press.

Blynn, G. (1966). *Agricultural trends in India, 1891–1947: Output, availability and productivity*. Philadelphia: University of Pennsylvania Press.

Bottrall, A. (1974). The McNamara strategy: Putting precept into practice. Development Policy Review, A7(1): 70–80.

Bowles, C. (1971). *Promises to keep: My years in public life*. New York: Harper and Row.

Bruton, H. (1998). A reconsideration of import substitution. *Journal of Economic Literature*, 36(2): 903–936.

Burnside, C., and Dollar, D. (2000). Aid, policies and growth. *American Economic Review*, 90(4): 847–868.

Chang, H.-J. (2002). *Kicking away the ladder: Development strategy in historical perspective*. London: Anthem.

Chenery, H., and Bruno, M. (1962). Development alternatives in an open economy: The case of Israel. *Economic Journal*, 72(1): 79–93.

Chenery, H., and Strout, A. (1966). Foreign assistance and economic development. *American Economic Review*, 61(4): 679–733.

Colombo Plan (n.d.). *History* [webpage]. Available at www.colombo-plan.org/index.php/about-cps/history/.

Cornia, G.A., Jolly, R., and Stewart, F. (1987). *Adjustment with a human face: Protecting the vulnerable and promoting growth: A study by UNICEF*, Vol. 1. Oxford: Oxford University Press.

Dandekar, V.M., and Rath, N. (1971). Poverty in India, dimensions and trends. *Economic and Political Weekly*, 6(1–2): 25; 106.

Desai, P. (1972). *The Bokaro steel plant: A study of Soviet economic assistance*. Amsterdam: North Holland Publishing Company.

Domar, E. (1946). Capital expansion, rate of growth and employment. *Econometrica*, 14: 137–147.

Eldridge, P.J. (1969). *The politics of foreign aid in India*. London: Weidenfeld and Nicholson.

Gershenkron, A. (1962). *Economic backwardness in historical perspective, a book of essays*. Cambridge, MA: Belknap Press of Harvard University Press.

Government of India (GOI) (1951–1976). *Five year plans* [database]. New Delhi: Planning Commission of India. Available at http://planningcommission.nic.in/plans/planrel/fiveyr/welcome.html. [Accessed 7 September 2015].

Hansen, H., and Tarp, F. (2000). Aid effectiveness disputed. *Journal of International Development*, 12: 375–399.

Harrod, R.F. (1939). An essay in economic theory. *Economic Journal*, 49: 14–33.

Hulme, D. (2009). The Millennium Development Goals (MDGs): A short history of the world's biggest promise. *Brooks World Poverty Institute Working Paper*, 100. BWPI, University of Manchester.

Kamath, S.J. (1992). Foreign aid and India: Financing the Leviathan state. *Cato Policy Analysis*, 170. Cato Institute, Washington, DC. Available at www.cato.org/pubs/pas/pa-170.html.

Krueger, A. (1978). *Foreign trade and economic development: Liberalization attempts and consequences*. Cambridge, MA: Ballinger Publishing Company.

Krugman, P. (1979). A model of balance-of-payments crises. *Journal of Money, Credit and Banking*, 11(3): 311–325.

Lele, U., and Agarwal, M. (1991). Four decades of economic development in India and the role of external assistance. In U. LeLe and I. Nabi (eds.), *Transitions in development: The role of aid and commercial flows*. San Francisco: ICS Press.

Lele, U., and Bumb, B. (1994). *South Asia's food crisis: The case of India*. Washington, DC: The World Bank Group Publishing.

Lele, U., and Goldsmith, O. (1990). The development of national research capacity: India's experience with the Rockefeller Foundation and its significance for Africa. *Economic Development and Cultural Change*, 37(2): 305–343.

Little, I.A.M., Scitovsky, T., and Scott, M.F.H. (1970). *Industry and trade in some developing countries*. Oxford: Oxford University Press.

Mahalanobis, P.C. (1953). Some observations on the process of growth of national income. *Sankhya the Indian Journal of Statistics*, 12(4): 307–312.

Mahalanobis, P.C. (1955). The approach of operational research to planning in India. *Sankhya the Indian Journal of Statistics*, 16(12): 3–130.

Mason, E.S., and Asher, R.E. (1973). The World Bank since Bretton. Washington, DC: Brookings Institution Press.

McNamara, R. (1973a). *Address to the Board of Governors (Nairobi, September 24)*. Washington, DC: The World Bank.

McNamara, R. (1973b). *One hundred countries, two billion people: One dimension of development*. London: Praeger.

Mellor, J.W. (1979). The Indian economy: Objectives, performance and prospects. In J.W. Mellor (ed.), *India: A rising middle power*. Boulder, CO: Westview Press, pp. 85–110.

Mosley, P. (1986). Aid-effectiveness: The micro-macro paradox. *IDS Bulletin*, 17(2): 22–27.

Mosley, P., Harrigan, J., and Toye, J. (1995). Aid and power: The World Bank and policy-based lending. London: Routledge.

Nurkse, R. (1953). *Problems of capital formation in underdeveloped countries*. Oxford: Basil Blackwell.

Organisation for Economic Co-operation and Development (OECD) (2015). *OECD stat* [database]. Available at http://stats.oecd.org/.

Pant, P. et al (1962[0][0]). *Perspective of development, 1961–1976, implications of planning for a minimum level of living*. New Delhi: India Planning Commission.

Parthasarathi, A. (2015). S&T in the industrial development of China: Comparison with and implications for India. In M. Agarwal and J. Whalley (eds.), *Sustainability of growth: The role of economic, technological and environmental factors*, vol. 1. Singapore: World Scientific, pp. 173–200.

Prebisch, R. (1950). The economic development of Latin America and its principal problems. *Economic Bulletin for Latin America,* 7: 1–12.

Ray, A.S. (2015). The enigma of the 'Indian Model' of development. *CTD Discussion Paper,* 15–01. Centre for Trade and Development, School of International Studies at Jawaharlal Nehru University, New Delhi.

Reserve Bank of India (1958–2006). *Database on India's economy; RBI's data warehouse* [database]. Available at http://dbie.rbi.org.in/DBIE/dbie.rbi?site=home.

Reserve Bank of India (2012). *Foreign direct investment flows into India* [webpage]. Available at www.rbi.org.in/scripts/bs_viewcontent.aspx?Id=2513.

Rosenstein-Rodan, P. (1943). Problems of industrialisation of Eastern and South Eastern Europe. *Economic Journal,* 53: 202–211.

Shields, M.P. (2007). Foreign aid and domestic savings: The crowding out effect. *Monash Economics Working Papers,* 35–07. Monash University, Department of Economics, Monash, Australia. Available at www.buseco.monash.edu.au/eco/research/papers/2007/3507foreignaid.pdf.

Singh, C.P. (1989). *Poverty alleviation policy under the plans.* New Delhi: Indus Publishing Company.

Streeten, P., Burki, S., Haq, M. ul, Hicks, N., and Stewart, F. (1981). *First things first: Meeting basic human needs in developing countries.* London: Oxford University Press.

Toye, J. (1987). *Dilemmas of development: Reflections on the counter-revolution in development theory and policy.* Oxford: Basil Blackwell.

Truman, H.S. (1949). Inaugural Address, January 20, 1949. Online by G. Peters and J.T. Woolley, *The American Presidency Project.* Available at www.presidency.ucsb.edu/ws/?pid=13282. [Accessed 29 October 2015].

Tseday, J.M., and Tarp, F. (2011). Aid and growth: What meta-analysis reveals. *Journal of Development Studies,* 49(4): 564–583.

United States Senate Committee on Agriculture and Forestry (U.S. Senate) (1976). *American foreign countries' food assistance public law 480 and related materials.* Washington, DC: US Government. Available at http://archive.org/stream/amereignf00unit/amereignf00unit_djvu.txt. [Accessed 7 September 2015].

Weisskopf, T. (1972). The impact of foreign capital inflows on domestic savings in underdeveloped countries. *Journal of International Economics,* 2: 25–38.

Williamson, J. (ed.) (1990). *Latin American adjustment: How much has happened.* Washington, DC: Peterson Institute for International Economics.

3 India's development cooperation through capacity building

Kumar Tuhin[1]

Introduction

The Indian Technical and Economic Cooperation (ITEC) Programme began on 15 September 1964, with the Cabinet decision to institute a bilateral program of governmental assistance. Born from the vision of India's first prime minister (PM), Jawaharlal Nehru, and formally launched under Lal Bahadur Shastri, the second PM, the creation of ITEC reflected their desire for relations of interdependence and mutual assistance between the countries of the world, based on commonly held ideas and aspirations. The spirit of shared knowledge would become the basis for technical and economic cooperation, considered an intrinsic component of India's foreign policy postindependence. India's development cooperation has since evolved to encompass partnerships with fellow developing countries under the framework of South-South cooperation. India's development compact highlights capacity building and technology transfers as key components and considers financial instruments such as lines of credit, investments, preferential trade financing, grants, and so forth as supplements to the array of available interventions (MEA 2015a).

ITEC came into existence just as countries in Asia, Africa, and Latin America gained independence from colonial rule. All these countries laboured under the retarding effects of colonialism and faced the challenge of advancing the social and economic well-being of their peoples. Most had major bottlenecks due to deficits in skilled labour, experts, financial resources, and technology transfers. Some faced such huge gaps that cooperation with developing countries mattered as much as assistance from developed ones or from international organisations. The ITEC program was India's earnest attempt to share its own experiences and achievements with other developing countries.

This chapter provides an overview of the history and profile of the ITEC. The first section will address its philosophy and background, including Indian efforts in capacity building prior to the creation of ITEC. This will lead to a discussion of ITEC's framework and operations (including its current statistical profile), and then a brief overview of the technical cooperation programmes of a few select countries – Malaysia, Thailand, and Brazil. The next section will touch on ways to improve ITEC's operations, before concluding with some reflections on its special role in South-South cooperation.

ITEC: philosophy and historical context

Although ITEC was formally launched in 1964, India has provided human resources assistance to developing countries since independence in 1947. For example, in 1949 the Indian government provided seventy scholarships to students from other countries, aiming to enhance cultural relations with (particularly) Asian and African countries while facilitating higher education cooperation (Kumar 1987). Scholarships and educational exchange remain a significant part of ITEC activity to this day.

The knowledge sharing has continued ever since. For example, the Green Revolution of the 1960s and the White (dairy) Revolution of the 1980s increased the demand among developing countries for Indian agricultural and dairy training. Various countries transitioning from communist to market economies received training at eminent Indian institutions such as the Entrepreneurship Development Institute (EDI) (Chaturvedi 2015). An outgrowth of similar historical and developmental circumstances, ITEC provided a platform to showcase India's solidarity with fellow developing countries. ITEC originated in India's own experience during and after its independence struggle, with the recognition that capacity building and technical cooperation play critical roles in a nation's economic growth and independent policymaking. It therefore provides technical cooperation that is bilateral in nature, demand driven, and focused on addressing the needs of developing countries (Nehru 1948).

India's assistance to developing countries between 1947 and 1964 took place through multilateral assistance frameworks under the auspices of the Commonwealth and United Nations. The former included the Colombo Plan for Economic Development and Cooperation in South and South East Asia (Colombo Plan), launched in 1950, and the Special Commonwealth African Assistance Programme (SCAAP) begun in 1960; the latter included contributions to the United Nations Development Programme (UNDP) (Chaturvedi 2012).

The SCAAP was created after the September 1960 meeting of the Commonwealth Economic Consultative Council, which resolved to expand the assistance outflow to African Commonwealth countries. These programmes provided India with strategic opportunities to engage with the newly independent countries of Asia and Africa. The Ministry of External Affairs of India played a significant role in shaping programmes and technical assistance under the SCAAP and the Colombo Plan. A unique turnaround in a matter of decades saw India – dependent on other countries for expertise until the 1950s – itself become an exporter of experts, training foreign nationals in various fields (MEA 2013). By 1966, it had emerged as the fifth largest contributor to SCAAP after the United Kingdom, Canada, Australia, and New Zealand (MEA 1971).

The 1950s saw India expanding its bilateral initiatives in education and technical cooperation, well before the creation of ITEC: several scholarship programmes brought Asian and African students to India, beginning as early as 1949 and increasing in numbers and scope in the early 1950s. These programmes included training in cottage industries as well as in various schools; much of the sharing and technology transfer occurred under the auspices of the Colombo Plan, of which India was a founding member in 1950. Afghanistan regularly received assistance during this period, welcoming Indian teachers, communications and meteorological equipment, and advisors on the development of cottage and small-scale industries – all aimed at transferring expertise and training (Colombo Plan n.d.; MEA 2015b). Similarly, 200 Indian doctors served in Myanmar in 1952 under terms approved by the Indian government; Nepal received slots in technical schools for around 200 nationals in 1954–1955, and one of its senior officials completed a six-month training residency in the Ministry of External Affairs (MEA 2015b). Such efforts represent the beginning of an assistance strategy that has since retained a strong neighbourhood focus.

Although in its present form ITEC has become synonymous with training and capacity-building programmes for foreign officials, it initially served as an arm of India's nascent development cooperation scheme – the means through which it channelled various forms of assistance. These included training in Indian facilities for foreign nationals; deputation of Indian experts abroad; and gifts of capital goods, equipment, drugs, and medicines.[2] Moreover, ITEC took on the financing of feasibility studies for development work in partner countries (as in Libya in 1972) and administered special projects in countries that had economic agreements with India. The latter included agricultural and hospital projects in Afghanistan and archaeological conservation efforts in Cambodia, Lao PDR, and Vietnam (MEA 1971).

Although such efforts reflected emerging economic realities and partnerships, India's educational cooperation actually has much deeper roots. Ancient India had numerous seats of learning that attracted scholars, students, and travellers from far-off countries, such as the Nalanda and Taxila monasteries; the latter has the distinction of being one of the oldest known universities in the world (Monroe 1918). Nalanda and Taxila assisted scholars and students through critical dialectics, discussions, and exchange of ideas (Scharfe 2002). In its own unique way, ITEC has continued this tradition by empowering many trainees from distant corners of the globe, developing human resources, and building bridges of friendship.

ITEC: framework and operations

ITEC framework of demand-driven partnerships

A crucial aspect of ITEC's assistance is that it responds to demand: it extends training programmes to nominees from recipient countries in the developing world in response to their specific requirements (MEA 2015a). The wide range of ITEC study programs – circulated annually among the partner countries in a comprehensive brochure – likewise reflects specific requests that have emerged over the years, including highly specialised ones. For example, India's own experiences in boosting rice production during the Green Revolution in the 1960s created better understanding of other developing countries' agricultural needs. Building on this experience, India began extending support to the Vietnamese agricultural sector in 1976–1977, offering ITEC scholarships in agricultural research and development.

Furthermore, ITEC response to specific training requests from Cambodia, Lao PDR, Myanmar and Vietnam (CLMV) has facilitated private-sector development and entrepreneurship in these countries. India has taken this opportunity to expand its commitment towards the Initiative for ASEAN Integration (IAI), an Association of Southeast Asian Nations (ASEAN)–led effort to reduce the gap between the advanced ASEAN members and the new ones from the CLMV region (OECD 2012). The Indian initiatives included the Laos-India Entrepreneurship Development Centre (LIEDC), Vientiane, created in 2004, followed by similar centres in Cambodia, Vietnam, and Myanmar. The Indian government has also announced entrepreneurship development centre initiatives for several African countries. In due course, some of these India-created centres have received additional support from multilateral agencies such as the World Bank (Chaturvedi 2015).

ITEC has traditionally had five components: (1) India-based professional training, covering topics such as trade, investment, and technology, with candidates chosen by the ITEC partner countries (this would include support for several training programmes conceived under multilateral processes)[3]; (2) projects and related activities, including feasibility studies and consultancy services; (3) deputation of Indian experts abroad; (4) study and fact-finding tours; and (5) assistance for disaster relief (Chaturvedi et al. 2014). However, ITEC's biggest strength remains its training for professionals from partner countries.

ITEC programs cover a truly impressive range of specialisations and engage both public and private institutions across India. ITEC-sponsored curricula include courses in accounting, audits, banking, finance and microfinance, and rural development; they also train visiting officials in diverse areas, such as public expenditure management, government accounts, and public-sector enterprise audits.[4]

Courses reflect India's technological and workforce strengths: curricula in information technology, telecommunication, management, and other technical fields have helped build the human resource capacity of the developing world. IT and telecommunication courses include multimedia and web design, telemedicine, database management, geographic information systems (GIS), and programming languages.[5] ITEC has expanded its list of panel institutions; for example, it recently added a one-year executive management course at the Indian Institute of Management at Ahmedabad.[6] Other special courses and training programmes address a range of specific partner-country requests.[7]

Exposure to varied global practices widens the opportunities for mutual learning, enabling partner economies to pursue best practices and design effective development policy architecture in their countries. Courses on security-related topics broaden understanding and also increase the scope of collective response to terrorism, fraud, and international crimes. Such forms of targeted intervention in capacity building – often in response to partner country requests – ensure dissemination of India's development narrative and help lay a firm foundation of solidarity among developing countries in global platforms. This in turn helps ensure that when India's ITEC partners engage with global institutions, they achieve optimum returns for their capacity-building and development efforts (MEA 2009).

Although India initially envisaged ITEC as an essentially bilateral programme, in recent years its resources have also gone to programs conceived in regional and inter-regional contexts, such as the Economic Commission for Africa, the Industrial Development Unit of the Commonwealth Secretariat, the United Nations Industrial Development Organization (UNIDO), and the Groups of 77 and 15 (Chaturvedi, Fues and Sidiropoulos, 2012). Lately, ITEC has also engaged with regional and multilateral organisations, including ASEAN, the Bay of Bengal Initiative for Multi-Sectoral Technical and Economic Cooperation (BIMSTEC), the Mekong-Ganga Cooperation (MGC), the African Union (AU), AARDO, the Pan-African Parliament, the Caribbean Community (CARICOM), the World Trade Organization (WTO), the Indian Ocean Rim-Association for Regional Cooperation (IOR-ARC) and the India-Africa Forum Summit (MEA 2015b). This expanded partnership scope suggests wider recognition for both India's role in SSC and the specific contributions of ITEC.

ITEC operations

India has laboured to give voice to the South in global decision making on financial and security architectures, as well as acting as a link between South and North in bodies such as the G20. As a result, India modified its stand on both accepting and giving aid in 2002–2003, adding nuance to its view of both roles (Chaturvedi et al. 2014). This shift in India's development cooperation policy resulted in a new division for managing assistance outflows (Srinivasan 2007), an important step. The government of India announced in 2007 that it would create the India International Development Cooperation Agency (IIDCA) to provide this unified administration; however, after long delays and a lack of consensus between ministries, the government dropped the idea of establishing a unique aid-coordinating body (Quadir 2013).

In January 2012 the MEA replaced the idea of an IIDCA with its own internal entity, the Development Partnership Administration (DPA). The DPA announcement appears for the first time in the 2012 MEA Annual Report. As the name indicates, this is not a freestanding agency, but rather one among several MEA divisions – apparently set up after considering the structure and functions of early Western aid agencies (Srinivasan 2007), and intended as something less than a fully autonomous development cooperation body.

Within DPA, DPA-I administers the lines of credit (LOCs) and all grant projects in Africa, DPA-II covers disaster relief, capacity-building schemes (including ITEC), and grant projects in certain global regions (neither African nor South Asian), and DPA-III oversees grant projects in India's neighbourhood. However, as of 2014–2015, the government of India's budget continues to report all development cooperation under the heading 'Technical & Economic Cooperation with Other Countries and Advances to Foreign Governments'; within this grouping, ITEC appears as a separate category. This official use of ITEC – at times representing only technical and economic training, and at others used synonymously with Indian development cooperation as a whole – reflects its evolution from a small initiative focused on training to a development cooperation programme with broad and increasing significance (Ranganathan 2012).

With the establishment of the DPA, India has pursued its emphasis on capacity-building cooperation and continues to stress human resource development as a tool of inclusive economic growth in developing countries. DPA's mandate is to ensure swift and efficient implementation of Indian development assistance programmes, which have expanded both in volume and in geography. This mandate includes streamlining and upgrading capacity-building programmes under ITEC and other schemes. In hindsight, this seems a far more balanced approach than what preceded it, as it better positions the MEA to link up the various divisions dealing with development cooperation and the evaluation of credit lines and projects (see Box 3.1).

Box 3.1 Capacity building through ITEC: a statistical profile

A review of successive budget figures provides a picture of long-term trends in ITEC activity – in particular, its financing and allocation of slots and the participation of partner countries.

Budget allocation

The budget allocated for technical assistance under the ITEC saw a jump from USD 900,000 in 1964–1965 to USD 1.34 million in the financial year 1971–1972. By 2013–2014, it had reached USD 34.51 million (ITEC plus SCAAP plus Colombo Plan) (MEA 2013). Figure 3.1 demonstrates

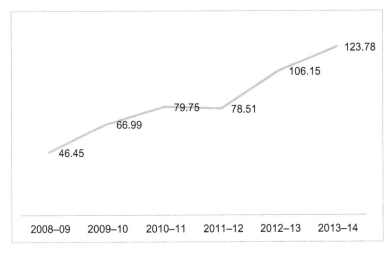

Figure 3.1 Growth in budget allocation for ITEC, fiscal 2008–2013

Table 3.1 Monetary allocations for LOCs versus ITEC, SCAAP, and TCS, fiscal 2008–2013

Year	Line of Credit (USD Million PPP)	ITEC/SCAAP/TCS (USD Million PPP)
2008–2009	1832.51	46.45
2009–2010	3343.21	66.99
2010–2011	6946.39	79.75
2011–2012	1714.42	78.51
2012–2013	609.45	106.15
2013–2014	5380.10	123.78

Source: MEA (2007–2013)

growth in budget allocation for ITEC over the past seven years in terms of purchasing power parity (PPP).

Over the same period (2008–2014), India's overall support for development in partner countries has also grown significantly. The monetary allocations for ITEC, SCAAP, and the Technical Cooperation Scheme (TCS) come into focus in comparison with India's LOC commitments (Table 3.1).

This demonstrates that technical cooperation and capacity building, despite their immense significance in India's assistance profile, account for a relatively small portion of total outflows. Nonetheless, they have tended to grow in line with the overall growth of India's portfolio.

Courses and slots

By the end of 1978, about 500 Indian technical experts were deputed abroad, and about 1200 foreign officials annually received training in various Indian institutions. This trend perfectly coincided with the 1978 Buenos Aires Plan of Action for Promoting and Implementing Technical Cooperation among developing countries, which in turn helped shape the course of the UNIDO strategy (UNIDO 2015). UNIDO's objective – providing rich and diverse opportunities for forging mutually beneficial South-South partnerships, thus promoting economic growth, industrial development, and poverty reduction – aligns precisely with the ITEC ethos.

In 2014–2015, the MEA (2015b) estimates that ITEC offered over 10,000 scholarship slots in diverse subjects (see 'ITEC framework of demand-driven partnerships'). Forty-seven empanelled institutions now conduct around 280 courses annually. Similarly, ITEC organises training programmes for defence personnel on security and strategic studies, defence management, marine and aeronautical engineering, logistics and management, marine hydrography, counterinsurgency, etc.; these take place in prestigious institutions such as the National Defence College and Defence Services Staff College, covering all three armed forces wings – Army,

Navy, and Air Force. Table 3.2 shows the distribution of civilian and security-related courses covered under ITEC.

The DPA-II division also handles allocations of slots to different countries, in consultation with the territorial divisions concerned; in 2012–2013, it managed over 8500 civilian and 1500 defence training slots, allocated to 161 partner countries under ITEC /SCAAP/[Columbo Plan] TCS. Figure 3.2 illustrates the growth in participant numbers since 2008. The latest statistics (Table 3.3) show that as of 2013–2014, the number

Table 3.2 Types of courses covered under ITEC, fiscal 2008–2013

Series	Name
1.	Accounts, Audit, Banking, and Finance Courses (across three institutes in India)
2.	IT, Telecommunication, and English Courses (across eight institutes in India)
3.	Management Courses (across four institutes in India)
4.	SME/Rural Development Courses (across four institutes in India)
5.	Specialised Courses (across twelve institutes in India)
6.	Technical Courses (across twelve institutes in India)
7.	Environment and Renewable Energy Courses (across four institutes in India)
8.	Technical Cooperation Scheme of Colombo Plan (across nine institutes in India)

Source: MEA (2007–2013)

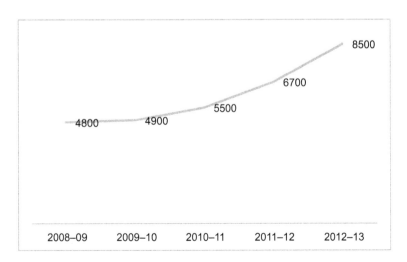

Figure 3.2 Growth in number of participants under ITEC/SCAAP/TCS, fiscal 2008–2012

of partner countries covered separately under ITEC, SCAAP, and TCS stands at 179.[8]

Although ITEC's partner countries come from all over the developing world, their geographical distribution reflects a closer association with neighbouring and African countries. Table 3.4 shows the regional distribution of the ITEC program, and Table 3.5 tabulates the top ten partner countries for ITEC/SCAAP from 2008–2013.

Table 3.3 Partner countries under ITEC/SCAAP/TCS, 2013

Name of the Scheme	Number of Countries
Indian Technical and Economic Cooperation (ITEC)	142
Special Commonwealth Assistance for Africa Programme (SCAAP)	19
Technical Cooperation Scheme of Colombo Plan Countries (TCS)	18

Source: MEA (2013)

Table 3.4 Regional distribution of ITEC programme participants, 2013

Region	Composition (share of slots in % terms)
Asia	44
Africa	44
Americas	4
Multilateral Agencies	2
Europe	2
Others	4

Source: MEA (2014)

Table 3.5 Top ten partner countries for ITEC/SCAAP civilian training slots, fiscal 2008–2012

Series	Country	2008–09	2009–10	2010–11	2011–12	2012–13
1.	Afghanistan	500	500	500	505	505
2.	Myanmar	100	100	140	145	430
3.	Tanzania	110	120	130	165	200
4.	Nepal	80	80	90	100	200
5.	Bangladesh	100	100	175	180	185
6.	Mauritius	65	80	90	135	170
7.	Nigeria	85	85	90	145	160
8.	Ethiopia	50	70	90	135	150
9.	Zimbabwe	50	60	90	110	150
10.	Sudan	130	130	130	150	150

Source: MEA (2008–2013)

Some overall trends worth noting: (1) the period since 2008 has witnessed a dramatic increase in both budgets and participants in capacity-
building programmes, solidifying their centrality in India's cooperation
strategy; (2) ITEC continues to account for the lion's share of course slots
and offerings, despite the contributions of the multilateral programmes such
as SCAAP and TCS; and (3) the geographical spread overwhelmingly leans
toward Asian and African partner countries, with Afghanistan and Myanmar at the top of ITEC slots. For all the global reach of ITEC, it retains a
neighbourhood core.

Technical cooperation by other emerging economies

We may better appreciate and assess India's development cooperation and partnership strategy through a review of similar capacity-building programmes in
other developing countries: Malaysian and Thai efforts in Asia, along with Brazil's work in Latin America and Africa. Although they share some common features, each of these efforts caters to specific priorities that differ from India's in
revealing ways.

Malaysia

Of the three countries, Malaysia's programme most closely resembles India's, and
may have taken it as a model to a degree. In the spirit of South-South cooperation, Malaysia shares its experiences and expertise with other developing countries through the Malaysian Technical Cooperation Programme (MTCP) (MFAM
2013). The MTCP initiative rests on the belief that the development of a country
depends on the quality of its human resources, an emphasis equally marked in
the case of the ITEC. The programme forms part of the Malaysian government's
commitment to promote technical cooperation and collective self-reliance among
developing countries, along with strengthened regional and subregional cooperation (MFAM 2013).

Both the Indian and Malaysian programmes share a background in Commonwealth platforms as well. The MTCP originated at the first Commonwealth Heads
of Government Meeting for the Asia-Pacific Region in Sydney in February 1978.
Its official launch took place on 7 September 1980 at the Commonwealth Heads
of State Meeting in New Delhi (MFAM 2013).

Similar in spirit to the ITEC, the MTCP focuses on the development of human
resources through training in various essential development fields: public administration, health services, education, sustainable development, agriculture, poverty
alleviation, investment promotion, information and communication technologies,
and banking. Most of the training occurs in about 100 short-term specialised
courses offered by seventy-nine MTCP training institutions, many of them recognised centres of excellence. Since its launch, more than 25,000 participants

from 140 countries have benefited from the various programmes offered under the MTCP (MFAM 2013). The programme's success, like India's, reflects an expansion beyond the original regional base and a strong emphasis on transfer of skills to partner countries.

Thailand

Through its Thailand International Cooperation Agency (TICA), Thailand has promoted technical assistance to its neighbours for over 30 years. Such assistance comes under various frameworks at the bilateral, subregional, regional, trilateral, and multilateral levels. Thailand has also implemented bilateral cooperation with other developing countries, following the adoption of the Buenos Aires Plan. TICA administers Thai international development cooperation projects, including the award of more than 1500 fellowships annually to developing countries. In the past, Thailand's bilateral programmes had mainly served immediate neighbours; more recently, the program has expanded to other developing countries such as Timor Leste, Sri Lanka, and some African countries (TICA 2013).

TICA programmes focus mainly on human resources development in three main areas: education, health, and agriculture. Activities cover training, dispatching of Thai experts, and provision of equipment; they include programmes tailored to partner country needs and identifying and designing special courses accordingly. A significant portion of Thai efforts are multilateral: TICA has also worked closely with traditional donors such as Japan and Canada at the bilateral level, and under the partnership frameworks of trilateral cooperation, including the Colombo Plan, UNDP, United Nations Population Fund (UNFPA), and the United Nations Children's Fund (UNICEF). Thailand also uses its technical cooperation resources to promote its multilateral initiatives such as the Ayeyawady-Chao Phraya-Mekong Economic Cooperation Strategy (ACMECS) and the Asia Cooperation Dialogue (ACD). In all these efforts, TICA stresses that Thai technical cooperation (TC) initiatives align with the eighth United Nations Millennium Development Goal and the Global Partnership for Development (TICA 2013).

In comparison to India, Thailand has only recently expanded its bilateral programmes to other developing nations and retains a somewhat narrower sectoral focus. Nonetheless, one should note the consonance between the demand-driven nature of TICA's scholarship/fellowship programmes and the ITEC stress on partner-country requirements.

Brazil

Brazil's technical cooperation characteristically operates through multiple agencies in the public sector and has primarily focused on three areas: agriculture, health, and industry and entrepreneurship. Public-sector agencies often include technical cooperation and capacity-building efforts with foreign partners, simply as another part of their normal operations. We might cite the examples of Embrapa, the Brazilian Agricultural Research Corporation; Fiocruz, the Oswaldo

Cruz Foundation; and SENAI (Serviço Nacional de Aprendizagem Industrial, or National Service for Industrial Training) (Leite et al. 2014).

The state-owned company Embrapa, created in 1973, has promoted Brazilian tropical agriculture and agribusiness through knowledge and technology generation and transfer since the early 2000s (Barbosa 2011). It has opened offices in Ghana (since 2008), in Panama (since 2010), and in Venezuela (in partnership with the Brazilian Agency for Industrial Development). Today, it is responsible for Brazil's three main 'structuring projects' in African agriculture: cotton growing in Benin, Burkina Faso, Chad and Mali; rice culture in Senegal; and agricultural innovation in Mozambique (Barbosa 2011).

The Brazilian Ministry of Health has designated Fiocruz as the focal point for Brazilian health-related South-South cooperation. Founded in 1900, Fiocruz now runs national activities including teaching, research, production, and technological development. It has developed a series of structuring projects in health, notably with South American and African partners.[9] These projects aim to foster 'capacity building for development' by strengthening partner-country health systems, combining concrete interventions with local capacity building, knowledge generation, and promotion of stakeholder dialogue. The foundation has also explored new collaboration opportunities with Nigeria, Burkina Faso, Mali, and Tanzania (Almeida et al. 2010).

SENAI, a professional education and vocational training company created by official decree in 1942, now operates under the management of industrial entrepreneurs; today, it runs 809 sites in Brazil offering 3000 courses. SENAI first began receiving foreign assistance from industrialised countries in the 1950s. Since the 1970s, it has also provided development cooperation in Southern countries, especially in the Americas (Colombia, Guatemala, Jamaica, Haiti, Paraguay, Peru, and Suriname) and in the CPLP. It implements official agreements coordinated by the Brazilian cooperation agency (ABC) and cooperates autonomously with partner organisations in developing countries (Gonçalves 2011). In 2011, SENAI had thirteen active TC projects and had received a further thirteen projects for consideration. It also had another five projects in autonomous negotiation, without the collaboration of any Brazilian governmental body (Leite et al. 2014).

These projects suggest a slightly different model for technical cooperation than India's; apart from the smaller scale, the relative decentralisation of development cooperation efforts and the strong ties to a global linguistic community also mark divergences. Given Brazil's collaboration with India in global platforms such as BRICS, one might anticipate that its model for TC and capacity building will draw further from India's in the future – and also vice versa.

Proposals and new practices under ITEC

A number of measures under current consideration would revisit ITEC practices and procedures to broaden the programme's long-range impact. ITEC would continue its present practice of giving a certificate of attendance to all students, but adding a new diploma certification for those who successfully pass a standardised test would encourage more comprehensive course assimilation. Furthermore, to encourage the participation of non-English speakers, the ITEC could consider providing a translation and interpretation system.

The other challenges that face the ITEC programmes are purely operational. The DPA has addressed the task of streamlining the application process through the creation of an online portal, which would handle not only the processing of applications but also bills and payments. This effort would unite the prospective participants and the institutes on a single technical platform (Price 2005). The DPA has already put the application portal into operation for 2015–2016. The new ITEC portal modules would significantly speed up MEA processing of proposals from partner institutes, because all ITEC institutions must now submit their course proposals online.

ITEC has already dealt with another difficulty that had arisen, namely that prior participants have found it hard to remain in touch with their training institutes. Through the portal, the 'umbilical cord' will remain intact: participants will remain in contact with the ITEC institutions that trained them, and their relationship with the institute faculties will continue even when they return to their home countries. The new portal requires the ITEC applicants to upload applications themselves. This should help them maintain contact with candidates even after their return from India, and also ease the workload on the Indian missions abroad, who have had to enter application details manually (Tuhin 2015). The DPA II division plans to have the portal provide a unified listing and processing of all courses available under various streams (ITEC, SCAAP, and TCS of Colombo Plan). As an advanced technical solution to a complex set of human problems, the portal not only assists those seeking to learn from India's capacity-building strengths; it embodies them as well.

Conclusion

Overall, the ITEC programme seeks an effective response to the capacity-building requirements of its partner countries. The evolution and expansion of ITEC since its inception strongly confirm its demand-driven nature, and the programme continues to adhere to this unique format.

India has always moved forward with an inclusive mind-set of solidarity, empathy, and connectedness with the larger developing world. As mentioned earlier, the MEA established the DPA to more effectively handle India's development cooperation projects through all stages, from conception to completion. In this spirit of co-creation, ITEC has enhanced India's development assistance programmes, even as it has expanded far beyond its origins – now offering around 10,000 scholarship slots to 161 developing countries in courses across a range of disciplines.

India and other developing countries have all worked to negotiate an equitable, inclusive, and balanced world order – one enabling all nation-states to effectively tackle a host of crosscutting security and development challenges. On the development side, we need multipronged global collaborative networks to address pressing challenges – poverty, global warming, and sustainable development. In negotiating solutions to these challenges, Southern perspectives must and will play a vital role. The South has to match its growing economic prowess with a more active discourse, one that promotes the making of the South by the South. It is here that India's ITEC programme has proven most effective, imparting focused and specialised training to professionals from the developing world; the capacity thus built will enable them to appreciate, promote, and nurture a Southern partnership in global negotiating platforms. Moreover, the demand-driven nature of these courses has ensured a direct impact on developmental strategies of the partner countries.

With 50 years of international participants benefitting from its courses, ITEC has a rich alumni list. Many have gone on to become ministers, senior diplomats, academics, government officials, and leading entrepreneurs. They and their countries have widely acknowledged India's competence as a provider of technical know-how and expertise. As we suggested at the outset, one hopes that ITEC, drawing from 'Vasudhaiva Kutumbakam,' the ancient Vedic ideal of 'One World, One Family,' will continue contributing towards this end.

Notes

1 The views expressed in the chapter are the author's and not that of the government of India.
2 In 1966–1967, India gave 1,000 milk buffaloes to Sri Lanka and donated cattle to the Philippines, seeds to Burma and Laos, sewing machines to a Laotian women's association, medicines to Indonesia, and books and drugs to the Maldives; in 1971–1972, gifts of medicines and hospital equipment went to the Children's Hospital at Kabul, and equipment valued at about USD 220,000 went to the Chardeh-Ghorband Irrigation Project (MEA 1971).
3 These include the Economic Commission for Africa, G77, the Afro-Asian Rural Reconstruction Organisation (AARRO), G15, and the Southern African Development Community (SADC).
4 Such courses take place at sites such as the Institute of Government and Finance in New Delhi and the National Institute of Bank Management in Pune. The rural development curriculum offerings include entrepreneurship development, small-business planning, women's empowerment, tourism and hospitality, and agribusiness, among others. The National Institute of Rural Development; the National Institute for Micro, Small and Medium Enterprises; and the Entrepreneurship Development Institute at Ahmedabad all offer training in these areas (MEA 2014).
5 These courses take place in public facilities such as the Centre for Development of Advanced Computing (Pune and Mohali), the University of English and Foreign Languages (Hyderabad), and private institutes such as NIIT and Aptech. Management courses cover leadership training, human resource management, and corporate governance at institutes such as the Administrative Staff College (Hyderabad) and the Institute of Applied Manpower and Research (New Delhi).
6 These include technical courses in specialised industries taking place at institutes such as the Central Institute of Tool Design in Hyderabad, the South India Textile Research Association in Coimbatore, and the Indian Institute of Remote Sensing, among others. In addition, the Indian Institute of Technology in Roorkee offers one-year diplomas and a two-year master of technology programme on hydrology and water resource management (MEA 2014).

7 These include election management (at the International Institute of Democracy and Election Management [IIDEM], in New Delhi), government performance management (with the cabinet secretariat), midcareer civil servant training (at the National Institute of Administrative Research/National Centre for Good Governance [NIAR/NCGG]), parliamentary studies (Bureau of Parliamentary Studies), urban infrastructure management (Human Settlement Management Institute), South-South cooperation, international economics, and development policy (Research and Information Systems for Developing Countries), WTO-related topics (Centre for WTO Studies, Indian Institute of Foreign Trade), and so forth. ITEC has also developed innovative courses for nonprofessionals, including one on solar technology at the Barefoot College, Tilonia, for semiliterate and illiterate grandmothers from least-developed countries (MEA 2014).

8 The actual number of countries included under these three major capacity-building schemes comes to fewer than 179 if we exclude the developed member countries of TCS and include other developing TCS countries in ITEC.

9 In South America, these operate through the Union of South American Nations (UNASUL) and in Africa, among the member states of the Community of Portuguese-Speaking Countries (CPLP): Angola, Cape Verde, East Timor Guinee-Bissau, Mozambique, and São Tomé and Príncipe (Barbosa 2011). In 2009, Fiocruz coordinated eighteen projects with CPLP countries and had a further ten projects under negotiation.

Works cited

Almeida, C., de Campos, R.P., Buss, P.M., Ferreira, J.R., and Fonseca, L.E.A. (2010). Concepção Brasileira de cooperação Sul-Sul estruturante em saúde. *RECIIS*, 4(1): 25–35.

Barbosa, P.H.B. (2011). *O Brasil e a Embrapa: O viés instrumental da cooperação técnica horizontal*. Master's thesis. Instituto Rio Branco, Brasilia.

Chaturvedi, S. (2012). India's development partnership: Key policy shifts and institutional evolution. *Cambridge Review of International Affairs*, 25: 557–577.

Chaturvedi, S. (2015). *Logic of sharing: Indian approach on South-South cooperation.* Cambridge: RIS and Cambridge University Press.

Chaturvedi, S., Chenoy, A., Chopra, D., Joshi, A., and Lagdhyan, K.H. (2014). Indian development cooperation: The state of the debate. *IDS Evidence Report*, 95. Institute of Development Studies, University of Sussex, Brighton.

Chaturvedi, S., Fues, T., and Sidiropoulos, E. (eds.) (2012). *Development cooperation and emerging powers: New powers or old patterns?* London: Zed Books. Available at http:// public.eblib.com/choice/publicfullrecord.aspx?p=914288.

Colombo Plan (no date). *History* [webpage]. Available at www.colombo-plan.org/index. php/about-cps/history/.

Gonçalves, F.C.N.I. (2011). *Cooperação Sul-Sul e política externa: um estudo sobre a participação de atores sociais*. Master's thesis. Instituto de Relações Internacionais, Pontifícia Universidade Católica do Rio de Janeiro, Rio de Janeiro.

Kumar, N. (1987). India's economic and technical cooperation with the co-developing countries. In G.R. Agrawal (ed.), *South–South economic cooperation: Problems and prospects.* New Delhi: Radiant Publishers.

Leite, I.C., Suyama, B., Waisbich, L.T., Pomeroy, M., Constantine, J., Aleman, L.N., Shankland, A., and Younis, M. (2014). Brazil's engagement in international development cooperation: The state of the debate. *IDS Evidence Report*, 59. Institute for Development Studies, University of Sussex, Brighton.

MEA (2007–2013). *Annual reports 2007–2008 through 2013–2014*. New Delhi: MEA, Government of India. Available at http://mea.gov.in/annual-reports.htm?57/Annual_Reports.

MEA (2009). *Civilian training programme Indian Technical & Economic Cooperation (ITEC) & Special Commonwealth Assistance for Africa Programme (SCAAP) 2009–2010*. New Delhi: MEA, Government of India.

MEA (2014). *Civilian training programme Indian Technical & Economic Cooperation (ITEC) & Special Commonwealth Assistance for Africa Programme (SCAAP) 2014–2015*. New Delhi: MEA, Government of India. Available at www.itec.mea.gov.in/?pdf2980?000. [Accessed 30 June 2015]

MEA (2015a). *About ITEC: Indian Technical and Economic Cooperation (ITEC) Programme*. New Delhi: MEA, Government of India. Available at http://itec.mea.gov.in/?1320?000. [Accessed 30 July 2015].

MEA (2015b). *50 years of ITEC*. New Delhi: MEA, Government of India. Available at www.mea.gov.in/Uploads/PublicationDocs/24148_REVISED_50_yrs_of_ITEC_brochure.pdf. [Accessed 30 July 2015].

Ministry of External Affairs (MEA) (1971). *Report 1971–72*. New Delhi: MEA, Government of India.

Ministry of Foreign Affairs of Malaysia (MFAM) (2013). *About MTCP: Malaysian Technical Cooperation Program 2013*. Kuala Lumpur: MFAM, Government of Malaysia.

Monroe, P. (1918). *A text-book in the history of education*. New York: The Macmillan Company (Republished 2000 by Genesis Publishing).

Nehru, J. (1948). Note on foreign policy. In S. Gopal and U. Iyengar (eds.), *The essential writings of Jawaharlal Nehru*, vol. 2. New Delhi: Oxford University Press, pp. 338–339.

Organisation for Economic Co-operation and Development (OECD) (2012). *Trade-related South-South co-operation: India*. Paris: OECD.

Price, G. (2005). Diversity in donorship: The changing landscape of official humanitarian aid India's official aid programme. *HPG Background Paper*, 9. Humanitarian Policy Group, Overseas Development Institute, London.

Quadir, F. (2013). Rising donors and the new narrative of 'South-South' cooperation: What prospects for changing the landscape of development assistance programmes? *Third World Quarterly*, 34(2): 321–338.

Ranganathan, T.C.A. (2012). Presentation on lessons from India's development cooperation at *Learning from National Experiences and Building Global Partnerships Workshop*, New Delhi, 22–23 June, RIS and The World Bank.

Scharfe, H. (2002). Education in ancient India. In *Handbook of Oriental Studies*, Section 2. Leiden: Brill Academic.

Srinivasan, G. (2007). Ministry keen to create agency for providing development aid. *Hindu Business Line*, 31 December.

Thailand International Cooperation Agency (TICA) (2013). *Thai International Cooperation Programme (TICP)*. Bangkok: TICA, Government of Thailand. Available at http://tica.thaigov.net/main/en/aid/40611-Thai-International-Cooperation-Programme-(TICP).html. [Accessed 8 July 2015].

Tuhin, K. (2015). India's developmental partnership outreach going digital. *India TV*, 19 March. Available at www.indiatvnews.com/business/india/india-s-developmental-partnership-outreach-going-digital-17956.html. [Accessed 12 September 2015].

United Nations Industrial Development Organization (UNIDO) (2015). *South-South and triangular cooperation*. New York: UNIDO. Available at www.unido.org/south-south.html. [Accessed 14 August 2015].

4 Towards health diplomacy

Emerging trends in India's South-South health cooperation

Sachin Chaturvedi

Introduction

In recent years, the South has emerged as a leading protagonist in international development cooperation, often in sectors previously dominated by developed countries. Health-related action provides one striking example. Emerging economies such as Brazil, India, China, and South Africa (BICS), along with other countries such as Cuba, have come forward to supplement global efforts in tackling various health-sector challenges. The growing magnitude of development assistance from BICS has given new hope for health-sector management efforts in developing countries (Chaturvedi and Thorsteindottir 2012a).

The BICS have played an important and crucial role, along with Russia, in the BRICS platform. With the adoption of the Sanya Declaration in 2011, the BRICS clearly emphasised health as an important area of cooperation within the group, a focus echoed at meetings of the BRICS Health Ministers in Beijing (2011) and Delhi (2013). Apart from dealing with specific Southern health challenges, the BRICS also called for greater participation from the developing world in reforming institutions, such as the World Health Organization (WHO), while promoting BRICS as an appropriate forum for coordination, cooperation, and consultation on matters related to global public health (Chaturvedi and Thorsteinsdóttir 2012a). The effort, it seems, has aimed to widen the narrative on global health governance issues with greater participation from the South. This also implies a greater Southern role in post-2015 global strategies: health-related development cooperation may assist the United Nation's Millennium Development Goals by reducing child mortality; improving maternal health; combating HIV/AIDS, malaria, and other diseases; and creating global partnerships for development.

South-South cooperation (SSC) in health therefore comes with a built-in element of diplomacy and raises questions about the agendas of participating countries. The present chapter analyses India's contributions to these actions and their implications for India's aid architecture in general. India's participation in the multilateral dialogue comes during a period of intensified effort in the health sector, both within and outside the country. This effort has focused on low-cost, often bilateral, projects in the areas of its growing domestic strength: health infrastructure, human resources, capacity building and enhancement, and education. Indian health professionals and researchers have shared expertise with other developing countries, and Indian entrepreneurs have shared products and other resources, thus promoting health research and capacity building alongside economic development.

The first section will address the emerging concept of global health diplomacy (GHD) and discuss the specific modalities that India has emphasised as elements of its development compact. The second section will situate Indian activity within the general framework of multilateral South-South cooperation in the health sector. We will then look at the traditionally bilateral, demand-driven character of India's development cooperation and its regional focus, now expanding to new developing countries and a greater role in multilateral platforms. We conclude with some of the challenges, as well as the most promising strategies, for future policy.

Theories of global health diplomacy and Indian engagement

The examples of South-South health cooperation noted earlier differ in significant ways from those of Organisation for Economic Co-operation and Development Development Assistance Committee (OECD-DAC) members. Several of the latter have issued policy statements on global health, where they usually distinguish policy-shaping processes through engagement of various actors – state, nonstate, or institutional. In case of several of the DAC members, such as the United Kingdom, Switzerland, and Norway, such specialised statements form the basis for action strategies.[1] None of the non-DAC emerging economies, such as China, Brazil, or India, have put such broad and sweeping frameworks in place. As a result, the trajectories for action, modalities of engagement, and volumes of assistance also differ sharply – as do concepts of the role of health aid in national foreign policies.

The literature on GHD largely emanates from the experiences of DAC members; as a result, its analytical frameworks reflect DAC policies and philosophical contexts rather than those of emerging economies.[2] In this context, the review of Blouin, Molenaar and Pearcey (2012) of African health diplomacy literature raises several important issues for analysts to consider – for example, what factors may influence the decision of states to collaborate and what variables may influence the implementation.[3] The authors in Bliss (2010) raise similar issues concerning the role of the BRICS. Such issues, as Blouin, Molenaar, and Pearcey noted, would benefit from theoretical frameworks woven around the broad policies each providing country follows in 'development partnerships' or 'aid'. Domestic achievements and geopolitical priorities play important roles in such engagements. National institutional architecture also plays an important role, but in some countries, like Brazil, multilateral institutions (chiefly UN related) lead initiatives in this area; this reflects the horizontality that Brazil emphasises in its Southern linkages (that is, bilateral relationships on equal footing, not the hierarchical donor–recipient dyad usually evident in DAC engagement). This approach enables Brazil to play a far more active role in global health programmes compared with other emerging economies such as India (Souza 2013).

India's approach to development cooperation has distinct characteristics of its own. Its theoretical underpinnings strongly reflect its experience as an aid recipient and have stressed win-win partnerships that embody shared challenges but distinct national priorities. India deploys a broad portfolio of modalities to increase the reach and effectiveness of its development cooperation, a flexibility that makes it much more attractive and appropriate for developing countries. This portfolio rests on five components: capacity building and skills transfer, technology (including technical assistance), trade and investment (including credit lines), development finance (further divided into concessional loans and lines of credit), and grants. These five components provide the basis of a development compact – something less than the articulated policies of the DAC members, but more than a string of unrelated aid programmes, and intimately related to broader economic strategies. The development compact supports growth by bolstering equitable access to trade, investment, and technology within the framework of South-South cooperation (Chaturvedi 2015).

In the case of health cooperation, India's membership in the multilateral platforms signalled earlier has allowed it to collaborate widely with other emerging partners and contribute strongly towards global solutions, as we shall see in the next section.

Dynamics of South-South cooperation in the health sector

The multilateral picture

SSC in health has evolved at various levels, with growing efforts to further consolidate it through global funds, the UN, and other agencies. The BICS together contributed nearly USD 200 million to global health initiatives during 2007–2008 alone, without including bilateral assistance in the same sector. These initiatives include the Global Alliance for Vaccines and Immunization (Gavi) and the global fund to fight AIDS, Tuberculosis, and Malaria (Global Fund) (Chaturvedi 2011). India contributed USD 3 million to Gavi in the last three years, and its donations to the Global Fund reached nearly USD 10 million from 2001–2010 and USD 7.5 million for 2011–2014 (Table 4.1).[1]

Additionally, efforts have emerged to build health systems across various developing countries; for example, the India, Brazil, South Africa (IBSA) initiative has established the IBSA Fund. IBSA experts and national partners have assisted the Burundi healthcare system to improve its fight against HIV/AIDS, using models and experiences from IBSA countries (IBSA n.d.). The BICS have also increased efforts to promote health through South-South collaboration. Typically, such initiatives involve government-to-government collaborations, although civil society engagement has also expanded (Chaturvedi 2011).

South-South cooperation has an additional advantage rooted in the common spectrum of diseases persisting in developing countries. Despite ongoing efforts to enhance control of infectious diseases, developing countries still face an undue burden in this area compared with developed ones. Additional challenges arise in

Table 4.1 India's contribution to global health funds (USD millions)

	Global Alliance for Vaccines and Immunization (Gavi)	Global Fund to Fight AIDS, Tuberculosis and Malaria
2008	–	2
2009	–	2
2010	–	2
2011	–	–
2012	–	–
2013	1.00	3
2014	1.00	4.5
2015	1.00	–

Source: Gavi (2015)

accurately identifying, diagnosing, and reporting infectious diseases due to the remoteness of affected communities and lack of transport and communication infrastructure. South-South cooperation can assist immensely in tackling these problems (Chaturvedi 2012).

The Indian collaboration

Such shared health concerns in developing countries drive India's South-South collaborations. In several cases, such as the HIV/AIDS virus, commonality in disease profile also spurs complementary research: at the global level, most of the research and development (R&D) focuses on subtype B, but India and Brazil, facing a heavier prevalence of subtype C virus, have launched joint projects of their own (Chaturvedi and Thorsteinsdóttir 2012b: 188). A similar drive led India and Bangladesh to collaborate on tackling infectious diseases that both countries confront. Cholera is a significant health problem in Bangladesh and Eastern India, spurring joint biotechnology research on its genome (Chaturvedi and Thorsteinsdóttir 2013). The National Institute of Cholera and Enteric Diseases (Kolkata, India) and the International Centre for Diarrhoeal Disease Research (Dhaka, Bangladesh), internationally recognised centres of excellence in diarrhoeal diseases, collaborate closely and work with international partners on the molecular pathogenesis of enteric disease agents (Chaturvedi and Thorsteinsdóttir 2012a) The International Centre for Diarrhoeal Disease Research has developed a vaccine candidate to prevent cholera in collaboration with the Indian firm Biological E (Hyderabad, India) (Chaturvedi and Thorsteinsdóttir 2012a).

Additionally, several formal South-South health networks have emerged. These networks show great potential for improving health, capacity building, and innovation. Developing countries may contribute on the basis of their respective strengths; this should enhance South-South R&D activities and lead to new healthcare products and services, aimed at fulfilling the countries' own needs.

Although IBSA-sponsored joint biotechnical research has yet to show substantive progress (Chaturvedi 2011), we should also signal that India has contributed widely to R&D collaborations. Indian researchers have increased their joint publication of papers with other Southern actors, from twenty papers in 1996 to eighty papers in 2008 (Figure 4.1). Notably, China is India's leading collaborator in health biotechnology, followed by Brazil, reflecting their BICS alignment noted earlier. Bangladesh comes in third, a noteworthy rank given the country's very recent exposure to the biotechnology sector. India chiefly collaborates with other developing countries in the subfields of genetics and heredity (sixty-four papers) and microbiology (thirty-four papers) (Chaturvedi and Thorsteinsdóttir 2012a).

Several examples of South-South health collaboration demonstrate how emerging economies may help others with similar socioeconomic and political backgrounds.[5] One collaboration that showcases capacity building (and also engages trade cooperation) has occurred between South African and Indian medical testing firms: East Coast Rapid Diagnostics (now split into Tulip South Africa and Life Assay) is a joint venture between the publicly funded LIFE Labs (South Africa) and the firm Indian Tulip Group Diagnostics (Bambolim, India) (Chaturvedi 2012). India also supports entrepreneurial collaborations with other developing countries (Figure 4.2). Once again, China has emerged as India's leading partner in this respect, followed by Brazil. The total number of collaborations was fifty-four, the third-highest number of South-South collaborations among all the countries examined in the study. In comparison, Brazil and South Africa each had over sixty South-South entrepreneurial collaborations (Chaturvedi 2012).

Although the multilateral collaborations cited here demonstrate an impressive range, they represent relatively recent trends in Indian cooperation. India's development compact in this sector has developed over decades, and historically has had a strong bilateral focus, as the next section will discuss.

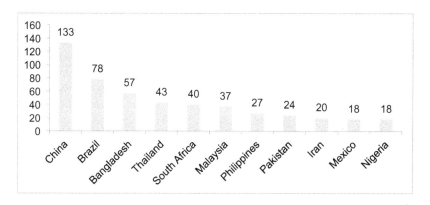

Figure 4.1 Co-authored papers from India, 1996–2009

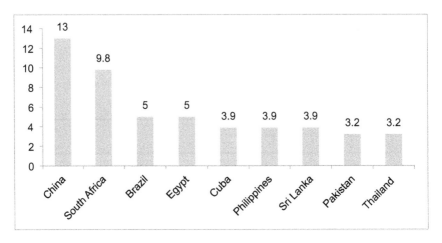

Figure 4.2 India's South-South health and biotech collaborations, 1996–2009

Indian engagement in South-South health cooperation

Institutionalisation and policy architecture

Under the energetic leadership of Jawaharlal Nehru, the Indian policy spectrum included a special focus on both science and technology and on South-South cooperation. He also helped catalyse the first meeting of the Southern economies, the 1955 Afro-Asian Conference at Bandung – in a way, the beginning of formal collaboration between developing countries (Chaturvedi and Thorsteinsdóttir 2012a). India pioneered SSC with the active participation of relevant ministries and agencies. The Ministry of External Affairs (MEA) has remained the key agency for extending bilateral and technical assistance; it generally approaches the Department of Economic Affairs of the Ministry of Finance with country-specific requests for disbursements (Chaturvedi 2012).

This basic architecture has allowed India to collaborate with other developing countries, particularly low-income countries (LICs), through various modalities, including grants and assistance, lines of credit, capacity building, and technology transfer. Since the beginning, such efforts emphasised training and scholarships through a structured programme called Indian Technical and Economic Cooperation Programme (ITEC) launched in 1964. The ITEC Programme is discussed extensively elsewhere in this volume,[6] but we should note here that it helped establish India's reputation as a country willing to share its development competencies, technical know-how, and expertise through training opportunities, consultancy services, and feasibility studies, as well as scholarships. In other words, it has proven a practical form of diplomacy that has generated considerable goodwill and many cooperation opportunities (Chaturvedi 2012: 173).

With the expansion of all forms of bilateral cooperation, especially since 2003 (GHSi 2012), and with India's increasing multilateral engagements, the government has moved to consolidate outgoing assistance through a new initiative (2012), the Development Partnership Administration (DPA), set up within the MEA to coordinate and implement programmes (Bliss 2010; Chaturvedi 2013). This agency aims at providing streamlining and greater transparency in India's growing foreign assistance program, a point to which we will return later.

Categories of Indian health cooperation and intervention

We have identified four major categories of Indian health support that have proven important historically and have broadened since 2003. Again, these chiefly reflect demand-driven, bilateral engagements pursued through the institutions and modalities discussed earlier.

Providing human resources for health and humanitarian assistance

From the time of its emergence as an independent state, India saw linkages with other developing countries as an important policy priority and promoted this by 'loaning' medical personnel (Chaturvedi and Thorsteinsdóttir 2012a), often in the form of health teams and paramedics. For example, in 1956, the government appointed 200 Indian doctors to posts in Burma (now Myanmar) to support its health sector management, and sent one doctor and two nurses to Ethiopia to work at the Gandhi Memorial Hospital at Addis Ababa. This hospital was itself built by the local Indian community to mark the birth anniversary of the Ethiopian king.

Afghanistan has proven one of India's chief recipients of medical aid over the years. In 1998–1999, a consignment of medical equipment, medical supplies, and medicines worth INR 400,000 went to the Indira Gandhi Institute for Child Health in Kabul, one of the first hospitals built with Indian support in Afghanistan. In 2004–2005, the institute also received medical equipment for rehabilitation and modernisation (MEA 2005: 2). India assisted humanitarian programmes over a number of years in five Afghan cities: Kabul, Herat, Mazar-e-Sharif, Kandahar, and Jalalabad. Through this programme, India has deployed fifteen healthcare providers and enough free medicines to treat 360,000 of Afghanistan's poorest patients annually (GHSi 2012: 50–53).

Similarly, India has also sent medical missions to Africa (GHsi 2012: 50–51) and provided wide-ranging assistance to a number of countries. Yemen provides one important case in which Indian partnership continued even during political and diplomatic crises. In light of the country's inadequate medical facilities, in 1971 India signed a unique agreement with its government, supporting travel for ten Yemeni patients every year to receive treatment in India. This number has multiplied over the years. Although India took a neutral stand at the outbreak of Yemen's civil war, Indian doctors and nurses continued to provide humanitarian services during the conflict.[7] After its successful conclusion in July 1994, the government of Yemen sought admission and medical treatment for over 150 war-wounded persons in Bombay hospitals (EOI 2015).

Other crisis-afflicted states have also benefited from Indian health assistance, provided through both bilateral and multilateral means. In 1957, the government of India sent a medical mission to work among Palestine refugees under the auspices of the United Nations Relief Works Agency for Palestine (Chaturvedi 2015). India also extended support to Indonesia and Malaysia in 1964–1965 when both countries faced an outbreak of cholera. In 1990–1991, India provided Cambodia with humanitarian assistance (medicines and artificial limbs) amounting to INR 10 million, and sent surgical instruments, appliances, and medicines worth INR 25,000 to Cambodian hospitals (Chaturvedi 2015). In 1994–1995, India also agreed to provide 100 doctors, engineers, and primary healthcare trainers to the UN mission in Haiti.

Health is probably the only sector where India has supported infrastructure building in addition to providing other services. India has financed and constructed hospitals and also provided operational support to run them. In Asia, this infrastructure building has focused most strongly on Afghanistan, followed by Nepal. India has undertaken similar programmes in a few African countries as well.

One should note, however, that the Indian approach to health infrastructure took rather different forms in Nepal and Afghanistan. What started in Afghanistan with the Kabul Children's Hospital (built in 1966) gradually expanded into several specialised clinics in different parts of Afghanistan, in addition to the highly specialised hospital at the original site, later named the Indira Gandhi Institute of Child Health (IGICH). In the case of Nepal, India took the reverse approach. The Indian Cooperation Mission (ICM) launched a major programme along the Sonauli-Pokhara Road, establishing five small medical units for essential medicine distribution and providing three mobile vans for the entire population in that area. This programme gradually expanded into a major health support initiative, leading to the establishment of major hospitals such as the B. P. Koirala Institute for Health Sciences in Dharan and Emergency and Trauma Centre and Bir Hospital in Kathmandu.

If we analyse the genesis and evolution of health programmes in Afghanistan and Nepal more closely, we may derive lessons for similar interventions in other countries. In Afghanistan, the Children's Hospital in Kabul started with 150 beds in 1966; it now has 350 beds, supported by several modern facilities, including a computed tomography (CT) scanner, magnetic resonance imaging (MRI) scanner, echocardiograph, electrocardiograph, and coloured X-ray scanner, purchased at a cost of USD 3 million (137,940,000 AFN)[8]. Other hospital specialisations include orthopaedic surgery and a premature birth ward; in 2010, IGICH also hosted a major workshop on malnutrition. Current proposals would link the IGICH with other Afghan hospitals through optical fibres, extending its existing links with two premier institutes in India at Chandigarh and Lucknow. This would improve the quality of expert consultation, and eventually may also contribute towards enhancing medical education (MEA 1967: 5).[9]

In Nepal's case, India launched several small missions for providing primary healthcare in different parts of Nepal. In 1973, a 15-bed hospital at Taulihawa opened its doors, the second of three that India supported at this scale, in addition to a chain of two 25-bed hospitals, one health centre, and six health outposts. In 1984, Bir Hospital in Kathmandu received INR 60 million for operating-theatre and other equipment, and in 2014 India added an Emergency and Trauma Centre. In 1994, India helped build the Institute for Health Sciences at Dharan, with an associated 300-bed hospital named the B. P. Koirala Institute for Health Science (BPKIHS). In 1999–2000, India established a Maternity and Neonatal Intensive Care Unit at Paropakar Hospital in Kathmandu. Not all Indian efforts focus on hospitals, however: between 1994 and 2013, India donated 382 ambulances to various organisations across seventy districts in Nepal, bringing healthcare services to several populations lacking access to health centres. According to a mission estimate, this contribution alone has reached nearly 60,000 patients (EOI 2013).

The supply of medicines crucially depends on availability of infrastructure for production and distribution. In Nepal, India provided support for installation of an iodisation plant at a cost of INR 20 million in 2015. Goitre prevention has been a major challenge in Nepal. In 1973, India signed a five-year agreement to distribute iodised salt throughout Nepal beginning in 1972–1973, at a cost of INR 10.25 million. This programme continued into the next decade, with a renewed agreement in 1982 (Chaturvedi, Kumar and Mendiratta 2013).

Outside of Asia, similar patterns – starting small and gradually building up institutions – have informed India's diverse African partnerships. In 1959, the Indian community in Ethiopia (backed by Indian government support) presented a fully equipped hospital to the king on the occasion of his silver jubilee celebrations. Similarly, in Kabwe (Zambia), India established the Mahatma Gandhi Memorial Clinic in 1983 (MEA 1983: 17). In 1994, India assisted Mozambique in building basic health infrastructure by presenting three ambulances and a mobile clinic for rural areas. India sent a consignment of ophthalmological equipment and medicines to the Victoria Hospital of Seychelles in June 2002, along with a credit line of USD 7.5 million to the Central Bank of Seychelles for purchasing vehicles and spare parts. Such efforts show that even smaller-scale assistance can contribute value to infrastructure building.

Broadening availability of medicines and vaccines

A growing number of South-South collaborations aim to expand the availability of more affordable drugs, vaccines, and diagnostics, and India has provided key support in this area. The 2010 Global Health Policy Report noted that Indian aid programmes had benefited from the low-cost AIDS drugs produced by Indian pharmaceutical companies (Bliss 2010: 28). Moreover, Indian manufacturers currently provide 80 per cent of all donor-funded HIV therapies in developing countries – drugs used by millions of patients (Waning, Diedrichsen and Moon 2010).[10] India also makes significant contributions through generic vaccine production. Eight manufacturers in India currently produce seventy-two WHO prequalified vaccines, more any other country. In addition, Indian companies manufacture between 60 per cent and 80 per cent of all vaccines procured by UN agencies, making India by far the largest provider of affordable, high-quality vaccines for developing countries. Estimates put India's vaccine industry revenues at approximately USD 900 million in 2011 and predicted 23 per cent growth from 2011 to 2012 (GHSi 2012: 50–53).

India has also ensured vaccine availability to developing countries in times of crisis. In the late 1950s and 1960s, when cholera broke out in several parts of Asia and other developing countries, India supplied vaccines and other drugs to Afghanistan, Nepal, Malaysia, Thailand, and the Philippines; it sent INR 1 million in medicines and a crisis medical team to Madagascar during its 2000 outbreak (MEA 2000: 47).[11]

Providing training and capacity building

India is well known for its large, highly educated cadre of healthcare professionals, and its multilateral initiatives have a strong focus on capacity building. Recognising this, other developing countries have approached India for help in strengthening their own healthcare workforce. India has established medical colleges and provided faculty support in a number of countries, particularly Bhutan and Nepal (GHSi 2012: 50–53). It has financed several important delegations from Iran for visits to Indian public health organisations and laboratories, and provided scholarships to students from different developing countries to attend medical colleges in India.

Apart from reserving slots at the technical institutions in the health sector, India has also leveraged the strength of the ITEC with a diverse range of health-sector courses. In recent years these have included advanced courses in healthcare technologies, telemedicine and medical informatics, and healthcare technology management and clinical engineering (offered by the Centre for Development of Advanced Computing, Mohali). The V. V. Giri National Labour Institute offered an international training programme on health protection and security, and the Central Scientific Instruments Organisation had a management development programme on biomedical equipment (ITEC 2015). Such initiatives reflect demand from development partners, as well as areas of recognised Indian competence.

Although it supports allopathic models and structures, India has also promoted traditional Indian medical practices such as yoga. The government invited a team of Ayurvedic experts from Burma (now Myanmar) to study relevant curriculum and literature in 1965 with the aim of creating an Ayurvedic college in Burma; following this exchange, India presented indigenous medicines to the Health Ministry in Burma. The potential for exporting these and other traditional practices merits further study; India has much to learn from China on this front (Chaturvedi and Srinivas 2014: 29). The Chinese experience reveals that traditional medicine can support developmental efforts, offering cheaper, effective treatment that could immensely benefit partner countries.

As noted earlier, India also takes part in multilateral initiatives aimed at encouraging South-South collaborations, including the International Centre for Genetic Engineering and Biotechnology (ICGEB), a UN initiative focused on strengthening research and training in molecular biology and biotechnology for developing-country needs (Chaturvedi and Thorsteinsdóttir 2012a). The WHO also arranges study tours and fellowships for developing-country health officials and personnel in Indian institutions on behalf of the Indian Ministry of Health. India possesses great scope for contributing to health biotech development in other countries that need it. As its own economy and its health biotech capacity have strengthened in recent years, India has increased its capacity-building support and its efforts to share technology.

Advocacy in global health governance and policy dialogue

India has played a key role in advancing the South-South dialogue on global governance in the realm of health. Indian contributions to the Trade-Related Aspects of Intellectual Property Rights (TRIP)–related debates have strongly influenced the discussion of intellectual property rights (IPR). At the 2001 Doha WTO Ministerial Conference, India forcefully advocated a TRIP- and public-health–related declaration that would recognise the supremacy of public health concerns over IPR and allow member countries some flexibility in this regard. This led to two important changes in the existing TRIP provisions. The first concerned least-developed countries and those without production capacity. The second clarified flexibilities in the TRIP agreement and assured governments' rights to exercise them in light of existing ambiguities. The change took legal effect on 30 August 2003 with the General Council's waiver of the provision; this allowed export of generics made under compulsory licenses to countries lacking production capacity, subject to certain conditions and procedures.

In tandem with other leading economies such as Brazil, India has formed coalitions to influence intellectual property–related debates across different fora, and has attempted to bring in the development dimension whenever possible. On 27 August 2004, the World Intellectual Property Organisation (WIPO) General Assembly (WO/GA31/11) saw a proposal from Argentina and Brazil for integrating the development dimension into intellectual property protection policy, in the specific context of the draft Substantive Patent Law Treaty (SPLT). The proposed treaty would considerably raise patent protection standards, creating new obligations that developing countries could scarcely meet. Throughout these discussions, developing countries (including India) also proposed amendments to improve the draft SPLT, making it more responsive to public interest concerns and the specific needs of developing countries (WIPO 2004).

This brings us full circle. India's advocacy in international fora clearly intersects with all the initiatives we have cited earlier: the financial and collaborative support for multilateral biotech and health research; the long history of bilateral health infrastructure and capacity building; the leveraging of its training strengths, pharmaceuticals manufacturing, and other forms of expertise to foster health and growth in other developing countries. The in-depth regional collaborations with Afghanistan and Nepal have now expanded to new development partners. In other words, we have ample evidence of health diplomacy, albeit of a distinctive South-South variety; what remains are the challenges that India will face in expanding it.

Conclusion

Developing economies have grown at a rapid pace in the past few years, with a consequent multiplication of SSC volumes. The Task Team on South-South Cooperation, supported by the OECD-DAC, has signalled the end of the era of one-way cooperation, as countries of the South engage in collaborative learning models and share innovative, adaptable, and cost-efficient solutions for development. The Task Team also mentioned that new arrangements among Southern countries have revolutionised the delivery and administration of assistance in socially relevant sectors, including health (TT-SSC 2011).

In this context, India has come to play a crucial role in promoting health cooperation with fellow developing countries by supporting their institutional and organisational capacity. This engagement, as we have seen, largely focuses on short- to medium-term needs of partner countries; what India now needs is to explore the broader potential for improved health, capacity building, and innovation. This may require enhancing their research and development activities to create new health products and services. Partner countries also need to invest more in their science, technology, innovation, and health-promotion plans. In tandem with other key Southern players, India should promote more dedicated funding for collaboration – allowing developing countries to address local health needs that high-income countries might overlook, thereby securing timely and affordable health products for improved global health.

Most importantly, joint research projects could ensure long-term gains for India and SSC in general. The current modalities may give short- to medium-term boosts for joint research and so create a true path forward. There is no substitute or shortcut for this. This may also help in ensuring quality medical exports from India or from other countries. In May 2004, the WHO recalled thirty-six Indian drugs from the market (mainly in Africa) because the Indian providers could not provide proof of bioequivalence. The onus for quality assurance rests with both providers and partner countries, and will test both the effectiveness of policy coordination and the ultimate collective gains.

Finally, several issues remain concerning cooperation effectiveness that may influence India's policy architecture. As India engages more deeply with global strategizing in the health sector, the historically demand-driven aspect of its cooperation may come up against the need for broader sectoral strategies. Moreover, cooperation delivery will require better alignment between the Ministries of Health and External Affairs, with the DPA as coordinator; timeliness and budgetary restraints may prove hurdles in this respect. India also lacks any evaluation mechanism for its cooperation programmes (notably, for gauging long-term ITEC effectiveness) and may well need to develop one specific to its experiences and aims. India may wish to consider re-orienting ITEC programmes in health sector to better facilitate adoption of new technologies by partner countries. For example, India spent enormous sums to establish the pan-Africa e-network programme, but has yet to offer participants ITEC courses dedicated to telemedicine or the other technology-intensive skills the initiative requires (Saran 2012). All these issues will, in some form or another, arise as India expands its development compact into something closer to a full-fledged, effective health diplomacy that will secure its place within global development strategies.

Notes

1 The United Kingdom issued its *Health Is Global: A UK Government Strategy 2008–11* in 2008, Switzerland announced its Health Foreign Policy in 2006, and Norway issued the Oslo Ministerial Declaration in 2007 (UKDH 2008).
2 Kickbusch and Kökény (2013) argue that four elements have contributed to the ascent of GHD for the G8 members: greater engagement by foreign affairs ministries in health cooperation (to leverage the 'soft power' for greater influence), security policy, trade agreements, and environmental and development policy.
3 Blouin et al. also signal the prevalence of case studies and the relative absence of theoretical frameworks on the subject.
4 BICS countries have both contributed to and received from these funds: although India had received USD 243.37 million as disbursements from Gavi during 2000–2015, the amount for China stands at USD 38.68 million for the same period; meanwhile, Brazil disbursed USD 1 million to Gavi in 2015, and China contributed nearly USD 35 million from 2003–2014 (Gavi 2015).
5 For example, the Kunming Institute of Botany (Kunming, China) and the Chinese firm SH-IDEA Pharmaceutical Company (Yuxi, China), which have worked with Thailand's Ministry of Public Health (Bangkok) on clinical trials of an HIV/AIDS treatment.
6 See Tuhin in this volume.
7 In 1978–1979, an eight-member Indian medical team went to the Peoples' Democratic Republic of Yemen under the ITEC programme, followed by a three-member medical specialist team visiting Aden (People's Democratic Republic of Yemen) for special treatment of patients in 1987–1988 (MEA 1978: 50)
8 AFN is the currency sign for Afghanis, the national currency of Afghanistan.
9 Security considerations may challenge further expansion. Seven Indian physicians working at this hospital died in February 2010 when Taliban-set explosions damaged the hospital. The nearby NATO hospital in the Kabul diplomatic area was the probable target.
10 In this connection, we signal the case of Cipla, a Mumbai-based drug manufacturing company, that in 2001 began producing triple-therapy antiretrovirals (ARVs) at a cost of USD 350 per patient per year – one-thirteenth of the standard price at that time. Ranbaxy's entry into the ARV drug market soon followed (Avert 2015).
11 In 1960, India supplied bleaching powder and 200,000 vials of cholera vaccines to Afghanistan; it worked with the Red Cross Society to furnish medicine and assistance to Nepal in 1958. It also provided 150,000 doses and 100,000 doses of anticholera vaccines to Malaysia and Thailand, respectively, in 1963–1964 (MEA 1964: 35) and 1985–1989 (MEA 1989: 25) and 10,000 vials to the Philippines in 1961–1962 (MEA 1962: 32).

Works cited

Avert (2015). *Antiretroviral drug prices*. Brighton, UK: Avert. Available at www.avert.org/antiretroviral-drug-prices.htm.

Bliss, K. (ed.) (2010). *The key players in global heath: How Brazil, Russia, India, China and South Africa are influencing the game*. Washington, DC: Centre for Strategic and International Studies.

Blouin, C., Molenaar, B., and Pearcey, M. (2012). Annotated literature review: Conceptual frameworks and strategies for research on global health diplomacy. *EQUINET Discussion Paper*, 92. Centre for Trade Policy and Law, Carleton University at University of Ottawa. Available at http://equinetafrica.org/bibl/docs/Diss92%20GHD%20Litrev%20 July2012.pdf.

Chaturvedi, S. (2011). South-South cooperation in health and pharmaceuticals: Emerging trends in India-Brazil collaborations. *RIS Discussion Paper*, 172. Research and Information System for Developing Countries, New Delhi.

Chaturvedi, S. (2012). India and development cooperation: Expressing southern solidarity. In S. Chaturvedi, T. Fues and E. Sidiropoulos (eds.) *Development cooperation and emerging powers: New partners or old patterns?* London: Zed Books.

Chaturvedi, S. (2013). External health aid and sustainable development: Emerging contours of Indian health diplomacy. *Presentation Made at World Health Summit (WHS), Regional Meeting*, 8–10 April, Singapore.

Chaturvedi, S. (2015). The development compact. In S. Chaturvedi (ed.) *Logic of sharing: Indian approach to South-South cooperation*. New Delhi: RIS and Cambridge University Press, pp. 45–75.

Chaturvedi, S., Kumar, S., and Mendiratta, S. (2013). Balancing state and community participation in development partnership projects: Emerging evidence from Indian SDPs in Nepal', *RIS Discussion Paper*, 183. Research and Information System for Developing Countries, New Delhi.

Chaturvedi, S., and Srinivas, K.R. (2014). Introduction: Health sector challenges, traditional medicines and India China collaboration. In S. Chaturvedi, M. Ladikas, G. Lifeng and K.R. Srinivas (eds.), *The living tree: Traditional medicine and public health in China and India*. New Delhi: Academic Foundation, pp. 27–31.

Chaturvedi, S., and Thorsteinsdóttir, H. (2012a). BRICS and South-South cooperation in medicine: Emerging trends in research and entrepreneurial collaborations. *RIS Discussion Paper*, 177. Research and Information System for Developing Countries, New Delhi. Available at www.ris.org.in/images/RIS_images/pdf/dp177_pap.pdf. [Accessed 17 September 2015].

Chaturvedi, S., and Thorsteinsdóttir, H. (2012b). A growing Southern agenda: India's South-South health biotechnology collaboration. In H. Thorsteinsdóttir (ed.), *South-South collaboration in health biotechnology: Growing partnerships amongst developing countries*. Ottawa: International Development Research Centre Academic Foundation, pp. 177–202.

Chaturvedi, S., and Thorsteinsdóttir, H. (2013). South–South cooperation and emerging economies: Insights from health sector cooperation between India and Brazil. In J. Dargin (ed.), *The rise of the Global South: Philosophical, geopolitical and economic trends of the 21st century*. Cambridge, MA: Harvard University Press.

Embassy of India (EOI) (2013). Gifting of ambulances, buses by Government of India to various organizations in Nepal on the occasion of the 64th Republic Day of India 2013, 26 January. Embassy of India, Kathmandu.

EOI (2015). *India-Yemen bilateral relations*. Saana: Indian Embassy. Available at http://eoisanaa.org/bilateral-relations/. [Accessed 1 September 2015].

Gavi (2015). *India: Proceeds to Gavi, the vaccine alliance from donor contributions and pledges (2011–2015) as of 30 June 2015*. Washington, DC: Gavi. Available at www.gavi.org/funding/donor-profiles/india/.

Global Health Strategies Initiatives (GHSi) (2012). *How the BRICS are reshaping global health and development*. New York: GHSi. Available at www.ghsinitiatives.org/downloads/ghsi_brics_report.pdf. [Accessed 10 September 2015].

India-Brazil-South Africa Dialogue Forum (IBSA) (No date). *Strengthening infrastructure to combat HIV/AIDS in Burundi*. New Delhi: IBSA. Available at www.ibsa-trilateral.org/component/content/article/9-uncategorised/331-strengthening-infrastructure-and-capacity-to-combat-hivaids-in-burundi.

Indian Technical and Economic Cooperation Programme (ITEC) (2015). *ITEC civilian training programme*. ITEC, Ministry of External Affairs, Government of India. Available at http://itec.mea.gov.in/?1396?000.

Kickbusch, I., and Kökény, M. (2013). Global health diplomacy: Five years on. Bulletin of the World Health Organization, 91: 159. Available at doi:10.2471/BLT.13.118596.

Ministry of External Affairs (MEA) (1961–2005). *MEA Annual reports 1961–2006*. New Delhi: MEA Library, Government of India. Available at http://mealib.nic.in/.

Saran, S. (2012). India and Africa: Development partnership. *RIS Discussion Paper,* 180. Research and Information System for Developing Countries, New Delhi.

Souza, A.M. (2013). Brazil's development cooperation in Africa: A new model. *Paper Presented at the Fifth BRICS Academic Forum,* 10–13 March, Durban, South Africa.

Task Team on South-South Cooperation (TT-SSC) (2011). *Recommendations: Unlocking the potential of South-South cooperation*. Paris: Organisation for Economic Co-operation and Development. Available at www.oecd.org/dac/effectiveness/46080462.pdf.

United Kingdom Department of Health (UKDH) (2008). *Health is global: A UK government strategy 2008–2011*. London: HM Government. Available at www.ghd-net.org/sites/default/files/UK%20gov.pdf. [Accessed 10 September 2015].

Waning, B., Diedrichsen, E., and Moon, S. (2010). A lifeline to treatment: The role of Indian generic manufacturers in supplying antiretroviral medicines to developing countries. *Journal of the International AIDS Society*, 13: 35. Available at doi:10.1186/1758-2652-13-35.

World Intellectual Property Organisation (WIPO) (2004). Thirty-first (15th extraordinary) session Geneva, 27 September–5 October, 2004, Proposal by Argentina and Brazil for the establishment of a development agenda for WIPO, WO/GA/31/11, 27 August. World Intellectual Property Organization, Geneva.

5 India's credit lines

Instrument of economic diplomacy

Prabodh Saxena

Introduction

On the eve of independence – despite centuries of neglect and impoverishment, despite scarce resources and enormous domestic needs – India affirmed its duty to support other poor countries. The Ministry of External Affairs (MEA) assumed guidance of India's developmental assistance agenda, and in 1966, the government of India (GOI) opened credit lines for friendly countries. The Department of Economic Affairs (DEA) in the Ministry of Finance (MOF), in collaboration with MEA, took on administration of these loans,[1] popularly known as LOCs, or lines of credit.

The subject has yet to receive scholarly attention. This chapter offers an 'insider's view' of institutional arrangements and improvements needed to raise the quality of India's LOCs, drawing on the author's experience as head of the DEA division responsible for LOCs from July 2010 to July 2012. During this time, the author consulted a cross-section of stakeholders representing all aspects of the LOC process, including upwards of fifty officers within the responsible ministries and divisions and their counterparts in partner countries, along with project administrators, personnel, and end users. For reasons of confidentiality, all informants remain anonymous.

The chapter will provide three background sections, addressing, respectively, the history of LOCs in India, the current composition of the LOC portfolio,[2] and the growing importance of Africa. The fourth and critical section will detail structural, implementation, and policy-related shortcomings and suggest remedial measures. The final section offers concluding remarks, stressing the vital role that LOCs may play in foreign and economic relations once quality control improves.

Background: the emergence of LOCs and the arrival of IDEAS

In the first phase of the LOC programme (1966–2003), the GOI signed credit agreements with the borrowing country; the relevant LOCs were directly charged to the budget and disbursed through the State Bank of India. During this period, the GOI extended eighty-three government-to-government LOCs to twenty-three countries, totalling LOCs worth USD 1,816.82 million in purchasing power parity

(PPP)[3] (for thirty-one LOCs in USD) and INR 5,862.1 million[4] (for fifty-two LOCs in Indian rupees).[5]

The Indian bilateral aid arrangement, both as recipient and donor, changed in 2003, opening the second phase of the LOC programme. The change reflected tensions with Western donors after the 1998 Pokhran nuclear test, the 1999 Orissa super-cyclone, and the 2001 Gujarat earthquake (Sinha 1999; Buck 2002; Hufbauer et al. 2008). The GOI found an opportunity to redraw its development cooperation paradigm after 2000, once India had achieved comfortable foreign exchange reserves and low domestic interest rates. Finance Minister Jaswant Singh, in his 2003–2004 budget speech (Union Budget 2003: Paras 66, 117 and 126), launched India as a significant 'donor' with its own distinctive path, while also drastically reducing the category of eligible bilateral partners.

That year saw the birth of the International Development Initiative, which allows India's Export-Import (Exim) Bank to extend LOCs to friendly foreign countries at the GOI's behest (DEA 2004). The GOI bears the interest equalisation support (IES), that is, the differential between the actual interest charged and Exim Bank's normative commercial interest rate. Such Exim Bank LOCs carry double guarantees: a sovereign one from the borrowing government and a counter-guarantee provided by the GOI. The programme was renamed the Indian Development and Economic Assistance Scheme (IDEAS) in July 2005.

IDEAS had several aims: boosting India's exports (especially of industrial goods), opening new markets for Indian companies, establishing India's reputation for high-quality goods and services, and, last but not least, increasing India's political influence and gaining goodwill among foreign countries. Of late, India's domestic requirements for natural resources, food, and energy security have also become important considerations in the scheme.

Initially proposed for five years beginning in fiscal year (FY)[6] 2005–2006, IDEAS received a five-year extension from the Cabinet (i.e., from FY 2010–2011 to FY 2014–2015) on 3 March 2011 (Table 5.1).

The administration of IDEAS comes under the guidelines issued by the DEA in 2007, revised and updated in July 2010 and September 2011 (DEA 2010; Para b [i]; 2011). The guidelines separately specify the operational guidelines and the bidding and procurement procedures (DEA 2010: Annex II; 2011).[7] The guidelines sort partner countries into three broad categories: heavily indebted poor countries (HIPC), low-income countries (LIC)/least-developed countries (LDC), and middle-income Countries (MIC), in accordance with United Nations (UN) definitions (World Bank 2012). The terms of credit appear in Table 5.2.

Unlike Organisation for Economic Co-operation and Development (OECD)–ordained concessional finance, the LOCs clearly serve to promote Indian business interests. The policy states this up front: a minimum of 75 per cent of the contract goods and services must come from Indian sources (DEA 2010; 2011). Exceptional circumstances (especially in civil construction projects) may permit a suitable relaxation (not exceeding 10 per cent), determined on a case-by-case basis.

As specified in the guidelines (DEA 2010: Para A[ii]; 2011), economic and infrastructure projects receive priority for LOCs, followed by specific sectors

Table 5.1 Annual phasing of IDEAS LOCs (in USD million [PPP])

	Broad Grouping	FY 2010–2011	FY 2011–2012	FY 2012–2013	FY 2013–2014	FY 2014–2015
i.	Normal credit lines to African countries and Regional Economic Communities (RECs) of Africa	1,367.40	1,395.65	1,618.12	1,793.36	–
ii	Additional credit lines to African countries and RECs of Africa	1,914.36	1,953.91	2,265.37	2,510.71	–
iii	Credit lines to African countries and RECs of Africa	–	–	–	–	4,372.97
iv.	Credit lines to non-African countries	1,367.40	1,395.65	1,618.12	1,793.36	1,822.07
v.	Total amount of LOCs	4,649.15	4,745.21	5,501.61	6,097.43	6,195.04

Source: CCEA (2011)

Table 5.2 Indian credit line terms and conditions

	HIPC	LIC/LDC	MIC
Rate of interest (%)	1.75	2.00	LIBOR + 0.5
Maturity (years)	20	10	8
Moratorium (years)	5	3	2
Grant element (%)	56.4	37.3	34.4

Source: Department of Economic Affairs (2010)

that may create bridgeheads for bilateral trade. In particular, LOCs target the export of essential goods and services to countries without an Indian presence, along with credit support for exporter facility networks.

However, IDEAS allows the borrowing country complete independence in identifying the target project, along with choosing the executing agency according to its local laws and procurement policies – provided that such selection is fair and transparent and does not contravene the guidelines. The Exim Bank oversees LOC implementation through all stages, from initial setup, loan documentation, contract approval, and disbursements to project monitoring and completion; it also ensures that the disbursements follow the parameters defined in the project reports.

Shifting priorities, shifting modalities: the growth of LOCs

We turn now to the overall profile of the LOCs, as well as their general distribution. As of 31 March 2014, the Exim Bank has signed 176 LOCs[8] covering sixty-two countries on five continents, with credit commitments aggregating USD 37.203 billion in PPP. Additionally, nineteen LOCs amounting to USD 2.91

billion PPP await implementation. Once they roll out, the total commitment will rise to 195 LOCs of USD 40.108 billion PPP in sixty-six countries. An overview appears in Table 5.3.

Over the last few years, the LOC portfolio has grown exponentially in all directions – in sheer volume, as a percentage of the entire bilateral assistance basket, and as a share of the Exim Bank balance sheet. Figure 5.1 summarises this growth, along with the increasing share of GOI-sponsored LOC in the total Exim Bank portfolio.

Sectorial distribution

Energy and transport, acute needs in any developing country, account for more than 50 per cent of the portfolio. Because investment also aims to generate

Table 5.3 Regional distribution of LOCs: numbers and credits in FY 2014–2015

Region	Number of LOCs	Credit Amount
		USD million (PPP)
Africa	127	22,848.75
Asia	33	13,348.48
Latin America and the Caribbean (LAC)	14	619.50
Commonwealth of Independent States (CIS)	1	204.07
Oceania	1	182.21
TOTAL	176	37,203.01

Source: Author calculations based on Exim Bank database (2014)

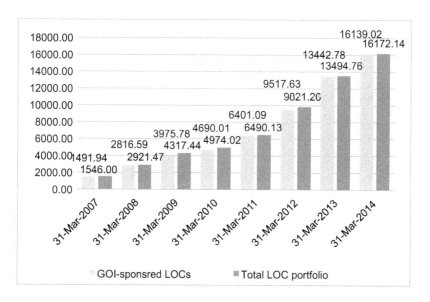

Figure 5.1 India: lines of credit – the growing portfolio

employment, the sugar industry (including plant rehabilitation) has also become a priority. In the last five years, the make-up of the portfolio has not changed much except for minor adjustments (Figure 5.2).

Distribution of LOCs across economic classifications

Figure 5.3 shows the allocation of LOCs by UN classification of the recipient countries. It demonstrates that the vast majority of LOCs go to the most indebted and least developed countries.

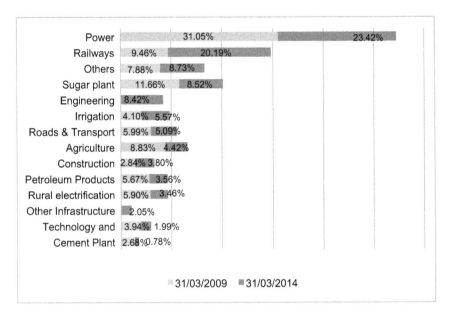

Figure 5.2 Distribution of LOCs by sector as of 31 March 2009 and 31 March 2014

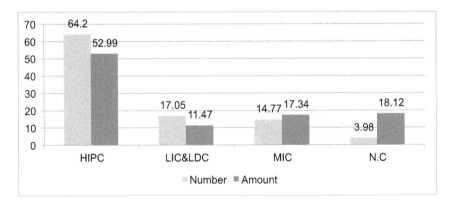

Figure 5.3 LOC approvals: numbers and volumes (%)

This general profile does not reveal many of the weaknesses that may afflict LOC projects. Many LOCs fall behind schedule; some never get off the ground. A large number of projects face challenging local conditions, and partner-government matching contributions (both financial and regulatory) may prove slow in coming. The situation may worsen when the projects themselves take too long to gestate. Other operational problems may lead to suboptimal disbursement performance: political instability in the partner country, poor contractor selection, institutional weaknesses, and contractual disputes, among other causes. The GOI's reluctance to cancel nonperforming LOCs for diplomatic reasons adds to the deadwood, pulling down the portfolio profile. We will return to these issues later; first, however, we will examine the newfound prominence of Africa in the LOC portfolio, which further illustrates long-range changes in LOC strategy.

Africa all over

India-Africa relations predate any governmental initiative. The colonial period saw substantial movement of Indians to Africa, particularly to the east. After India attained independence, its African diaspora grew substantially. Long before China evinced its interest in the region, Indian foreign policy sincerely cultivated relations with Africa (see Beri in this volume).

India has a broad commercial engagement with Africa, encompassing both aid and trade; LOCs form a significant component of both. Table 5.3 shows the regional breakdown of the Indian LOC portfolio.

This growing engagement received a huge boost with the launch of the India-Africa Forum Summit, first convened in 2008. At the Addis Ababa Summit in 2011, Indian Prime Minister Manmohan Singh announced LOC commitments to Africa aggregating USD 13,956.49 million PPP LOCs over the following three years – a transformational initiative.

In the last few years, then, Africa has moved to the centre of the circle. In the 6 years from FY 2008–2009 to 2013–2014, 91 LOCs out of 121 LOCs (74.38 per cent) went to African countries. In other credit allocations during the same period, USD 14,380.50 million PPP (62.23 per cent), out of a total allocation of USD 23,073.21 million PPP, went to the continent (see Table 5.1). The 5-year allocation approved by India's Cabinet Committee on Economic Affairs (CCEA) in 2011 earmarked 70.5 per cent of the total (USD 19,191.85 million PPP out of USD 27,188.44 million PPP); in FY 2012–2013, almost the entire allocation went to Africa. In fact, the 2011 Addis Ababa announcement has simply accelerated and targeted these increases. It has also opened the possibility of big-ticket projects with continental reach. Africa's increasing share appears in Table 5.4.

India's African LOCs have catalysed projects in diverse sectors, such as agriculture, construction, roads, railways and transportation, irrigation, energy generation and transmission, rural electrification, technology (parks and training centres), sugar industry rehabilitation, and so on. An illustrative list of African LOC projects appears in Table 5.5.

Table 5.4 Africa's share of all Indian LOCs

Financial Year	Signed LOCs					
	Total	Africa	Percentage	Total	Africa	Percentage
	No.	No.		USD million (PPP)	USD million (PPP)	
2008–2009	23	14	60.87	2,071.82	1,270.10	61.30
2009–2010	20	16	80.00	1,934.73	1,364.41	70.52
2010–2011	21	15	71.43	5,885.91	2,156.91	36.65
2011–2012	17	13	76.47	4,128.27	2,195.66	53.19
2012–2013	16	14	87.50	2,697.70	2,620.03	97.12
2013–2014	24	18	75.00	6,354.78	4,773.39	75.11
Total :	**121**	**90**	**74.38**	**23,073.21**	**14,380.50**	**62.33**

Source: Author summary of data from Exim Bank (2014)

Table 5.5 India LOC-financed African projects: a representative sample

Projects/Sectors Financed	Countries
Agricultural Projects	Angola, Benin, Burkina Faso, Cameroon, Chad, Côte d'Ivoire, the State of Eritrea, The Gambia, Ghana, Madagascar, Malawi, Mali, Mozambique, Senegal, Sierra Leone, Sudan, Tanzania, Togo
Construction Projects	Gabon, Ghana
Irrigation	Angola, Democratic Republic of the Congo, Lesotho, Malawi, Mozambique, Senegal, Zimbabwe
Power Generation, Transmission, and Distribution	Burundi, Central African Republic, Côte d'Ivoire, Comoros, Democratic Republic of the Congo, Ethiopia, Kenya, Mali, Mozambique, Niger, Sudan, Zambia
Rural Electrification	Chad, Ghana, Mali, Mozambique, Democratic Republic of the Congo, Senegal, Togo
Railway Rehabilitation	Angola, Benin, Ghana, Mali, Senegal
Roads and Transport	Central African Republic, Côte d'Ivoire, Ghana, Niger, Senegal, Tanzania
Technology (Parks and Training Centres)	Angola, Côte d'Ivoire, Democratic Republic of the Congo, Mozambique, Senegal, Swaziland
Sugar Industry Rehabilitation	Ethiopia, Malawi, Sudan

Source: Exim Bank (2014)

Africa's increasing share in the LOC portfolio testifies to India's general influence on potential 'suitor' countries. Numerous stakeholders interviewed for this chapter attested to this. India has pushed its African connection, not simply to score diplomatic points, but also to achieve a foothold in an energy- and mineral-rich region. Africa brings an essential chapter to India's quest for energy security, and LOCs offer a prominent vehicle for realising it. Increased LOC engagement has not only added to both 'hard' and 'soft' physical infrastructure, but has also spurred notable job creation, institutional development, capacity building, and technology and skill transfer, all while enhancing reciprocal trade relations. Despite the challenges of operating in Africa noted earlier, India sees a great opportunity for the partnership in boosting LOCs, and IDEAS presents the perfect vehicle for seizing the moment.

Re-energising LOCs: removing constraints and adding value

In the initial years of IDEAS, the majority of its LOCs consisted of supply contracts. More recently, the scope and profile of LOCs have expanded considerably. Now LOCs not only finance localised civil projects (e.g., building construction), but go to projects with an enhanced focus on capability creation, thus contributing to sustainable development. Although core physical infrastructure projects still occupy the prime share of the portfolio, borrowing countries have grown more confident in demanding knowledge-based credit lines. Notably, the GOI has decided to cover the complete cost of a few high-visibility projects, lest the borrowing country's budgetary constraints or capacity profile threaten to dilute their impact.

However, despite numerous individual success stories (see e.g., CII 2010; Quadri and Singhal 2014; Exim Bank 2015a), the recently increased volumes and range of LOCs make this an appropriate moment to reflect on their status and consider possible policy corrections. This section will address necessary reforms through five interlinked topics, again buttressed by the author's observations and commentary from anonymous stakeholders across the LOC process. First, we identify three policy questions that may present structural hurdles to LOC performance. Second, we look at the key administrative questions that arise in LOC project selection (including the pre- and postselection phases). Third, we look at the two most widely utilised LOC types: traditional supply contracts and information technology transfers. The latter in particular informs the fourth topic: the development of knowledge and value through LOC projects. After this overview, we will finally address changes to the guidelines needed to enhance LOC effectiveness and relevance, both in India and in the partner countries.

The policy issues

First, the quintessential policy debate has focused on whether India's LOCs can match their Chinese counterparts. Borrowing countries, particularly resource-rich ones, often play India and China against each other, sometimes even after the end of documentation and negotiations. They insist on relaxing terms and waiving conditions. Due to 'strategic reasons' or commitments/announcements made at higher levels, the GOI has granted quite a number of relaxations and, worryingly, they appear on the rise; thirty-seven LOCs have received modifications as of 31 March 2014 (Table 5.6) pertaining to rate of interest, repayment period,

Table 5.6 Sample relaxations under GOI-supported LOCs, March 2014

Recipient of LOC	Amount of LOC (USD million)	Project/Contract	Variance Approved for Change in Indian Content
Government of Gabon	14.50	Construction of an integrated neighbourhood unit on the plot of Bikele, Gabon	Reduction in Indian content to 65%
Government of Afghanistan	50.00	Export of goods and services and project exports	Repayment in 24 years (inclusive of 5 years moratorium) as compared to 20 years (inclusive of 5 years moratorium) applicable for HIPC
Government of Vietnam	45.00	NAM Chien Hydropower Project (200 MW) at Son La Province	Rate of interest reduced to 1.75% from LIBOR+.50%, difference of LIBOR–1.25% being borne by MEA
Myanmar Foreign Trade Bank	198.96	Sixteen ongoing irrigation schemes and two rehabilitation schemes in the irrigation project in Myanmar	Reduction in Indian content to 50%; rate of interest at 1.75% as compared to LIBOR+.50% as applicable to MIC countries. Repayment period 15 years (inclusive of 5 years moratorium); Waiver of management fee.
Senegal	19.00	Fisheries Development Project in Senegal	Increase in moratorium period to 6 years from 5 years. Tenure remains at 20 years.

Source: Author's notes (unpublished) (2014)

moratorium, Indian content, and so on. Besides their severe financial implications, such relaxations threaten the guidelines' universality and predictability.

The debate's roots lie in the opposed positions of the MEA and DEA. Are LOCs financial products or diplomatic instruments? The DEA maintains that LOCs exist to promote India's commercial interests; political goodwill is an incidental by-product. The MEA regards India's development cooperation as primarily serving strategic interests, and fears that financial intransigence will blunt the sharp edges of the diplomatic tool.

It seems clear, at any rate, that India cannot compete with China, lacking the latter's flexibility and resource bucket; attempts to do so will simply complicate Indian aid architecture. Enhancing proven strengths seems a more appropriate focus. A borrowing country desires an efficiently delivered project conforming to its expectations, even if it proves at times somewhat more costly than the alternatives. With the guidelines in the public domain, borrowers are fully aware of Indian terms and conditions. Frequent and indiscriminate discretionary actions can destroy both the transparency and credibility of the guidelines.

Second, the absence of a professional agency poses a major structural hardship. In fact, the MEA's attempt to create a specialised agency has a chequered history, with two failed attempts in 2007 and 2011. As a compromise, an umbrella division called the Development Partnership Administration (DPA) came into existence on 1 January 2012, uniting all assistance programmes under a single roof. It has proved a positive development, but has not added noticeable value in requisite skills, expertise, and knowledge. The change is more of form than of substance.

Third, the financial viability of LOCs requires steady, protective vigilance. With the moratorium of the first large LOCs about to expire, the honeymoon period will come to a close. Sudan, a major client of Indian LOCs, supplies a cautionary example. Since the oil-rich South Sudan region seceded in 2011, Sudan has been unable to honour payments due and has defaulted. This in turn has triggered interest penalties and caused setbacks to the financial health of the portfolio (especially during FY 2010–2011 to 2012–2013).[9] If push comes to shove, Exim Bank may invoke the GOI counter-guarantee against the defaulted debt. Realistically, however, this seems unlikely; it would set an undesirable precedent, encourage potential defaulters, and affect budgetary resources. In a business-as-usual scenario, the Exim Bank alone will have to face the brunt, raising serious concerns about the financial health of the Indian LOC product.

Mentoring the entire life cycle of projects

The efficiency of project delivery depends on as much on effective implementation as on diligent preapproval processes. The professionalism has to commence at the outset, with high-quality field- and desk-level appraisals. In 2011, MEA created a standing committee for streamlining LOC approvals and monitoring (MEA 2011). Surprisingly, the committee does not include the Exim Bank, the administrator with the broadest ground-level knowledge of LOC operations – a serious omission that undermines the committee's effectiveness. Despite the semblance of due diligence, much remains to be accomplished; we will return later to potential improvements within the existing institutional regime.

Project conception: the sine qua non of the reliable detailed project report

Although the guidelines require a detailed project report (DPR), a type of feasibility study, project authorities generally lack the capacity to conceptualise project ideas or transform them into fundable entities. Anecdotal evidence from reputable bidders[10] indicates that in some cases, borrowers will submit a low-quality report based on minimal data (reliable data often proving nonexistent anyway) and conduct investigations designed to support the desired outcome. Often, the project request will include an outdated, rehashed report prepared by some aid consultant without relevant experience.

The DPR's quality aside, in some cases project realities differ from those in the report (e.g., river water flow patterns for hydropower, or power/raw material availability for industrial projects), with time then wasted in reconciling the two. Such variations require GOI approvals, resulting in more lost time.

The Central African Republic (CAR) offers a particularly egregious case: in July 2008, the GOI approved an LOC for USD 80.66 million PPP for a cement plant.[11] In August 2011, it approved further LOCs of USD 72.88 million PPP and USD 110.79 million PPP for limestone mining and the plant's power supply, respectively. By definition, a cement plant requires a proximate source of limestone and access to power. In the absence of both, it defies understanding that the initial DPR could not foresee that the plant would immediately become a white elephant.

In a few cases, allegations have arisen that agencies hoping to receive the finalised contract have (unofficially) prepared the DPR themselves.[12] This very serious conflict of interest calls into question the integrity of both the numbers offered and the bidding process itself. Paid front-end support should therefore expand to include activities beginning with project identification. For projects not selected, the paid consultancy becomes a grant; for those approved, it becomes part of the project cost, covered by the LOC. Alternatively, the GOI may direct the Exim Bank to set aside a small sum from its annual profits (by reducing the 'dividend' payable to GOI or its profit targets) to provide coverage for such costs.

The Exim Bank plans to model project preparation on an experimental basis. In partnership with Infrastructure Leasing and Financial Services, Ltd. and with equity support from the African Development Bank, it launched an innovative joint venture in Africa in July 2015. Known as the Kukuza Project Development Company, the entity will provide specialist project development expertise, preparing quality project dossiers for contracting parties; these will include the DPR, financial and technical feasibility, resettlement and environment plans, and so on (Exim Bank 2015b). However, this venture cannot substitute for a well-defined protocol, as suggested earlier.

One caveat: LOCs must retain their speed for effectiveness, and DPRs thus should only facilitate and not obstruct. Therefore, whereas a hydro project necessarily requires a detailed DPR, a feasibility study will usually suffice for an agricultural development project.

Preselection and selection: nothing but the best

Well begun is half done. Procurement and contracting concerns with Indian bidders often loom large in selection. Unlike multilateral development banks and major bilateral partners, the guidelines recognise the country procurement system for all project sizes. Weak institutional systems, high tolerance for corruption in governance, and unstable political conditions in a few borrowing countries influence outcomes as well. Regrettably, the existing selection procedures have not attracted the best of companies.

To prevent LOCs from becoming a zero-sum game, India needs to impose strict selection without offending the systems and sensitivities of the borrowers. A credible DPR will prepare the ground for a sound selection. In this context, appointing a project management consultant (PMC) will facilitate a good start and should invariably form part of approval conditions. The PMC must ensure prequalification of all bidding companies – that is, grading them on their financial strength, international and national experience, past performance, and labour pool. Prequalification may also give extra weight to companies already operating in the partner country.

The selection process must also bind the contractor to doing the job well and on time. One might achieve this by requiring the Indian contractor to furnish a performance guarantee covering (say) 10 per cent of the contract value, refundable upon timely project completion according to all specifications (or if delayed for causes beyond the company's reasonable control). Alternatively, the Exim Bank might withhold (say) 5 per cent of each invoice, released to the Indian contractor in the same manner as the performance guarantee. The Exim Bank might also employ a money-retention system, holding a percentage of funds until the buyer's final acceptance of works executed.

Industry leaders have also criticised the practice of large advance payments to all companies, regardless of credentials; they believe that this prompts weak and insincere parties to join the fray. Such large advances may be diverted to other purposes, to the project's detriment. One possible solution would link the value of preselection advances to the nature of the underlying activities (initial design, procurement of long-lead items, long manufacturing cycles, and so forth) in order to separate the wheat from the chaff.

Reducing the idle-time lag

The approval process needs simplification. Currently, the Office of the External Affairs Minister (OEAM) within the MEA initially approves LOC proposals; afterwards, they go to the MOF for approval at the finance minister level. Although the MEA approves the country and project, the DEA ensures that each proposal conforms to the guidelines, with budgetary provision for the IES and the guarantee.

After this approval and the proposal's return to the OEAM, the latter sends a formal LOC offer to the borrowing country. Inordinate delays may occur at this phase, for various reasons (not all are in the public domain); the MEA may choose to wait for an impending diplomatic visit or other opportunity to derive additional benefit from the offer. The MEA understandably wishes not to publicise the LOC until the OEAM can write a formal letter of offer. At times, this gives rise to asymmetry of information. Because proposals may circulate between desks for a considerable period, sometimes companies get wind of important project information, giving them an unfair competitive advantage at the bidding stage. Proper and transparent bidding therefore requires drastic reduction of the time lag at each approval phase. Professionalism should prevail over posturing and protocol in decisions of significant commercial importance.

Regular and strict monitoring

The guidelines (Para 12) require borrowing governments to set up suitable moni-toring mechanisms involving representatives of Exim Bank and Indian embassies. But the GOI has not activated its own monitoring committee as envisaged in the guidelines, and embassy oversight appears conspicuous by its absence. MEA and DEA officers also rarely make overseas visits, leaving periodic review and onsite inspections exclusively to the Exim Bank (which has its own limitations in deal-ing with foreign governments and Indian embassies). A few interministerial del-egation visits took place in 2012,[13] but thereafter, the practice abruptly stopped.

This absence prevents the MEA and DEA from taking any systemic ownership of IDEAS and betrays the general protocol of developmental cooperation. India's biggest bilateral partner, Japan International Cooperation Agency (JICA), pro-vides a sharp contrast: in addition to frequent interactions, structured dialogues occur regularly between the GOI and JICA, as well as the GOI and the govern-ment of Japan. There is no reason why India, having committed such enormous resources, should shy away from such interactions. If anything, India should for-mally establish regular and periodic consultations and follow-up visits at LOC project sites and pursue relevant dialogue with the borrower countries.

Ex-post evaluation

No ex-post evaluation practice currently exists for LOCs. IDEAS urgently needs such a process, one that would assess project outcomes through reputable agencies against the DPR objectives within 2 years of project completion. Initially, evalu-ations could be done for all major projects, with random assessments becoming the rule once a protocol comes into effect. Needless to say, all specialised bilat-eral partners do this as a mandatory part of their portfolio. Postevaluation funding could take several forms: as part of the project cost, as a GOI budget item, or as an arrangement worked out with the Exim Bank. Lack of resources, in other words, should not appear as a barrier here, nor do the guidelines stand in the way; rather, proper evaluation requires proactive and creative solutions.

Ensuring comprehensive supply contracts

Any holistic discussion of LOC protocol streamlining must include supply con-tracting. At first glance, supply LOCs (the common term for goods-only credit lines) appear the easiest to disburse and deliver; on closer examination, however, they prove the most difficult. In the absence of adequate backward-and-forward linkages, they do more harm than good.

The demand for supplies should normally form part of a larger intervention, but many borrowing countries prefer to secure them on a standalone basis. This creates numerous problems. In the Democratic Republic of the Congo (DRC), a director-level site visit (February-March 2012) found that a USD 46.63 million PPP LOC for cement machinery had essentially gone to waste. The machines have stood idle for an unjustifiably long period while the host government struggles to set up the plant, having changed the project site as many as five times. In such

LOCs, the construction schedule should synchronise with supply orders and actual delivery. Shipment of goods should not occur before site readiness; otherwise, the Indian company may dispatch the goods, claim the payment under line of credit, and wash its hands of the project with impunity. At the same time, fairness requires some provision to compensate the Indian exporter if the site handover faces delays; otherwise, exporters risk losses through no fault of their own.

Questions also persist about the capabilities and intentions of Indian contractors. One might address this by restricting these supply contracts to original manufacturers. General suppliers or trading companies sometimes simply procure, install, do minimal handholding for operators, station some spares, and disappear from the scene. They may act as fly-by-night operators – unlike manufacturers, who have full wherewithal to deliver services and reputations to guard. Although vested interests may hamper such a policy change, the perception and delivery of supply LOCs would improve spectacularly with more rigorous contracting.

The challenge: increasing demand for 'soft projects' that transfer knowledge and enhance skills

A dysfunctional project not only wastes precious resources, but also constitutes a permanent slur on Indian cooperation. Many projects have lost their viability soon after handover; we should exercise caution concerning these 'soft' projects, in particular information technology (IT) and 'knowledge park' initiatives. Many developing countries deeply admire India's IT prowess and seek to replicate its success. To date, these efforts have not entailed significant LOC amounts, but recently the number of requests has risen (Exim Bank 2014).[14]

In May 2012, the author had the opportunity to visit one such project as part of an interministerial delegation: the Technology Development and Innovation Centre at Science and Technology Park, Maluana, about 30 kilometres from Mozambique's capital, Maputo. The project comprises a state-of-the-art, IT-intelligent building, with a support system including an 'incubator' research and development facility, a technology park, and administrative offices. The vendor is a civil contractor – an infrastructure specialist – who outsourced the essential tech handholding to IT professionals. This selection of a single executing agency for hardware and software appears problematic, creating a 'turnkey' situation unlikely to lead to the best outcomes in knowledge-based projects. Only time will show whether the project will succeed in transferring skill sets and managerial capabilities to the host country.

The GOI should only offer these types of LOCs after assessing the capacity and human resource skills of the borrowing country. This becomes even more critical in Francophone countries, where serious linguistic constraints often impede training and capacity building. Recently, the GOI has added a requirement to obtain details of the project's sustainability and operational viability throughout its life cycle; these now form part of the LOC agreement, – a small step in the right direction. Notional 'training', casually built into feasibility reports, will not do any good; the GOI and its partners should view long-term building of organisational skills as part of the intervention.

The LOC process also needs to ensure that the borrowing government supply a road map for building its own manpower capabilities. The GOI could insist upon a commitment to adequate budgetary supports where needed. Ultimately, sustainability should give the benchmark for measuring the success and relevance of a delivered project.

Technical assistance: the gift of solution

All developmental partners, whether multilateral or bilateral, actively encourage technical assistance (TA) related to their projects (Chaturvedi 2014). India has proved the most notable exception. It has all the credentials to transfer knowledge, offer solutions, present international best practices, and build and augment capacities in borrowing countries. India is in a unique position to offer a Triple A advantage to borrowers: technology that they can Afford, Appropriate to their developmental level, and Adaptable to their particular conditions.

To complete its development cooperation profile, India must introduce TA programmes, whether as standalones or in conjunction with investment projects (or both). Typically, such programmes take the form of grants; they will bring India into the legal, policy, management, governance, and regulatory spaces of its partner countries. Not only will this enhance the quality of LOCs, but it will also enable the borrowing country to receive them more efficiently, consequently improving their capacity and skill base. It would also serve to entrench awareness and recognition of Indian capabilities, and perhaps lead to future commercial opportunities.

Guiding the guidelines

From these procedural issues, we now turn to specific reforms in the IDEAS guidelines – last revised, as noted, in July 2010 with some modifications in September 2011. Changes in the global economic situation since then (particularly the continued low-interest regime in Western international capital markets), as well as early programme implementation experiences, have raised concerns among borrowers. In brief, the guidelines must suitably respond to the following issues:

1   For the past 5 years, HIPC and LIC/LDC have paid higher fixed interest (1.75 to 2.00 per cent) compared with MIC (LIBOR + 50 basis points (bps) = 0.88 per cent as in March 2014). The LIBOR will likely remain 'soft' for at least another few years, perpetuating this anomaly. This has underpinned many borrowing-country demands for relaxation, and makes a strong case for revising credit terms. The classification systems of multilateral development banks may offer guidelines here. Furthermore, the GOI must offer appropriate incentives to foster graduation from more concessional to less concessional brackets. Currently, there is a sharp fall in concessional parameters from HIPC (20 years with 5 years' grace) to LIC/LDC and MIC (10/8 years and 3/2 years). This unintentionally penalises HIPC countries that do well enough to graduate to the higher category. A case exists for making the transition gentler.
2   Baldly stated, the country procurement system does not always follow international standards. We would propose a monetary limit (say, projects of USD

72.88 million PPP and above), above which all LOC procurement requires Exim Bank review. Smaller projects would not require the same close monitoring. This resembles the World Bank's prior and ex-post review mechanism; the Asian Development Bank follows a similar practice (see e.g., World Bank 2013).

3   India's robust portfolio now permits greater liberality with the local contents/ production threshold. Borrowing countries should not feel excluded from capital formation. We need to precisely define the Indian content and encourage professional certification of added value. At the same time, LOC policy should strictly discourage third-country imports, except in rare (and documented) cases where Indian manufacture proves unfeasible.

4   Calculation of the grant element often comes into question. The grant element essentially represents the difference between the present value (PV) of debt servicing and the face value of the LOC. High discount rates, long credit periods, higher moratoriums, and related permutations will upwardly bias the PV; the reverse conditions will push it downward. IDEAS currently envisages a grant discount rate of 10 per cent (OECD formula). This seems reasonable in an Indian context with bank base rates over 10 per cent, but materially out of line for a USD credit with LIBOR at less than 1 per cent and the borrowing rate at less than 2 per cent. Applying current interest rates would reduce relaxation requests that call for discretionary concessions.

These essentially technical matters, in addition to the procedural reforms already outlined, would go far toward reassuring partner countries and maintaining the fiscal health of the LOC portfolio.

Conclusion

Over the past decade, India has become a significant provider of development assistance. In fact, current trends suggest that the country will become a net exporter of development assistance sometime in the next few years. This transformation reflects India's perception of itself as an emerging power and its competition with China for global political and economic influence. LOCs have also given a contextual framework for building relationships with key resource-rich countries.

Undeniably, IDEAS has put a strong Indian signature on the South-South platform; several informants testified to its immense value across the range of borrowers. LOCs have proved a safe financing option for Indian exporters, especially small and medium enterprises, and serve as both an effective market entry tool for Indian exporters and as a means to strengthen Indian development partnerships. They have enabled Indian exporters to penetrate new markets with minimal risks. Apart from generating export revenue for Indian firms, LOCs have also created goodwill; enhanced India's political presence; demonstrated Indian project execution capabilities; and supported India's long-term economic interests in the new emerging markets of Africa, Asia, Latin America, and the Commonwealth of Independent States (CIS) (see Agarwal, Chaturvedi, and especially Beri in this volume). LOCs have also helped other countries implement their development projects – using Indian technology, goods, services, and scientific know-how – at relatively low cost and interest rates, with long repayment periods, and without any prescriptive policies on the use of such funds. In a limited manner, they have also served to counterbalance the growing influence of China in many African countries (see also Li and Zhou in this volume). Not surprisingly, OECD partners have also shown interest in learning about the Indian LOC product.

Although empirical studies do not yet exist,[15] our informants broadly concurred that the increased access that LOCs provide generates new opportunities for Indian companies, often prompting them to stay in host countries after completing LOC-funded projects. The ultimate success obviously rests with the incremental business these companies secure on commercial terms after initial market entry through LOCs – a point that future research may confirm.

LOCs have undeniably become potent instruments in the international architecture of both development cooperation and finance. The major challenge lies in steering the LOC protocol from its current deficiencies to a more professional, transparent, and appropriate platform, from preapproval through postevaluation. Once IDEAS graduates to a position attracting the best and the most professional Indian companies, it will achieve an enhanced success; this chapter has offered some essential steps toward that end. A professionally delivered credit line will also nullify the debate between so-called strategic and commercial objectives.

India's policy planners must recognise the necessity of transforming LOCs into a world-class instrument, conforming to the best international practices. The full potential of this instrument will blossom with the untying of its artificial shackles. A product subject to the rigors of professional scrutiny, standards, and universally acknowledged safeguards will certainly prove India's most effective and visible envoy.

Notes

1 The exceptions are the LOCs for Bangladesh, Bhutan, and Nepal, administered from the MEA budget as per the 1961 Allocation of Business Rules (official delegation of responsibilities to ministries) (GOI 1961).
2 'Portfolio' here and throughout this chapter refers to the GOI LOCs implemented through the Exim Bank (and excludes the latter's own portfolio of LOCs).
3 India's PPP conversion factor of 0.03 is based on the 2011 World Bank International Comparison Program (World Bank 2015).
4 Approximately USD 350.60 million PPP.
5 As of 31 March 2014, there are twenty-one outstanding LOCs covering eight countries, for a total of about USD 366.6 million PPP (eleven LOCs in US dollars) and about INR 32.17 million (ten LOCs denominated in Indian rupees) (Exim Bank 2014).
6 In India, the fiscal year runs from 1 April to 31 March of the succeeding year.
7 After this chapter was written, the DEA issued revised Guidelines on 7 December 2015 (No. 21/3/2015-IDEAS). The 2015 Guidelines correct or improve many deficiencies discussed in this chapter, such as using IMF-prescribed minimum binding concessional requirements for country classifications, introducing more liberal terms of credit (Para 3), improving the committee's effectiveness, and appointing a lending-bank engineer for independent project monitoring (Para II (iv)). The 2015 Guidelines also add a separate section on ethics and integrity (Para 15), allow grant funds for project identification, proposal, appraisal, evaluation, assessment including consultancy charges and

provides that an amount not exceeding 1% of the LOC will be utilized for preparation of the DPR para 14), recommend appointing a project management consultant (Para 12 (iii)), and introduce proactive and creative solutions to a number of issues. In addition, the 2015 Guidelines introduce evaluation of projects of USD 50 million or above by the lending Bank or an independent agency (Para 12 (iii)). The 2015 Guidelines also extend more liberal tenor and moratorium periods and better interest rate differentiation among different categories of countries. (Para 3) to the LOC terms. The editors recommend readers view the contents of this chapter in light of the 2015 Guidelines (DEA 2015).

 8 Only three LOCs have been fully repaid: Ghana for USD 54.66 million PPP, Senegal for USD 54.66 million PPP, and Ceylon Petroleum Corporation (Sri Lanka) for USD 546.62 million PPP.
 9 In July 2013, the GOI rescheduled Sudan's outstanding payments, substantially reducing the overdue amount. The GOI further moved to capitalise the interest in arrears on all LOCs until December 2013 (USD 164.62 million PPP), with repayment in six half-yearly installments. The solution, albeit temporarily, gives relief to the balance sheet of Exim Bank. On the downside, no cash has actually come into the system; the resolution remains only a book entry. See also Sudan Tribune (2013).
10 Personal communications, 2012.
11 Site visited by an interministerial delegation in February-March, 2012.
12 Personal communications, 2012.
13 Senior-level delegations visited Tanzania, Mozambique, and Sudan, and director-level delegations visited Central African Republic, Gabon, and Democratic Republic of Congo. The author was the DEA representative in the senior-level delegation and separately visited Ethiopia.
14 As of 31 March 2014, the commitment of six LOCs amounts to USD 386.28 million PPP, including USD 92.93 million PPP to Mozambique. Other lines include USD 18.22 million PPP to Cape Verde (not yet accepted), USD 92.93 million PPP to Côte d'Ivoire, USD 36.44 million PPP to Senegal, USD 72.88 million PPP to Swaziland, and USD 72.88 million PPP to Mongolia (as of June 2015, not implemented as of this writing).
15 In 2009, the DEA selected a consulting firm (name withheld) to do an independent assessment of the IDEAS and to assess the symbiotic relationship (or lack of it) between LOCs and the growth of Indian business and export markets in borrowing countries. Unfortunately, the study was prematurely terminated in 2011 because of unsatisfactory progress and failure to identify sources.

Works cited

Buck, R. (2002). A tale of two disasters: A comparison of earthquake relief efforts in Gujarat, India and El Salvador. *The Monitor,* 8(2). Available at http://web.wm.edu/so/monitor/issues/08–2/6-buck.htm.

Cabinet Committee on Economic Affairs (CCEA) (2011). *Extension of Indian Development and Economic Assistance (IDEA) scheme.* New Delhi: Press Information Bureau, Government of India. Available at http://pib.nic.in/newsite/PrintRelease.aspx?relid=70441.

Confederation of Indian Industry (CII) (2010). Indian success stories in Africa. New Delhi: CII. Available at www.oialliance.com/images/indian_success_story_in_africa__oia_.pdf.

Chaturvedi, S. (2014). Entrepreneurship development, capacity building and economic integration: The case of Indian-ASEAN engagement across the CLMV region. In A. Mulakala (ed.), *The rise of emerging Asian providers: new approaches to development cooperation in Asia?* Paris: AFD, pp. 168–180.

Department of Economic Affairs (DEA) (2004). Terms and conditions and procedure to be adopted in respect of Government of India (GOI) Supported Exim Bank Lines of Credit (LOCs). O.M. No 5/8/2002-CIE-II, 23 January. Ministry of Finance, Government of India, New Delhi.

DEA (2010). Terms and conditions and procedure to be adopted in respect of Government of India (GOI) Supported Exim Bank Lines of Credit (LOCs). F.No.21/6/2008-CIE-II, 23 July. Ministry of Finance, Government of India, New Delhi. Available at www.eximbankindia.in/sites/default/files/C.pdf.

DEA (2011). Terms and conditions and procedure to be adopted in respect of Government of India (GOI) Supported Exim Bank Lines of Credit (LOCs). O.M. No 21/6/2008-CIE-II (Vol. III), 23 September. Ministry of Finance, Government of India, New Delhi.

DEA (2015). Guidelines on Lines of Credit extended by the Government of India to various countries under the Indian Development and Economic Assistance Scheme (IDEAS), Number 21/3/2015-IDEAS, enacted 7 December 2015. Ministry of Finance, Government of India, New Delhi.

Export-Import Bank of India (Exim Bank) (2014). *Government of India supported lines of credit (Database)*. New Delhi: DEA, Government of India. Available at www.eximbankindia.in/lines-of-credit.

Exim Bank (2015a). *Annual report 2014–2015*. New Delhi: DEA, Government of India. Available at www.eximbankindia.in/sites/default/files/AR%202013–14%20English%20for%20web%20New.pdf.

Exim Bank (2015b). EXIM Bank co-promotes a project development company in Africa, 24 July. DEA, Government of India, New Delhi. Available at www.eximbankindia.in/press-releases?release_date=2015–07.

Government of India (GOI) (1961). The Government of India (Allocation of business) Rules, 1961, January 14/Pausa 24, 1882(S). Cabinet Secretariat, GOI, India. Available at http://cabsec.nic.in/allocation_order.php.

Hufbauer, G.C., Schott, J.J., Elliott, K.A., and Oegg, B. (2008). Case studies in sanctions and terrorism: Case 98–1, US v. India (1998: Nuclear weapons proliferation). In *Economic Sanctions Reconsidered*. Washington, DC: Petersen Institute for International Economics.

Ministry of External Affairs (MEA) (2011). MEA ID No AC/202/171/2007, dated 3 June. MEA, Government of India, New Delhi.

Quadri, A., and Singhal, R. (2014). Development and diplomacy through lines of credit: achievements and lessons learnt. *ORF Occasional Paper*, 53. Observer Research Foundation, New Delhi.

Sinha, A.K. (1999). *Report on recovery and reconstruction following the Orissa super cyclone in October 1999* [webpage]. Kobe: Asia Disaster Reduction Center. Available at www.adrc.asia/publications/recovery_reports/pdf/Orissa.pdf.

Sudan Tribune (2013). India agrees to reschedule Sudan's lines of credit over 'difficult economic situation', *Sudan Tribune*, 26 July. Available at www.sudan4jesus.com/2013/07/india-agrees-to-reschedule-sudans-lines.html.

Union Budget (2003). *Union budget and economic survey*. New Delhi: Ministry of Finance, Government of India. Available at http://indiabudget.nic.in/ub2003–04/ubmain.htm. [Accessed 19 October 2015].

World Bank (2012). *Newest country classifications released* [webpage]. Washington, DC: The World Bank Group. Available at http://data.worldbank.org/news/newest-country-classifications-released.

World Bank (2013). *Operational manual. BP 11.00, Annex D – Mandatory prior review thresholds for RPMs and the OPRC*. Washington, DC: The World Bank Group. Available at http://go.worldbank.org/VMGNKC1EX0.

World Bank (2015). *Price level ratio of PPP conversion factor (GDP) to market exchange rate [International comparison program database]*. Washington, DC: The World Bank Group. Available at http://data.worldbank.org/indicator/PA.NUS.PPPC.RF.

6 Civil society organisations and Indian development assistance

Emerging roles for commentators, collaborators, and critics

Emma Mawdsley and Supriya Roychoudhury

South-South cooperation (SSC) is characteristically organised around government-to-government relations, with most Southern partners having relatively low levels of engagement with domestic or partner-country civil society organisations (CSOs) (Mawdsley 2012).[1] This reflects postcolonial commitments to state sovereignty, institutional infrastructures, and geoeconomic imperatives. Nevertheless, the shifting character of twenty-first century SSC raises questions about evolving relations between Southern bilateral partners and CSOs – domestic, partner-country, or transnational – and the implications for economic growth, social well-being, and political inclusion (Tomlinson 2013; Vaes and Huyse 2013; Poskitt, Shankland and Taela forthcoming).

In this chapter we analyse factors shaping India's nascent engagement with CSOs in its official development cooperation partnerships. We contend that such an analysis cannot uncouple the domestic and the international and that complex state–CSO relations within India shape how CSO roles may evolve in external development cooperation. We propose a typology of CSO–state *relationships* (rather than *organisations*), comprising independent activists, critical engagers, and government partners. Within this framework, we discuss the implications for whether and how CSOs might engage with Indian development cooperation in the future. The analysis draws from interviews conducted with relevant stakeholders in 2014.[2]

India has a diverse and richly populated civil society sector, which includes a wide array of associational forms, such as caste-based and religious organisations, social and sports clubs, village and neighbourhood committees, grassroots movements, and trade unions. In this chapter we focus on universities, think tanks, and nongovernmental organisations (NGOs) concerned with rights-based advocacy, welfare provision, and humanitarian assistance.[3] We use CSOs as our preference throughout, although at some points we use NGOs, specifically where we (or the commentators we cite) refer to this subset. Of course, it is itself a very diverse category, varying in origin, size, form, funding, motivation, personnel, and agendas (Tandon 1987; Kamat 2002; Chandhoke 2003; Jenkins 2010).

Changing state–CSO relations

Sen (1999) provides a valuable historical overview of state–NGO relations, although he is clear that this general picture conceals a wide plurality of contexts, organisations, and individuals. The immediate postindependence period, broadly speaking, saw good state–NGO relations, built on the shared experience of anticolonial struggles across the political activist spectrum and a sense of common and urgent development goals. However, during the 1960s and 1970s antagonism emerged, as NGOs and social action groups gradually came into conflict with the state. As the Congress Party hegemony eroded and Indira Gandhi embraced more authoritarian approaches, many NGOs and social movements found themselves in an increasingly politicised terrain. For example, many saw the creation of the Foreign Contribution Regulation Act (FCRA) in 1976 as a means of surveillance and control of dissenting voices (Jenkins 2010). The 1980s and 1990s witnessed the shift towards an increasingly formal incorporation and professionalisation of NGOs within national development, particularly in welfare, local participation and growth, and rights-based empowerment and advocacy. At the same time, NGOs struggled to overcome differences and divisions to establish stronger collective platforms and to defend themselves against charges of weak accountability, corruption, and ineffectiveness. In the 2000s, many international NGOs 'federated' to produce Indian chapters of transnational networks, thus strengthening Indian voices in the national and international development community.

CSOs and the state continue to inhabit a somewhat dualistic relationship. Increasingly, the state invites CSOs into the formal realm of national policy formation; CSOs also serve as significant humanitarian actors and welfare service providers and helped to catalyse a number of progressive legislative initiatives, such as the Right to Information Act (2005). Some Indian CSOs have increased their engagement with multilateral policy processes, such as the G20, BRICS, and the post-2015 development agenda processes (United Nations 2013), fuelled in part by the paradoxical nature of India's trajectory: it has become a global economic powerhouse that simultaneously houses one-third of the world's poor.

However, notwithstanding these positive interactions, the sector continues to face considerable distrust from some within the state. Some have accused CSOs of incompetence and corruption, but also, controversially, of subversion, illegally representing 'antinational', terrorist, criminal, or foreign interests. In June 2014 the Intelligence Bureau submitted a report to the Prime Minister's Office suggesting that Western states had strategically funded NGOs to raise 'people-centric' issues – such as human rights, violence against women, caste discrimination, religious freedom, and indigenous rights – in order to 'actively stall' Indian growth and development (Ranjan 2014). The Modi government has since faced accusations of suppressing civil society voices in a number of contexts (e.g., Dhawan 2015; Vijetha 2015).

The vast literature analysing the civil society sector in India understandably emphasises the domestic context. However, we would contend that this complex interplay of state–CSO relations at home must also inform any analysis of CSO roles, present or future, in India's development cooperation abroad. In the next section, we draw these parallels by analysing debates over the role of Indian CSOs in its development cooperation policies and programmes.

CSOs and Indian development cooperation

India exemplifies the predominance of state-state relations in SSC (Mawdsley 2015). Although there are early examples of the government working with CSOs to deliver assistance (e.g., Chaturvedi 2012: 172–173), it is evident that CSOs have played an almost negligible role in the last decade's considerable expansion of Indian development cooperation. Exceptions include support to NGOs in Afghanistan (MEA n.d.) and certain training and educational organisations empanelled by the Indian Technical and Economic Cooperation Programme (ITEC), although even here the state appears to prefer companies and state-led agencies (Agrawal 2007). We noted some of the 'official' reasons at the outset; they centre on the commitment to state sovereignty strongly expressed at the Bandung Conference, which continues to animate foreign policy statements today (Raghavan 2013; Akbaruddin 2014).

Moreover, the Ministry of External Affairs (MEA) and the wider foreign policy establishment comprise the part of government least open to dialogue and cooperation with nonstate actors (Wulf 2013). Unlike the majority of government ministries and national policy agencies, India's foreign policy mandarins tend to be insulated from domestic party politics and publics (Malone 2011). Additionally, the small size of India's foreign service may slow or limit more innovative development cooperation approaches (Agrawal 2007; Markey 2009; Chanana 2010), including engagement with CSOs. In their analysis of humanitarian assistance, for example, Meier and Murthy (2011: 6) observe a 'reactive rather than proactive logic' within an overstretched MEA. India's humanitarian and development assistance institutions have also not tended to engage with the wider international development sector, limiting exposure to the idea of working with CSOs. Finally, the MEA may lack appropriate information on the CSO sector – the spectrum of its activities, knowledge of its achievements and weaknesses, and which organisations to approach as reliable and effective partners.

On the other hand, domestic issues and demands have tended to fully engross Indian civil society organisations, to the exclusion of external engagement. Some Indian CSOs have participated in nonstate networks, building solidarities and partnerships in a variety of contexts, from Via Campesina to Slum/Shack Dwellers International to various United Nations (UN) forums. But until recently, they generally had neither been invited nor sought to act as formal partners in Indian development cooperation. Meier and Murthy (2011) note that when in 2008–2009 the state government of Tamil Nadu channelled funding to Sri Lanka via the International Committee of the Red Cross, the government of India (GOI) did not follow suit. Similarly, the GOI rarely directs funds to CSOs in partner countries, although there have been occasional exceptions (see e.g., Oglesby 2011).

The weak enlistment of CSOs in development cooperation arises not only from preference, but also from legal constraints. The May 2015 earthquake in Nepal, for example, revealed the difficulties faced by Indian CSOs seeking to provide assistance to their neighbours. Among other things, income tax authorities required a cumbersome process of special clearance to permit CSOs spending in Nepal, a barrier that has led to calls for change (Mukul 2015).

Clearly, both supply and demand constraints limit CSO engagement in official Indian development partnerships. However, as India's development assistance footprint has grown alongside that of other SSC partners, this has become an issue of debate. Chaturvedi et al. (2014) observe that a number of Indian and international CSOs have initiated studies and public seminars around development cooperation, including the Institute for Defence and Strategic Analysis, the Observer Research Foundation, and the Centre for Policy Research. The government side has also seen growing receptiveness to the idea of CSO cooperation. Dr. Syeda Hamid, a senior member of the (former) Planning Commission, noted that the government needed to find systems to work with voluntary organisations, both in India and abroad, 'based on mutual trust and respect and with shared responsibility' (quoted in Tomlinson 2013: 314). Importantly, the recently established Development Partnership Administration (DPA) appears aware of the gap; in 2012, its deputy secretary acknowledged the absence of dialogue with CSOs on Indian development cooperation (Raghavan, quoted in Chaturvedi, Kumar and Mendiratta 2013).

The creation of the Forum on Indian Development Cooperation (FIDC) in early 2013 therefore marks substantial progress. This platform brings together a steering committee comprising academics, select Indian CSO representatives, and officials from the DPA to discuss strategic issues relating to Indian development cooperation. Hosted by Research and Information Systems for Developing Countries (RIS), FIDC organises seminars and public discussions on various thematic aspects of Indian development cooperation (RIS 2015). These are frequently attended by civil society. In the past, they have also dealt with issues relating directly to CSOs' experiences with Indian development cooperation. CSO representatives of the FIDC's steering committee welcome the opportunity it presents to tactically influence the policies of Indian development cooperation.[4]

Several forms of state–CSO interaction can coexist within development cooperation. First, national and partner-country CSOs might act as local service-delivery contractors – providing, for example, vaccine programmes or training in microfinance. Second, policy forums might invite CSOs to contribute to shaping principles, programmes, and strategies, including those involving other actors, such as regional banks and the private sector. FIDC provides one such example. Third, CSOs might receive government recognition to enable them, along with their in-country partners, to act as independent advocates on behalf of the marginalised – even when this means confronting established political and corporate power. Many see this role as essential to democratic functioning, especially in populations with large segments of the poor and relatively powerless. As we have seen earlier, however, the establishment may feel threatened by such dissent, interpreting it, not as contributing to negotiations around the benefits and costs of 'development', but as 'antinational'. We return to this range of competing/complementary possibilities later.

In the following section we develop an analytical typology for CSOs currently engaged in Indian development cooperation, a framework that also provides a way of conceptualising future state–CSO relations within this context.

The spectrum of CSO–state relations in development cooperation

Only a tiny percentage of CSOs have any interaction with India's official development cooperation policies and programmes. For those that do, we contend that relations tend to fall under three categories: independent activists, critical engagers, and government partners. This typology does not intend to describe specific organisations or propose watertight categories; distinctions may prove fluid, particularly in this still-evolving context.

Independent activists

Independent activists tend to see Indian development cooperation in terms of a mercantilist agenda (Chaturvedi et al. 2014). Historically opposed to the deepening penetration of neoliberal economic globalisation, these CSOs have protested domestically against the activities of foreign and national multinational corporations (MNCs), such as Coca-Cola, POSCO, Arcelor Mittal, and Vedanta (Padel and Das 2010). More recently, activist organisations such as the National Alliance of People's Movements (NAPM) and the Indian Social Action Forum (INSAF) have extended this critique to Indian MNCs operating overseas (including state-owned enterprises). In light of activities that increasingly support natural resource extraction, trade, and investment by outward-looking companies, many view Indian development cooperation as an extension of neocolonial policy (Chaturvedi et al. 2014).

Indian corporate investment abroad has grown significantly in the last decade (Cheru and Obi 2011; Mawdsley and McCann 2011), in some cases drawing upon official development financing in the form of lines of credit (LOCs) (Mullen 2013; Chaturvedi et al. 2014). In addition, the government has encouraged overseas private-sector investment, most notably in agriculture (Cheru and Modi 2013). In 2014, for example, the government proposed the Asia-Africa Agribusiness Forum as an 'initiative of South-South cooperation' (Mukherjee 2014). According to the former head of the DPA, it aimed to combine development assistance with the 'commercial perspectives' of Indian businesses in order to increase its 'developmental impact in our partner countries' (Raghavan 2013).

For supporters, this demonstrates the value of Indian development cooperation: the provision of scarce investment, appropriate technology, and mutually beneficial economic benefits. However, Indian activist organisations such as Kalpvriksha challenge the premise that agribusiness and other forms of investment-led economic growth will automatically improve citizen welfare (Oakland Institute

2013). They argue that the state supports models and vehicles of growth that neglect equity, rights, and sustainability (Rowden 2011). They assert that India does not act in its own 'national' interests or those of its partner countries, but on behalf of capital and the transnational wealthier classes in both.

Further criticisms of development cooperation policy concern the official claims to noninterference; some of our interviewees see this principle as a smokescreen permitting the Indian state to act with impunity. They argue that the government should not have the sole power to assess what this means, on the basis that the high ideals of demand-driven aid come into question when partner government rationales do not accord with local community interests.

Several activist organisations hold these positions. NAPM, INSAF, Kalpvriksha, and the South Asian Farmers' Committee, for example, have drawn attention to the relationship between domestic and external development politics. At a *sangharsh* ('struggle' in Hindi) organised by NAPM in New Delhi in 2011 to protest the proposed (Indian) Land Acquisition Act, Medha Patkar – a prominent activist leader sometimes disparaged by officials and elites – also raised the problem of Indian companies involved in overseas land acquisition, asserting a crisis shared by citizens in India, Africa, and Southeast Asia (Rowden 2011: 35). In 2013, the Oakland Institute collaborated with Indian Social Action Forum (INSAF), PEACE, and Kalpvriksha at a joint meeting addressing Indian private investments in Ethiopia. The organisers brought members of Ethiopian indigenous communities and popular movements to New Delhi, who accused the Indian government of complicity in exploitative land acquisition, furthered through incentives such as import tariff reductions and double taxation avoidance agreements (Oakland Institute 2013). Another alliance critical of Indian policy took place between the international NGO Genetic Resources Action International (GRAIN), the international social movement Via Campesina, and the South Indian Coordination Committee of Farmers' Movements. In 2012, the Kenya Revenue Authority ruled that the India-based multinational Karuturi Global had used transfer mispricing to avoid paying the government of Kenya corporate income tax, to the tune of nearly USD 11 million. One of the activist networks interviewed for this study laid claim to raising public visibility of this issue in India.[5]

However, as of this writing, no recent similar transnational civil society meetings have addressed the role of Indian private investments overseas. One representative of an activist network stated that organising international meetings requires clearances at multiple levels, including from the Ministry of Home Affairs, the Ministry of External Affairs, and the nodal ministry concerned.[6] Given the sensitivity of this issue and current challenges around the FCRA legislation, it remains to be seen whether the Indian government will allow or block such meetings. One should note that India is not alone in this suppression of CSO dissent; Ethiopia, for example, also stringently regulates its CSOs. Partner-country governments and elites also may not welcome a stronger role for Indian CSOs in some cases, especially perhaps in alliance with their own CSOs.

To conclude, these organisations represent varying degrees of political radicalism, and in general they choose not to engage directly in state-facilitated platforms such as FIDC, which they regard as a form of co-optation by the Indian government. Many policy and business elites in India see no legitimate role for these adversarial voices and tactics, and resist attempts to link domestic development politics and pathways to international impacts and activities. We would argue for the legitimacy of dissenting voices, who question the precepts of mainstream development, both in India and abroad.

Critical engagers

The majority of Indian CSOs involved in some form or another with Indian development cooperation are 'critical engagers'. Three types of CSOs cluster under this category: national organisations and networks, academics and think tanks, and international nongovernmental organisations (INGOs). They broadly share a perception of SSC as an important component of Indian internationalism, which ideally signifies a more politically equitable era in international relations. They are open to dialogue with the government, but nevertheless, still question and critique elements of the official discourse on SSC. They seek a stronger role, arguing for the specific skills, dispositions, and safeguards brought by the CSO sector. Critical engagers also tend to welcome the possibility for synergies between SSC and North-South cooperation, particularly as it relates to cross-learning and exchange of developmental best practices.

A number of national networks and organisations – such as the Voluntary Action Network of India (VANI), the Participatory Research Institute in Asia (PRIA), and Wada Na Todo Abhiyan (WNTA) for example – have increasingly engaged with concerns about Indian development cooperation. There are several reasons for this. First, as one national network argued the government must account for taxpayer money used for India's overseas engagements, addressing how such global engagements affect India's own development trajectory, as well as poorer countries and peoples elsewhere.[7] Second, these organisations question the primacy of the state in Indian development cooperation interventions. They argue that Indian CSOs have had a long and rich history in piloting innovative development models and leading advocacy movements for progressive legislation – achievements meriting a stronger role for them in policymaking. Third, as recipients of aid themselves, these CSOs argue that they have the knowledge to deliver effective development cooperation assistance. Elements of this view appear consistent with the DPA's own interpretation of the role envisioned for Indian CSOs (Raghavan 2013, quoted in Piccio 2013). As a first step, in 2013 VANI and PRIA, in collaboration with the DPA, created a directory documenting the names of CSOs and their areas of expertise. It provides a reference document to match Indian expertise against requests from partner countries and serves to showcase the breadth and diversity of CSOs operating in India. However, no evidence has appeared at time of writing confirming whether the DPA has made use of this directory.

National CSOs have also pushed for a clearer and more enabling regulatory environment to facilitate CSO engagement in Indian development cooperation. As seen in the case of the Nepal earthquake, FCRA rules prohibit Indian organisations from working internationally (although some still do). A senior representative from an environmental NGO argued that this prevents Indian CSOs from engaging in development cooperation without government mediation of their efforts. CSOs tasked with implementing training programmes have also argued that they should screen their own candidates for slots, because they are the best placed to gauge profiles and suitability.[8]

National organisations and networks have tended to adopt a 'constructive insider' approach with regard to their state engagement. Although they remain aware of the dangers of co-option, this does not preclude them from working with the government where they find it useful and strategic to do so. Thus, these networks support institutionalising FIDC to ensure that the mechanism stays intact, regardless of which government is in power. At the same time, they also raise questions around the principles of demand-driven and unconditional aid, if generally in less oppositional ways than the independent activists. They stress the challenges implicit in introducing good governance mechanisms in partner countries, such as the political participation of civil society, while also recognising the danger of such Western-donor–style conditionalities.[9]

NGO networks and organisations such as VANI and PRIA have strong connections to CSO platforms in partner countries. Although Indian development cooperation has primarily taken place at the bilateral level, they recognise an opportunity for the Indian government to work directly with partner communities via their national CSO platforms. To date, however, these organisations and networks have apparently not directly addressed the issue of private sector–led development cooperation and its overseas impact, although they recognise that any evidence of lax regulation should come under public scrutiny.

The second group in this category includes universities and think tanks. For example, individuals from Jawaharlal Nehru University (JNU), the Institute for Defence Studies and Analysis, the Centre for Policy Research, and RIS have played a substantial role in the FIDC process. As country and region specialists, several of these researchers and analysts have conducted field-based research in addition to their practical experience in government departments, multilateral financial institutions, and donor agencies (e.g., Cheru and Modi 2013; Mullen 2013). In this way, they bring their expert knowledge and experience to the formulation of Indian development cooperation policy. The steering committee governing FIDC comprises several academicians and think-tank participants.

Research organisations have also collaborated with foreign universities and international CSOs to conduct joint research studies and joint workshops. In 2013, the Observer Research Foundation partnered with Saferworld, an international advocacy organisation, to support a round-table discussion on Indian development cooperation in conflict areas (Saferworld 2013). RIS, JNU, and the Institute for Development Studies in the UK have conducted workshops and research studies on the current 'state of the debate' on Indian development cooperation

(Chaturvedi et al. 2014); moreover, the present volume itself represents a collaboration between the RIS and The Asia Foundation. Thus, North-South and South-South partnerships hold a recognised significance within the context of information, ideas, and knowledge exchange on India's development cooperation.

Collaboration on SSC issues among think tanks and advocacy organisations across the global South has evolved in interesting and innovative ways. April 2014 saw the launch of the Network of Southern Think Tanks (NeST), envisioning a 'global platform . . . to collaboratively generate, systematise, consolidate and share knowledge on South-South Cooperation' (South-South Opportunity 2015). The network's secretariat is based at the RIS in India, and its members include the China Agricultural University (CAU), Instituto de Pesquisa Econômica Aplicada (IPEA) in Brazil, the South African Institute on International Affairs (SAIIA), and the Wits School of Governance (WSG) in South Africa. NeST also invites participation from universities, research institutes, and NGOs, although the specific role of NGOs from SSC-delivering countries appears somewhat less clear from the available literature (South-South Opportunity 2015). It is too early to say whether and how Indian NGOs and the FIDC will engage with NeST's proposal to develop an analytical framework for SSC.

Although knowledge production remains a key function of think tanks and their partners, some Indian CSO representatives have questioned the *kind* of knowledge they produce and prioritise, as well as the *ends* served through its use. The line between constructive engagement and co-option may prove blurry for individuals and institutions alike. A different critical concern arises from the restricted dissemination of the knowledge thus far generated, which has tended to exclude CSOs, social movements, and grassroots networks, and thus widened the gulf between them and the policy elite.

The INGOs are the last of these 'critical engagers'. They generally tend to represent members of the larger global federations and confederations, and view SSC from an internationalist perspective. Much of the world's economic growth and trade vitality now centres in the South, requiring close engagement from those concerned with inclusive growth and just development. INGOs do not necessarily view SSC as neocolonial, but believe that it could result in the destruction of local livelihoods and the violation of social and environmental rights if not properly managed and regulated. These international organisations act as facilitators, brokering relationships and linkages between their domestic members and global networks – aiming, among other goals, to build transnational solidarity across groups and movements. Through these platforms and alliances, issues of particular relevance to the global South reach the policy hubs of the North, where much of the decision making related to global development partnerships continues to occur. The relationships held by these INGOs with their Northern affiliates also increases their access to information on traditional Organisation for Economic Cooperation (OECD) Development Assistance Committee (DAC) models and practices, which they can then contribute to domestic-level conversations on Indian development cooperation. Their networks, linkages, and significant resources allow them to commission evidence and often field-based research studies that examine specific impacts of emerging-economy investments in partner countries.

Western donor interest in this area has also increased. A number of OECD governments and private foundations have invested in policy research and advocacy work with Northern-based INGOs in support of SSC-related advocacy and capacity building in their Southern affiliate offices. Support has also grown for research on the post-2015 agenda, India's role in the G20 and the BRICS, and the role of rising powers as development partners. At the same time, Northern donors appear to be shifting toward the development investment model, as practiced by their Southern counterparts (Mawdsley, Savage and Kim 2014). Although this may seem to demonstrate a fruitful convergence and emerging collaborative approaches, some commentators have warned that these efforts essentially aim to co-opt South-South partnerships (e.g., Abdenur and Fonseca 2013).

Government partners

Notwithstanding the general pattern of state primacy, a few CSOs have received official and direct state support to carry out developmental activities abroad. They operate within the parameters laid down by the government of India and generally work in service delivery. Examples include the Barefoot College in Rajasthan, which offers solar engineering programmes to rural women from South Asia, Africa, and Latin America; Jaipur Leg, which provides artificial limbs in Afghanistan and Sri Lanka; and the Self-Employed Women's Association (SEWA), which provides vocational training programmes to women in Bhutan, Nepal, and (since 2005) Afghanistan.

The SEWA Afghanistan programme is, to our knowledge, the most substantial interaction between the Indian government and an Indian NGO in development cooperation, complementing India's very substantial investments in mining, road building, and energy (among other infrastructure projects), as well as educational scholarships and humanitarian assistance (Sachdeva this volume; MEA n.d.; Mullen 2013). SEWA launched in 2005 with initial funding of USD 1.4 million, aimed at training Afghan women in ecological regeneration, food processing, and garment manufacturing. It has since expanded and now includes support and training for managerial and market skills. In keeping with the stated principles of Indian development cooperation, the Afghan Ministry of Women's Affairs identifies the trainee candidates. It appears that SEWA manages to harness its substantial domestic experience and success in service of some of the neediest and most vulnerable people in Afghanistan; it can claim, with some justice, to better understand and support these women than many Western organisations.

Despite limited CSO engagement elsewhere, several reasons may prompt the Indian government, and more specifically the MEA, to fund CSOs in the Afghan context. First, India's strong strategic interest and engagement with Afghanistan make it one of its largest and best-supported partners in financial, institutional, and personnel terms. India thus has not only the interest but also the capacity to support this programme. Second, providing for vulnerable women and children plays well with domestic and overseas audiences; like other development partners, India enhances its regional and global image through such work. Third, India – to an unusual degree – has coordinated its development-partner presence in Afghanistan with the OECD-DAC donor community, a factor that may have encouraged a stronger role for CSOs. In launching the programme, India's ambassador to Afghanistan spoke of engaging with the 'international community' on gender empowerment and mainstreaming (Mojumdar 2008). Finally, SEWA does not advance systemic critique, domestically or abroad. Although unquestionably meeting certain needs, SEWA does not embody a more challenging rights-based approach (towards the state, that is; in some cases, it may indeed unsettle local social hierarchies). Nor does it support indigenous or project-displaced communities that might act to 'stall' development (in the view of the Intelligence Bureau report cited earlier). Not surprisingly, organisations contracted by the Indian government tend not to criticise its development agendas and modalities, whether at home or abroad.

To date, the small number of Indian government–sponsored CSOs operating abroad have not received much attention or analysis beyond the anecdotal, although Chaturvedi, Kumar and Mendiratta (2013), evaluating the Small Development Projects in Nepal, includes scrutiny of Indian and Nepalese CSO involvement. The operations of these CSOs still raise many questions, including whether they manage to bring specific skills and experiences to bear in promoting effective development outcomes; how they negotiate some level of autonomous decision making with different parts of the Indian state; if they are accountable to clients and local representative institutions, as well as to funders; and whether they use their ground-level experiences to engage in wider policy and critical reflection. One might also ask how Indian personnel and programmes experience similarities and differences with partner contexts and cultures, including at the interpersonal level. Notwithstanding the high-level, bilateral language of fraternity and empathy, how do class, caste, religion, ethnicity, gender, and so forth shape cross-border, on-the-ground relations between individual stakeholders?[10]

Conclusion

We have argued that domestic civil society–state relations play a role in shaping the place of CSOs in external development cooperation, and proposed an analytical framework for thinking about current and potential relations. We recognise that these are not watertight categories; independent activists, for instance, may choose at some point to engage with the FIDC, whereas critical engagers may choose to appropriate mass mobilisation techniques or become quasi-partners of the government's official programmes in development cooperation.

As Indian civil society seeks to move forward in this arena, it will need to address a number of challenges. The state's implicit preference for strengthening the role of service-delivery NGOs in official cooperation (as opposed to rights-based advocacy organisations) manifests in the kinds of programmes it currently supports, as well as the technical and administrative barriers it maintains. Limiting civil society's engagement in this way deters a more substantive role in shaping the policies and strategies of Indian development cooperation, and arguably, the effectiveness of its country-level and local efforts. Notably, successive governments have failed to seek civil society input on aligning development cooperation with transparency and accountability (Chaturvedi et al. 2014).

The significance of SSC within the global development architecture continues to grow. Many Southern governments assert that this will create a more multipolar world, and impel faster and better development in partner countries. Many CSOs, on the other hand, express concerns about the nature of current growth strategies, often asking what these changes in the global order might mean for the world's poor. In their response to the Planning Commission's Twelfth Five-Year Plan Draft Approach paper, Indian civil-society progressives have called for a domestic framework 'that is livelihood-based, people-centric, pro-poor, and owned by the people themselves, as these are the foundations of truly inclusive and sustainable development' (WNTA 2013). Looking within India and beyond, we concur with Neera Chandhoke, who recognises the imperfections but also asserts the necessity of civil society:

> Civil society might not be the best solution to the problems of the world, but . . . [w]e simply have no choice. The democratisation of the global order of governance is desirable for a number of reasons, but the democratisation of countries belonging to the category of rising powers is equally significant.
>
> (Chandhoke 2009: 306)

A progressive development model that differs structurally from that of the neoliberal paradigm – whether driven by the Western powers or India, China, and Brazil – calls for both national and transnational civil society activism. Only when this occurs will we see the realisation of South-South cooperation in its truest sense.

Notes

1   The DAC/non-DAC comparison has a number of conceptual and methodological flaws. 'Aid' is not equivalent to 'development assistance', and 'donors' cannot be equated with (Southern) 'development partners'. We fully appreciate this category error and use the comparison here in the spirit of an imperfect but not entirely illegitimate discursive device.

2   This chapter is based on semistructured individual interviews conducted by Roychoudhury from March to August 2014 in New Delhi. They included twenty respondents from various backgrounds: NGOs, research organisations, grassroots networks, national networks, multilateral organisations, and academic institutions. For obvious reasons, all respondents and some organisations remain anonymous.

3   Civil society and CSOs have been extensively theorised with little resulting consensus (Jenkins 2010). This chapter deploys a simple vernacular usage of 'CSOs' as 'third-sector' organisations that do not fall within the categories of state, private sector, or family.

4   Anonymous interviewee, 2014.

5 Anonymous interviewee, 2014.
6 Anonymous interviewee, 2014.
7 Anonymous interviewee, 2014.
8 Anonymous interviewee, 2014.
9 Anonymous interviewee, 2014.
10 For a domestic corollary, see Ramanujam, Sing and Vatn (2012).

Works cited

Abdenur, A.E., and Fonseca, J. (2013). The North's growing role in South–South cooperation: Keeping the foothold. *Third World Quarterly*, 3(8): 1475–1491.

Agrawal, S. (2007). *Emerging donors in international development assistance: The India case*. Ottawa: International Development Research Centre. Available at www.idrc.ca/EN/Documents/Case-of-India.pdf. [Accessed 19 May 2015].

Akbaruddin, S. (2014). United Nations adopts anti-Lanka resolve, India abstains. *Deccan Chronicle*, 4 April. Available at www.deccanchronicle.com/140328/world-neighbours/article/united-nations-adopts-anti-lanka-resolve-india-abstains. [Accessed 19 May 2015].

Chanana, D. (2010). *India's transition to global donor: Limitations and prospects* [webpage]. Madrid: Real Instituto Elcan. Available at www.realinstitutoelcano.org/wps/portal/web/rielcano_en/contenido?WCM_GLOBAL_CONTEXT=/elcano/elcano_in/zonas_in/ARI123–2010#.VVB1Ce1TE20. [Accessed 19 May 2015].

Chandhoke, N. (2003). *The conceits of civil society*. New Delhi: Oxford University Press.

Chandhoke, N. (2009). Putting civil society in its place. *Economic and Political Weekly*, 44(7): 12–15.

Chaturvedi, S. (2012). India and development cooperation: Expressing Southern solidarity. In S. Chaturvedi, T. Fues and E. Sidiropoulos (eds.) *Development cooperation and emerging powers: New partners or old patterns?* London: Zed Books, pp.169–189.

Chaturvedi, S., Chenoy, A., Joshi, A., and Lagdhyan, K. (2014). Indian development cooperation: The state of the debate. *IDS Evidence Report*, 95. IDS, Sussex.

Chaturvedi, S., Kumar, S., and Mendiratta, S. (2013). Balancing state and community participation in development partnership projects: Emerging evidence from Indian SDPs in Nepal. *Research and Information System for Developing Countries Discussion Paper*, 183. RIS, New Delhi.

Cheru, F., and Modi, R. (eds.) (2013). *Agricultural development and food security in Africa: The impact of Chinese, Indian and Brazilian investments*. London: Zed Books.

Cheru, F., and Obi, C. (2011). Chinese and Indian engagement in Africa: Competitive or mutually reinforcing strategies? *Journal of International Affairs*, 64(2): 91.

Dhawan, H. (2015). NGOs protest in Delhi against 'coercive' state action. *The Times of India*, 8 May. Available at http://timesofindia.indiatimes.com/city/delhi/NGOs-protest-in-Delhi-against-oercive-state-action/articleshow/47200948.cms. [Accessed 19 May 2015].

Jenkins, R. (2010). Indian politics and NGOs. In N. Jayal and P. Mehta (eds.), *Oxford companion to politics in India*. Oxford: Oxford University Press, pp. 423–440.

Kamat, S. (2002). *Development hegemony: NGOs and the state in India*. Oxford: Oxford University Press.

Malone, D. (2011). *Does the elephant dance? Contemporary Indian foreign policy*. Oxford: Oxford University Press.

Markey, D. (2009). Developing India's foreign policy software. *Asia Policy*, 8:73–96.

Mawdsley, E. (2012). *From recipients to donors: Emerging powers and the changing development landscape*. London: Zed.

Mawdsley, E. (2015). India's Role as an international development Actor. In K.A. Jacobsen (ed.), *Handbook of contemporary India*. London: Routledge, pp. 146–148.

Mawdsley, E., and McCann, G. (eds.) (2011). *India and Africa: Changing geographies of power and development*. Oxford: Famahu.

Mawdsley, E., Savage, L., and Kim, S.-M. (2014). A 'post-aid world'? Paradigm shift in foreign aid and development cooperation at the 2011 Busan High Level Forum. *Geographical Journal*, 180(1): 27–38.

Meier, C., and Murthy, C. (2011). India's growing involvement in humanitarian assistance. *Global Public Policy Institute Research Paper*, 13. GPPI, Berlin.

Ministry of External Affairs (MEA) (No date). *India and Afghanistan: A development partnership*. New Delhi: Government of India. Available at http://mea.gov.in/Uploads/PublicationDocs/176_india-and-afghanistan-a-development-partnership.pdf. [Accessed 19 May 2015].

Mojumdar, A. (2008). SEWA brings hope to Kabul. *Civil Society*, 12. Available at www.civilsocietyonline.com/Archive/aug08/dec0844.asp. [Accessed 19 May 2015].

Mukherjee, P. (2014). Speech by the President of India, Pranab Mukherjee at the Inauguration of the Asia-Africa Agri-Business Forum, 4 February. Government of India, New Delhi. Available at http://presidentofindia.nic.in/speeches-detail.htm?29. [Accessed 19 May 2015].

Mukul, J. (2015). Oxfam India says time to review policy on permission for working overseas. *Business Standard*, 2 May. Available at www.business-standard.com/article/current-affairs/oxfam-india-says-time-to-review-policy-on-permission-for-working-overseas-115050100341_1.html. [Accessed 19 May 2015].

Mullen, R. (2013). *The state of Indian development cooperation: A report*. New Delhi: Centre for Policy Research.

Oakland Institute (2013). Report as it happened. *Indian-Ethiopian Civil Society Summit on Land Investments*, New Delhi, 5–7 February. Available at www.oaklandinstitute.org/it-happened-indian-ethiopian-civil-society-summit-land-investments. [Accessed 19 May 2015].

Oglesby, R. (2011). *India's evolution from aid recipient to humanitarian aid donor*. Unpublished Master's thesis. University of Cambridge, Cambridge, UK.

Padel, F., and Das, S. (2010). Cultural genocide and the rhetoric of sustainable mining in East India. *Contemporary South Asia*, 18(3): 333–341.

Piccio, L. (2013). *India's foreign aid program catches up with its global ambitions* [webpage]. Available at www.devex.com/news/india-s-foreign-aid-program-catches-up-with-its-global-ambitions-80919. [Accessed 19 May 2015].

Poskitt, A., Shankland, A., and Taela, K. (forthcoming). *Civil society from the BRICS: Emerging roles in the new international development landscape*. Sussex, UK: IDA.

Raghavan, P.S. (2013). *Round-table mapping experiences around international development cooperation new challenges and opportunities*. Available at www.observerindia.com/cms/sites/orfonline/modules/report/ReportDetail.html?cmaid=49081&mmacmaid=49082. [Accessed 19 May 2015].

Ramanujam, R.V., Singh, S.J., and Vatn, A. (2012). From the ashes into the fire? Institutional change in the post-tsunami Nicobar Islands, India. *Society and Natural Resources*, 25(11): 1152–66.

Ranjan, A. (2014). Foreign-aided NGOs are actively stalling development, IB tells PMO in a report. *The Indian Express*, 7 June. Available at http://indianexpress.com/article/india/

india-others/foreign-aided-ngos-are-actively-stalling-development-ib-tells-pmo-in-a-report/. [Accessed 19 May 2015].

Research and Information Systems for Developing Countries (RIS) (2015). *Forum for Indian Development Cooperation (FIDC)* [webpage]. New Delhi: RIS. Available at http://ris.org.in/events/fidc.html. [Accessed 24 September 2015].

Rowden, R. (2011). India's role in the new global farmland grab: An examination of the role of the Indian Government and Indian companies engaged in overseas agricultural land acquisitions in developing countries. *Brief*, 103. GRAIN and Economics Research Foundation, New Delhi.

Saferworld (2013). *Roundtable in Delhi explores India's development cooperation in a changing global environment* [webpage]. Available at www.saferworld.org.uk/news-and-views/news-article/609-roundtable-in-delhi-explores-indias-development-cooperation-in-a-changing-global-environment. [Accessed 19 May 2015].

Sen, S. (1999). Some aspects of state–NGO relationships in India in the post-independence era. *Development and Change,* 30(2): 327–55.

South-South Opportunity (2015). *The South-South opportunity* [website]. Available at www.southsouth.info. [Accessed 24 September 2015].

Tandon, R. (1987). The relationship between NGOs and government. Mimeo paper presented to the *Conference on the Promotion of Autonomous Development*, PARIA, New Delhi.

Tomlinson, B. (2013). *Working with civil society in foreign aid: Possibilities for South-South cooperation?* Beijing: United Nations Development Programme China. Available at www.undp.org/content/dam/undp/documents/partners/civil_society/publications/2013_UNDP-CH-Working-With-Civil-Society-in-Foreign-Aid_EN.pdf. [Accessed 19 May 2015].

United Nations (2013). *National consultation report: Post-2015 development framework, India.* New York: United Nations. Available at http://in.one.un.org/img/uploads/National_Consultation_Report_29Nov2013.pdf. [Accessed 19 May 2015].

Vaes, S., and Huyse, H. (2013). *Emerging powers' South-South cooperation with Africa-African civil society perspectives.* Leuven, Belgium: HIVA Research Institute for Work and Society at University of Leuven. Available at www.cid.org.nz/assets/2015-South-South-Cooperation-African-CSO-perspectives-2013.pdf. [Accessed 19 May 2015].

Vijetha, S.N. (2015). Court relief for Greenpeace activist. *The Hindu,* 13 March. Available at www.thehindu.com/todays-paper/tp-national/court-relief-for-greenpeace-activist/article6988140.ece. [Accessed 19 May 2015].

Wada Na Todo Abhiyan (WNTA) (2013). *Equity unaddressed: A civil society response to the draft approach paper 12th five year plan.* New Delhi: Wada No Todo Abhiyan. Available at www.in.undp.org/content/dam/india/docs/equity_unaddressed_a_civil_society_response_to_the_draft_approach_paper_12th_five_year_plan.pdf. [Accessed 19 May 2015].

Wulf, H. (2013). India's aspirations in global politics: Competing ideas and amorphous practices. *Institut für Entwicklung und Frieden*, 107. INEF Faculty of Social Sciences of the University of Duisburg-Essen, Germany. Available at https://inef.uni-due.de/cms/files/report107.pdf. [Accessed 19 May 2015].

7 Prosper thy neighbour

India's cooperation with Nepal

Bishwambher Pyakuryal and Sachin Chaturvedi

Introduction

This chapter approaches India–Nepal South-South cooperation (SSC) in the broadest sense, encompassing aid, trade, investments, and political and security ties. It situates the bilateral relationship within a context shaped by numerous factors: South Asia's challenging regional relations, India's recognised asymmetrical political and economic power in the region, the geostrategic interests of India and China (the region's other superpower), and complex and shifting bilateral trade arrangements. The discussion will contrast development cooperation efforts – comparatively both more successful and less politicised – with the countries' more politically incompatible trade and investment relations. Finally, the chapter will consider the bilateral relationship in a new era of South Asian governance.

Lost opportunities in regional economic cooperation and integration

The South Asian region has great potential for growth, given the relative strengths of the different economies. Pakistan's dairy products have a comparative advantage in South Asian countries, and it can market cheeses in the United States and Europe. Bangladesh has rich natural gas reserves and produces cotton textiles, and Nepal's advantages lie in hydropower. India has competitive edges in iron and steel, machinery, engines, apparel, cotton, and other manufactures. Other countries in the region also have comparative advantages that could shape meaningful relationships within and outside the region.

The South Asia Association for Regional Cooperation (SAARC) supplies a key vehicle for enhancing cooperation and connectivity among its members. Although SAARC member nations have promising average growth rates, such growth has failed to add value to their expanding economic cooperation. Bilateral relations between India and its neighbours often have a political dimension, creating a 'trust deficit' that extends to other aspects of bilateral and regional relations. This mistrust and political squabbling, both bilaterally and regionally, have slowed down prospects for increased intraregional trade. As we shall see, India and Nepal have faced significant political fallout in the past over such issues, even to the point of economic crisis.

Some feel that the cost of SAARC institutionalisation outstrips the concrete economic benefits. Given the nonbinding nature of SAARC agreements, the low rate of compliance should come as no surprise. Despite the loud and clear voices in support of economic integration (Parthasarathy 2015), intra-SAARC trade accounts for less than 5 per cent of total regional trade. Unfortunately, South Asia in general must contend with serious political or economic problems – disputes over boundaries or shared water resources, among other more or less intractable differences. An effective SAARC has the potential to transform the region economically, but this depends first on the recognition and development of new forms of mutual trust and confidence between India and the rest of the SAARC nations. In this context, also, regional relationships with China may play a significant role.

The India–China–Nepal relationship

Chinese Premier Li Kequiang observed in 2013 that Beijing and New Delhi 'must shake hands' to make Asia an 'engine of the world economy' (Karl 2013). The statement implies that a relationship of mutual cooperation would accelerate regional development. The Asian region offers enormous opportunities for both giants, and therefore both often leverage their weight to gain advantage. India has accelerated economic and security cooperation with Southeast Asia through its 'Look East' (now 'Act East') policy, in hopes of countering China's increasing dominance in the region (Maini 2013). China's maritime neighbours, concerned about possible boundary disputes, also view India as a critical balance in the region. Although China has significant influence in the South China Sea, India has made progress toward closer defence and security ties with Vietnam. India has also worked toward closer relationships with Thailand, Myanmar, and Japan. Singapore's senior statesman Lee Kuan Yew has noted that India should be 'part of the Southeast Asia balance of forces' and 'a counterweight [to China] in the Indian Ocean' (Suryanarayan 2011).

Nepal shares an approximately 1000-mile border with Tibet in the north, a proximity that recently has enhanced its China trade. High-profile Chinese visits by senior officials (such as Ai Ping, the vice minister of the International Department for South Asian Affairs) have recently become more frequent, signalling a visible increase in China's regional influence. The Qinghai-Tibet railroad links the Tibetan capital Lhasa to Shigatse; extensions to the same railway should link Nepal and China via the Tibetan city of Kerung by 2020, and continue to Yatung County, on the border of India and Bhutan (China Daily 2015). The distance from Kerung to Rasuwagadhi on the Nepalese border is just 35 kilometres, and from Kathmandu to Rasuwagadhi 118 kilometres. The entry into Kerung, the largest Tibetan trade centre, will considerably ease Nepal's connection to Tibet and presumably contribute to the development of trade and tourism in both Nepal and China.

In short, the rail network expansion will play a crucial role in promoting economic, cultural, and tourism growth in South Asia as a whole. Chinese geopolitical influence across South Asia should grow with its gradual increase in investments, including the infrastructure loans it readily makes available to partners. China's engagements in diversified economic areas thus underscore the geopolitical importance of India's strategic relationship with Nepal.

The evolution of the Nepal–India relationship

Within this context, Nepal and India experience a unique economic interdependence not found amongst other SAARC member countries. The 1415-kilometre-long open border allows unrestricted and free movement between the territories, strengthening their integration through interpersonal contact. Although diplomatic relations began on 1 June 1947, the relationship became more visible and meaningful after the signing of India-Nepal Peace and Friendship Treaty in 1950.

The importance of intangible factors: trust and political leadership

All aspects of the Nepal–India relationship, whether trade, economic assistance, or security, stand or fall at any given time through the level of mutual trust and the will and efforts of national leaders. The high-level visits exchanged by Nepali and Indian statesman, often occurring during periods of political uncertainty in Nepal, tend to arouse suspicion. The majority of Nepalis believe that their leaders have visited India – especially during the political stalemate – seeking fulfilment of their own interests, through Indian influence on Nepali authorities. Many Nepalis also believe that high-level Indian visits often mask intended intervention in Nepal's domestic affairs (DNA India 2015).

In 1988, during the Panchayat regime, Indo-Nepalese relations came under threat when Kathmandu signed a weapons-purchasing agreement with Beijing; this accord also gave China the contract to build the Western sector road linking China with Nepal. Indian officials suspected that this decision might jeopardise their country's security. They responded by imposing an economic blockade on Nepal from March 1989 to June 1990, upon expiry of the 1978 Trade and Transit treaty on 23 March 1989 (Singh 2009). India closed all but two customs points, cutting off Nepal's links to Kolkata port.[1] At the time, many commentators and journalists reported that Nepal viewed this blockade as contrary to the spirit of Article 7 of the 1950 Treaty (see e.g., Crossette 1989).

Nepal's enormous trade deficit with India has fuelled another key source of misunderstanding (Kantipur Daily 2014). Kathmandu expects Delhi to take proactive steps, removing nontariff barriers to reduce the trade imbalance. Similarly, India's high-level visits have sought assurance that Nepal will depoliticise economic issues. India has also expressed concern over the security threat from Nepal's open border, seeking a guarantee that Nepali territory not serve as a base for anti-India activities (Subramanian 2004).

These issues reflect mistrust and suspicion. During periods of political stability and with no visible anti-Indian interest groups active in Nepal, the countries have had no problem in cooperating. For instance, after Nepal reinstated democracy in the early 1990s, Nepal's interim Prime Minister K. P. Bhattarai made an official visit to India. India duly acknowledged Bhattarai's role in strengthening bilateral relations, and subsequently removed the economic blockade and re-established the special security relationship between New Delhi and Kathmandu. Similarly, after Nepal ratified its new constitution and held general elections, the Nepali Congress leader G. P. Koirala became prime minister; he further strengthened the bilateral relationship with an official visit to India in June 2006, where both countries signed separate trade and transit treaties and a host of other economic agreements (MEA 2006). These events underscore the importance of political leadership in the bilateral relationship.

Trade and investment

Trade has proven the most pivotal factor in the India–Nepal partnership. Indian capital (Table 7.1) began flowing into Nepal before the end of the Rana regime (in 1950) – especially after the promulgation of the Company Act in 1936, with the availability of cheap raw materials and labour as a prime attraction. Nepal offered Indian investors a climate free from the complicated customs and tax law of the Indian government under British rule. Early individual Indian projects included Nepal's then-largest jute factory (established 1936), its largest rice mill (1937), a cotton mill (1942), and a sugar mill (1946) (Pyakuryal and Bhattarai 1991).

Table 7.1 Nepal trade volumes with India, 2003–2013 (INR 000)

Fiscal Year	Exports	Imports	Balance (Nepal)
FY 2003/04	30,777,100	78,739,500	– 47,962,400
FY 2004/05	38,916,900	88,675,500	– 49,758,600
FY 2005/06	40,714,700	107,143,100	– 66,428,400
FY 2006/07	41,728,800	115,872,300	– 74,143,500
FY 2007/08	38,555,700	142,376,500	– 103,820,800
FY 2008/09	43,574,482	165,119,002	– 121,544,520
FY 2009/10	39,902,811	214,261,109	– 174,358,298
FY 2010/11	42,868,108	259,162,277	– 216,294,169
FY 2011/12	50,933,222	321,346,419	– 270,413,196
FY 2012/13	51,788,460	397,957,920	– 346,169,460

Source: TEPC (2014)

Constraints to effective trade relations

Historical market dependency

Imports dominate Nepal's trade. As the larger economy of the two, India has been a critical market for Nepal exports. With luxury goods and other items restricted in India in the early 1990s (just before the economic liberalisation), Nepal became an entry point for such imports. This in turn generated revenue in Nepal for purchasing its own Indian imports. A study by Pyakuryal (1995) showed that Nepal had financed the payments disequilibrium by selling convertible currencies to India. But after India launched aggressive economic reform programmes through deregulation and delicensing in 1991, the facilities established in Nepal for Indian re-exports – electrical, steels, and polythene-based assembly plants – closed down one after another (Pyakuryal 1995).

This situation changed following Prime Minister I. K. Gujral's official visit to Nepal in June 1997, when he promised Indian aid in developing a strong Nepali industrial base through investment and trade-treaty concessions. The Indo-Nepal Trade Treaty of 1996 provided duty-free access to all products manufactured in Nepal, based on certificates of origin issued by authorised Nepalese institutions. This treaty had even removed value-added criteria. Statistics reveal a five-fold jump in exports by during 1996–2001 (Ojha 2012). After the treaty, the rate of growth of Nepal's trade with India, both in exports and imports, surged higher than its total exports and imports.

However, after the treaty's renewal in 2002, India introduced a value-addition norm of 30 per cent together with a set quota on certain 'excess' Nepali exports (vegetable ghee, acrylic yarn, copper products, and zinc oxide), as exporters had used the initial quota-free provisions to dump these products in India, thus injuring domestic production (Yogi 2002). In recent years, in the absence of proper rules of origin, Nepal has become a re-export point for the products from China and other South Asian countries. India's Ministry of Micro, Small and Medium Enterprises (MMSME) has particular concerns about the impact on small and medium-sized industries of cheaper imports, especially those coming from China via the Nepal and Myanmar borders (MMSME n.d.).

The new trade agreement of 2009 aims to benefit traders on both sides through elimination of nontariff barriers and other facilities. The treaty provides that Nepali merchants trading in Indian currency will receive excise and all other facilities enjoyed by traders using convertible currency. Some provisions have worked less well, and hurdles remain. For example, the law no longer requires exporters of Nepali tea, cardamom, ginger, and other agricultural products to present quality certification from Indian laboratories in Kolkata or Patna; nonetheless, this practice continues. On the other hand, the new treaty has expanded bilateral trade via air cargo and four new land routes.

Trade barriers

Complex procedures and documentation, slow and inefficient customs clearances, and inadequate transport infrastructure constrain Nepal in maximizing its trade relationship with India. Transportation and logistics have restricted Nepal's opportunities to explore regional and global markets as well. This has significantly increased the cost of doing business and adversely affected growth, employment, and poverty reduction. Nepal's chief challenge therefore lies in overcoming transit and transport-related hurdles, thus reducing pilferage, loss/damages, and transit time.

The government of Nepal has identified three keys to trade facilitation: uninterrupted railway movement, efficient cargo exchange between gateway ports and inland container depots (ICDs), and introduction of multimodal transport systems (GON 2012). According to some estimates, movement of cargo to and from the ICD could reduce transit costs by 30 to 40 per cent, given the diversion from roads to rail (IMF 2006). However, Nepal has made less than satisfactory progress in developing integrated physical facilities at its four inland custom stations: Biratnagar-Jogbani, Birgunj-Raxaul, Bhairahawa-Sunauli, and Nepalgunj-Rupaidiha (Pyakuryal 2005). Integration requires efforts to streamline transportation by diversifying transit corridors and reducing costs. Despite the construction of a dry port in a strategic location (Sirsiya district village committee, in the District of Parsa) and the completion of a broad-gauge railway line, Nepal has not yet succeeded in improving logistics and introducing multimodal transport systems.

Although India provides duty-free access for almost all Nepali products, the barriers related to special additional duty (recently scrapped), quarantine, and infrastructure have deterred Nepal from increasing its Indian exports (Sharma et al. 2014). Moreover, Nepal has failed to produce goods that the Indian market demands, either in terms of quality or quantity. Priority export products have declined recently, including zinc oxide, vegetable ghee, toothpaste, copper wire rod, mild steel pipe, and mustard and linseed. Nepal's export earnings only suffice to fund one-third of its petroleum imports. This reflects its poor infrastructure, long power outage hours, weak access to finance, and bad road conditions (Kathmandu Post 2012).

Observers see quantitative restrictions, product disqualification, and uneven treaty implementation by individual Indian states as major obstructions to Nepal's international trade (USAID 2005). Efforts to overcome these barriers have already begun. To make trade less import-centric and more comprehensive and mutually beneficial, India has offered to enter into a memorandum of understanding (MOU) for a comprehensive economic partnership agreement (Pyakuryal 2005). This would expand the trade in goods to trade in services and investment as well. Nepali labour is also not cheap. Manufacturing carries a high average labour cost per worker, with low productivity and low added value per unit of labour. Moreover, the comparative advantage indicator – that is, labour cost per unit of output – remains relatively high compared with Nepal's other South Asian neighbours (Astha Rai 2015).

Trade facilitation

The development of and adherence to various trade treaties and agreements between India and Nepal have shaped the high and lows of the bilateral trade relationship.

Some significant trade facilitation measures have included:

• The Comprehensive Economic Partnership Agreement (CEPA). The CEPA has four pillars: trade liberalisation, regulatory convergence, economic precedents for an international system, and trade security. The agreement remains unsigned pending Nepali review.

- Nepal's new 2010 Industrial Policy and the Board of Investment Act 2011, both aimed at attracting foreign direct investment (FDI).
- Nepal's soon-to-be-finalised 2014 Foreign Investment Policy. Milestones of this investment regime include a legal commitment against nationalising private industries and a proposed intellectual property policy.

Investment

A World Trade Organization study (Blackhurst and Otten 1996) revealed strong positive and self-reinforcing relationships between bilateral trade and FDI flows, because trade induces FDI and FDI induces trade. The government of Nepal has prioritised five areas for foreign investment: hydroelectricity, infrastructure and development, agroprocessing and herbs, tourism and other services, and minerals and mining-related projects. Although both India and China have investment interests in Nepal, it still ranks second to last in FDI among South Asian countries after Bhutan. Nepal's foreign trade dependence on India accounts for 56 per cent of its total, ranging between 50 and 55 per cent (Nepal Rastra Bank 2014), but the FDI inflow is just 0.05 per cent (Table 7.2).

Political party–affiliated labour conflicts, allegedly an outgrowth of Indian investment, have apparently created enough insecurity to account for declining interest – at least in India if not elsewhere (Afram and Salvi Del Pero 2012; Tandon 2012).

According to the Department of Industry of the government of Nepal (Global Times 2014), 4129 Chinese nationals have expressed interest in investing in Nepal, accounting for 30 per cent of the total number of potential foreign investors. Indians number 708, securing the second position in this pool. In terms of investment size, however, India leads China with commitments amounting to INR 125 billion, as compared with INR 16 billion by the Chinese (MCI 2014).

Nepal entered into a Bilateral Investment Promotion and Protection Agreement (BIPPA) with India on 21 October 2011. Informal discussions with Nepal's private sector reveal that they expect a protective, predictable, hospitable, and profitable climate to develop under BIPPA (Kumar 2011). The agreement provides for fair and equitable treatment, with dispute resolution mechanisms in place (FNCCI 2011).

Hydropower opportunities

India prioritises the energy sector in its regional cooperation. One might argue, in fact, that India's development support for this sector in neighbouring countries serves to secure its own energy supply. For example, between 2006 and 2013, over 95 per cent (approximately INR 84 billion) of Indian energy-sector grants and loans went to South Asian countries (IDCR 2015). Not surprisingly, energy concerns also play a significant role in India's cooperation with Nepal.

Out of 42,000 megawatts (MW) of technically and economically viable hydropower potential, Nepal has harnessed only about 1 per cent (705 MW).

Table 7.2 India and other countries' FDI to Nepal, 2003–2013 (INR billions)

Fiscal year	2003–04	2004–05	2005–06	2006–07	2007–08	2008–09	2009–10	2010–11	2011–12	2012–13
Total FDI	0.00	0.14	− 0.47	0.36	0.29	1.83	2.85	6.44	9.20	9.08
India	0.00	− 0.03	− 0.05	0.36	0.13	− 0.32	0.04	0.00	1.67	0.05
Other	0.00	0.17	− 0.42	0.00	0.16	2.15	2.81	6.44	7.53	9.03

Source: Nepal Rastra Bank (2014)

The peak domestic demand is 950 MW, with a growth projection of 7.5 per cent annually through 2020 (Bergner 2013). This suggests a strong potential for surplus to export.

As Nepal completes surveys to license an additional 4700 MW of hydroelectric power, it has also begun negotiations with India to construct a high-capacity cross-border transmission line, connecting Lamki in Nepal and Raybareli in India. In addition, the government of Nepal has almost completed a draft request to India, seeking either (1) a grant (50 per cent) plus concessional loan (50 per cent), or (2) a mix of 33 per cent each for direct aid, concessional loan, and commercial loan. Either package would finance 900 MW of capacity for the proposed Arun III revival (detailed project report already completed). Finally, the Upper Karnali hydropower project in far western Nepal, expected to generate 900 MW of river-run electricity, should reach completion in 2021; India's GMR (an infrastructural company founded by Grandhi Mallikarjun Rao in 1978 and headquartered in Bangalore) will negotiate for the power purchase agreement. Such negotiations will assume particular importance after 2016, when Nepali private producers estimate that the country will have achieved a power surplus (Parashar 2014).

India and Nepal have also signed the revised terms of reference (TOR) for the Pancheshwor Development Authority. This will allow work to begin immediately on the 6500-MW multipurpose project, and thus allay public suspicions about the extent of benefit accruing to the developer and the government of Nepal. The TOR stipulate that the Authority must start project construction within a year. On 4 August 2014, Nepal's foreign minister announced that Nepal and India would finalise a deal on the power trade agreement (PTA) and Upper Karnali Project Development Agreement within 45 days (Setopati 2015). As of this writing, both agreements are still pending.

Widespread media coverage in Nepal has focused on a long-pending government proposal for an Indian hydro project (Avinah 2014); after 4 years' wait, the government of India recently responded, stating that it would allow electricity exports from projects with Indian investment. This may limit the entry of other investments, including those from China; it has also spurred pro-Chinese groups in Nepal to organise greater support for Chinese assistance. In fact, Nepal's Ministry of Energy failed to do its homework, missing a win-win collaboration opportunity. As with any business proposal, the ministry should have assessed the merit of the Indian project and discussed it with the Indian government before making the text public. However, the August 2014 visit of Indian Prime Minister Narendra Modi has allayed these suspicions and opened the door for meaningful negotiation on these points (Avinah 2014; Shrestha 2015).

Development cooperation: history and current sectoral profile

Indo-Nepalese cooperation in the field of modern economic development began as early as 1951. As a leading donor country, India helped mobilise assistance through the Colombo Plan after Nepal's adoption of democracy in 1951. Indian

Prime Minister Nehru's visit to Kathmandu in June 1951, 4 months after the revolution in Nepal, set a landmark in the history of Nepal–India cooperation. Initial projects included the construction of Kathmandu's airport and the Tribhuvan Highway from Kathmandu to the border town of Raxaul in western Nepal (begun in 1953) (Mihaly 1965). This launched a relationship aimed at developing Nepal's road and air links; notably, requests for both projects originated with the government of Nepal, inaugurating a trend of recipient-driven projects.

On her visit to Nepal in 1966, former Prime Minister Indira Gandhi emphasised that India's role in Nepali economic development would focus on grants and cooperation. Morarji Desai affirmed this by adding 'whatever may be our difficulties, it will be our duty to contribute our utmost to the economic development of Nepal' (Pyakuryal, Dahal and Adhikari, 2004). Such statements appeared to underscore India's emotional stake in the well-being of Nepal and the respect that Indians have for its people. And one must acknowledge India's aid in a critical period of Nepalese history – the 1950s, with the advent of democracy and Nepal's entry into the community of nations (Acharya 2002). Although India did help Nepal develop and improve physical and infrastructural facilities, its assistance did more: it created intangible assets of goodwill, difficult to quantify in monetary terms.

Development cooperation became institutional with the 1954 establishment of the Indian Aid Mission in Kathmandu. The name changed in 1966 to the Indian Cooperation Mission, reflecting the extension of aid into cooperation. Since 1984, it has become the Economic Cooperation Wing of the Indian Embassy (Pyakuryal, Dahal and Adhikari, 2004).

In practice, most Indian assistance rests on local needs, assessed through community participation and local governmental bodies. Development efforts therefore reach the beneficiaries directly. Such efforts include schools, multidisciplinary campuses, nursing campuses, specialised training institutes, primary health posts, maternity centres, rural electrification, micro-hydro projects, rural/urban roads, bridges, and so on. The grant assistance system also includes gifts of books, school buses, ambulances, medical vans, and equipment (Pyakuryal, Dahal and Adhikari, 2004).

Whether in small-scale or large projects, Indian cooperation has had a significant impact on Nepal's human resource development – notably in the health services sector. Examples include a five-storey outpatient centre-cum-ward at Bir Hospital; a 200-bed emergency and trauma centre in Kathmandu costing INR 149 billion (approximately USD 20.1 million); BP Koirala Institute of Health Sciences in Dharan, built for INR 200 billion (approximately USD 26.7 million); and the Bakhtawari Hari Eye Hospital in Krishnanagar, Kapilvastu, established at a cost of INR 40 billion (approximately USD 5.4 million) (Pyakuryal, Dahal and Adhikari, 2004).

The health services of Nepal Netra Jyoti Sangh (NNJS), a central coordinating body for technical manpower, are acknowledged widely both in India and Nepal. Its chair, Dr. Tirtha Mishra, has stated that Indian support of NNJS provides an ideal example of meaningful bilateral assistance (Box 7.1). The NNJS program coordinator has noted that Indian nationals account for 'almost 60 per cent of their total patients' (Republica 2014).

Box 7.1 Indian assistance: a quest for confidence-building

Nepal Netra Jyoti Sangh (NNJS) was established in 1978. It is a pioneering charitable and nonprofit nongovernmental organisation dedicated to eye care services in Nepal. It aims to reduce the incidence of preventable blindness by creating eye health awareness and appropriate healthy behaviour. Since its establishment, Nepal has seen both quantitative and qualitative improvement in eye service delivery programs.

Historically, cataracts have been the major cause of blindness in Nepal. They accounted for 66.8 per cent of blindness in 1981, a figure that dropped to 52.9 per cent during 2006–2010. Creating human resources for eye services has had a visible impact on eye health. In 1981, Nepal had only 7 ophthalmologists, increasing to 76 in 2000 and 175 in 2012. Similarly, it had no optometrists in 1981 and 1995, but acquired 20 by 2000 and 36 by 2012. The same period has seen noteworthy growth in hospital managers and biomedical technical personnel.

With the help of the government of India, NNJS has now twenty eye hospitals, over fifty-six eye centres, more than 1000 dedicated employees, and 1000 social workers. It conducts over 300,000 surgeries per year and more than 2.7 million consultations per year, both in Kathmandu and outside the valley via mobile screening centres. NNJS provides eye care services to almost 90 per cent of the country's people. Many view these services as a flagship program of bilateral cooperation between India and Nepal. In recent years, efforts have gone beyond quantitative achievements alone, seeking to enhance the quality of surgery, compliance with standard protocols, and regular medical and surgical audits in eye care programs.

These efforts contribute to both the national and global initiative 'Vision 2020: The Right to Sight' (IAPB 2013). The NNJS also needs to improve eye care services in terms of quality and patient satisfaction. This necessitates strengthening coordination at the community, district, regional/zone, and national levels. Such efforts should give a sense of ownership to the governmental, nongovernmental, and community-level stakeholders.

Indian support began in 2001–2002 with funding for cataract procedures; after an encouraging response from the community, beneficiaries, and government, the number of examinations has grown to 425,000, with 87,000 surgeries performed in NNJS mobile camps. Indian assistance has now totalled INR 21.1 billion. In 2007, NNJS launched a new eye health care programme in schools. More than 27,000 students have since received optical devices. In developing eye services with India's financial and technical assistance, NNJS has created a network of eye care infrastructures, more accessible and affordable for the poor than standalone facilities. It has also established a quality assurance system in service delivery.

The Embassy of India, Kathmandu, and NNJS signed their latest MOU on 17 December 2013. It provides NNJS with INR 33.9 million of Indian grant assistance for eye care programs in various districts of Nepal. The MOU will cover the cost of conducting 15,000 cataract surgeries through mobile screening camps. Other support will include access to buses and ambulances, an outpatient building for Geta Eye Hospital in Kailali (far-western Nepal), and a plan for a new ophthalmologic hospital in Krishnanagar, western Nepal.

Source: NNJS (2013).

Another key example of SSC between India and Nepal, facilitated by the United Nations Environmental Programme (UNEP), is in the area of agricultural biomass (Box 7.2).

Box 7.2 South-South cooperation: technology transfer for converting waste agricultural biomass into energy

The United Nations Environmental Programme (UNEP), in partnership with local institutions, local government, and businesses, implemented a project in Madhyapur Thimi Municipality in Nepal from July 2009 to September 2010. The project demonstrated technologies for converting waste agricultural biomass (crop residues) into energy. To ensure local ownership, the coordinators engaged the local community throughout the project's duration. This has helped build local capacity and has facilitated replication at the national level. The UNEP has initiated similar projects in Pakistan, Philippines, Cambodia, India, and Sri Lanka.

Especially significant in an agriculture-based economy, the project has demonstrated a viable process for converting waste agricultural biomass into energy. UNEP has provided USD 40,000 in technology procurement costs. The municipality provided land as an in-kind contribution, along with USD 20,000 towards technology procurement. In addition to training Nepali operators, the Indian technology provider offered a package bio methanation plant, complete with a digester, gas containment, and necessary control systems. Although the initial technology transfer rested on a one-time procurement, the supplier also pursued a local business partnership to expand the technology delivery.

Transfers of this kind become extremely useful in a least-developed country like Nepal, one suffering from a lack of indigenous technology. Aid practitioners have realised that, compared to technology transfers from developed countries, technologies from nearby developing countries often prove more economical; moreover, the cultural similarity between South-South countries enables better adaptation – and hence greater sustainability.

Source: UNEP (n.d.)

Looking forward

All the various South-South partnership arrangements between India and Nepal have proven instrumental in Nepal's development trajectory. The powerful position that India holds in South Asia, and the relative ineffectualness of SAARC in managing relations amongst its member states, often leave countries like Nepal in a weak bargaining position. If India's primary foreign policy concentrates on its neighbourhood, then Nepal should be one of its strategic priorities.

Recently, the potential for increased economic cooperation with India has grown, with expanded economic opportunities and a more dynamic investment and trade climate. For Asian countries to take advantage of this, they will need better and more accessible information on the region's raw materials, utilities, infrastructure, development potential, human resource capabilities, products, and markets. The challenge for SAARC will be to find ways of addressing these needs.

The change in India's governance may bring some promise in this direction. Prime Minister Narendra Modi's recent visit to Nepal (August 2014) may signal the beginning of a new era of confidence building, openness, and strengthened bilateral cooperation. In his key speeches, Modi has summarized the 4 C's of bilateral relations: cooperation, connectivity, culture, and constitution (India Today 2014). Modi's emphasis on enhanced integration and connectivity amongst South Asian neighbours holds great potential. His trade-and-investment–led agenda should help increase both forms of development within the region. He has also clearly indicated that India has no interest at all in 'micro-managing' Nepal's internal affairs. Modi's commitment – to timely completion of existing projects, settlement of border disputes, and development of the PTA and hydropower initiatives with credible timeframes – reflects a number of policy adjustments. These include restructured institutional mechanisms, continuity in bilateral consultation techniques, and successful leadership, ultimately building increased confidence between the two countries. These adjustments presume, in his view, 'little government but more governance' (Daily Mirror 2014). It remains to be seen how the two countries will realise this vision.

The India–Nepal bilateral relationship revolves around cultural, economic, and security factors. The relationships have always remained close, cordial, stable, and mutually beneficial, despite occasional turbulence created by mistrust and suspicion. The understanding that developed after Modi's official visit in August 2014 reveals that more frequent bilateral interaction may open up avenues of cooperation in broader areas of complementarity. Confidence building between countries may lead them to address even politically sensitive and vulnerable issues, if the desire for partnership outweighs the prejudices and misconceptions.

Note

1   One key issue was Nepal's delay in responding to the bilateral trade agreement renewal after its expiry on 23 March 1989. In less than a month, 90 per cent of Nepal's industries closed down; 7,126 laborers became unemployed, and industrial production dropped as low as NPR 850 million per month, down from NPR 1700 million (Poudyal 1993).

After the restoration of democracy in 1990, India–Nepal relations improved, and India relaxed restrictions during the interim period led by Nepali Congress Prime Minister, K. P. Bhattarai.

Works cited

Acharya, M.R. (2002). *Nepal culture shift.* Pinnacle Technology: New Delhi.

Afram, G.G., and Salvi Del Pero, A. (eds.) (2012). *Nepal's investment climate: Leveraging the private sector for job creation and growth.* Washington, DC: The World Bank Group.

Astha Rai, O. (2015). Zero-cost migration. *Nepali Times,* 28 June. Available at www.nepalitimes. com/blogs/thebrief/2015/06/28/zero-cost-migration. [Accessed 12 August 2015].

Avinah, C. (2014). Will a PTA really give the boost needed for India-Nepal hydropower trade? *The Economic Times,* 10 August. Available at http://articles.economictimes.indiatimes. com/2014–08–10/news/52648198_1_pta-hydropower-power-exchanged.

Bergner, M, (2013). *Developing Nepal's hydroelectricity resources: Policy alternatives.* Charlottesville, VA: University of Virginia. Available at www.stimson.org/images/ uploads/research-pdfs/Developing_Nepals_Hydroelectric_Resources_-_Policy_ Alternatives.pdf. [Accessed 5 September 2015].

Blackhurst, R., and Otten, A. (1996). *Trade and foreign direct investment.* Geneva: World Trade Organization. Available at www.wto.org/english/news_e/pres96_e/pr057_e.htm.

China Daily (2015). Qinghai-Tibet railway to reach Nepal in 2020. *China Daily,* 7 April. Available at www.chinadaily.com.cn/china/2015–04/07/content_20016574.htm. [Accessed 12 August 2015].

Crossette, B. (1989). Nepal's economy is gasping as India, a huge neighbor, squeezes it hard. *New York Times,* 11 April. Available at www.nytimes.com/1989/04/11/world/ nepal-s-economy-is-gasping-as-india-a-huge-neighbor-squeezes-it-hard.html.

Daily Mirror (2014). Which way modified India? *Daily Mirror,* 23 May. Available at www. dailymirror.lk/47464/which-way-modified-india. [Accessed 12 August 2015]

DNA India (2010). Prachanda suspicious about India's role in Nepal's politics. *DNA India,* 18 January. Available at www.dnaindia.com/india/report-prachanda-suspicious-about- indias-role-in-nepals-politics-1336084. [Accessed 12 August 2015].

Federation of Nepalese Chambers of Commerce and Industry (FNCCI) (2011). *Agreement between the Government of Nepal and the Government of India for the promotion and protection of investments.* Kathmandu: Government of Nepal and FNCCI. Available at www. fncci.org/downloads/nepal_india_bipa_agreement.pdf. [Accessed 5 September 2015].

Global Times (2014). China tops foreign investors in Nepal. *Global Times,* 11 April. Available at www.globaltimes.cn/content/853919.shtml. [Accessed 12 August 2015].

Government of Nepal (GON) (2012). *Trade policy review WT/TPR/G/257.* Kathmandu: Secretariat, Government of Nepal. Available at https://docs.wto.org/dol2fe/Pages/FE_ Browse/FE_B_S005.aspx?MeetingId=96799&Language=1&StartDate=&EndDate=&S ubjectId=&SearchPage=&&CatIds=60072,86583,82919,85064,44851,88107,75527,53 465,93702,35285&languageUIChanged=true#.

India Today (2014). PM Narendra Modi winds up Nepal visit with slew of sops. *India Today,* 4 August. Available at http://indiatoday.intoday.in/story/narendra-modi-winds- up-nepal-visit-slew-of-sops-sushil-koirala/1/375558.html. [Accessed 12 August 2015].

Indian Development Cooperation Research (IDCR) (2015). *Trends in Indian development assistance in the energy sector.* New Delhi: Centre for Policy Research. Available at http://idcr.cprindia.org/blog/trends-indian-development-assistance-energy-sector. [Accessed 25 July 2015].

International Agency for the Prevention of Blindness (IAPB). (2013). *Vision 2020 global action plan 2014–2019: 'Universal Eye Health'*. Geneva: World Health Organisation. Available at www.iapb.org/vision-2020. [Accessed 12 August 2015].

International Monetary Fund (IMF) (2006). *Nepal: Selected issues and statistical appendix.* Washington, DC: International Monetary Fund.

Kantipur Daily (2014). Nepal's trade deficit with India continues to grow steeply. *Kantipur Daily*, 5 August. Available at www.ekantipur.com/2014/08/05/business/nepals-trade-deficit-with-india-continues-to-grow-steeply/393168.html. [Accessed 24 July 2015].

Karl, D. (2013). India: Asia's geopolitical darling. *Fair Observer*, 24 June. Available at www.fairobserver.com/region/north_america/india-asias-geopolitical-darling/. [Accessed 25 July 2015].

Kathmandu Post (2012). Non-tariff, supply barriers hindering Nepal's exports to India, experts say. *The Kathmandu Post*, 24 March. Available at www.ekantipur.com/the-kathmandu-post/2012/03/23/money/non-tariff-supply-barriers-hindering-nepals-exports-to-india-experts-say/232998.html. [Accessed 12 August 2015].

Kumar, S. (2011). *India-Nepal BIT* [blog] Available at https://ilcurry.wordpress.com/2011/10/31/indianepalbit/. [Accessed 5 September 2015].

Maini, T.S. (2013). *India's north-eastern states essential to India's Southeast Asia policy* [webpage]. East Asia Forum, New Delhi. Available at www.eastasiaforum.org/2013/08/13/indias-northeastern-states-essential-to-indias-south-east-asia-policy.

Mihaly, E.B. (1965). *Foreign aid and politics in Nepal.* Oxford: Oxford University Press.

Ministry of Commerce and Industry (MCI) (2014). *India's trade*. New Delhi: MCI, Government of India.

Ministry of External Affairs (MEA) (2006). Joint press statement, official visit of Rt. Hon'ble Girija Prasad Koirala, Prime Minister of Nepal to India from 6–9 June 2006. MEA, Government of India, New Delhi. Available at www.mea.gov.in/bilateral-documents.htm?dtl/6203/Joint+Press+Statement+Official+Visit+of+Rt+Honble+Girija+Prasad+Koirala+Prime+Minister+of+Nepal+to+India+from+69+June+2006. [Accessed 9 September 2015].

Ministry of Micro, Small and Medium Enterprises (MMSME) (No date). *Issue of imports coming from Nepal route*. New Delhi: MMSME, Government of India. Available at www.dcmsme.gov.in/emerge/nepal.htm. [Accessed 24 July 2015].

Nepal Netra Jyoti Sangh (NNJS) (2013). *Profile*. Kathmandu: NNJS.

Nepal Rastra Bank (2014). *Current economic situation*. Kathmandu: Nepal Rastra Bank. Available at www.nrb.org.np/ofg/macroeconomic_new.php.

Ojha, P. (2012). Overview of trading system in Nepal. Kathmandu: Ministry of Commerce, Government of Nepal.

Parashar, U. (2014). Power trade deal: Nepal's focus on Modi visit. *Hindustan Times*, 30 July. Available at www.hindustantimes.com/world-news/for-nepal-power-trade-agreement-major-focus-of-modi-visit/article1-1246406.aspx. [Accessed 12 August 2015].

Parthasarathy, G. (2015). Look East for economic integration. *The Tribune,* 12 August. Available at www.tribuneindia.com/news/comment/look-east-for-economic-integration/101160.html. [Accessed 12 August 2015].

Poudyal, S, (1993). Industrial development in Nepal. *FNCCI Annual Souvenir*. Federation FF Nepalese Chambers of Commerce and Industries, Kathmandu, Nepal.

Pyakuryal, B. (1995). *Impact of economic liberalization in Nepal.* Kathmandu: Evergreen Expo (P), Ltd.

Pyakuryal, B. (2005). Trade facilitation: Nepal's priorities. In N.N. Pandey (ed.), *Trade facilitation: Nepal's priorities.* Kathmandu: Institute for Foreign Affairs, pp. 10–14.

Pyakuryal, B., and Bhattarai, N. (1991). *Strategy for the development of industrial sector in Nepal.* Panama: Tribhuvan University, Nepal and International Center for Economic Growth.

Pyakuryal, B., Dahal, M.K., and Adhikari, D. (2004). *Partnership in development: An Enquiry into the Indian aid policy to Nepal.* Kathmandu: B.P. Koirala India Nepal Foundation, Embassy of India.

Republica (2014). Nepal Netra Jyoti Sangh celebrates 36th anniversary, *Republica,* 27 March. Available at http://myrepublica.com/portal/index.php/twb/milto?action=news_details&news_id=71700. [Accessed 24 July 2015].

Setopati (2015). Nepal, India to conclude PTA within 45 days, *Setopati,* 4 August. Available at http://m.setopati.net/news/2577/. [Accessed 9 September 2015].

Sharma, B., Adhikari, S., Bhusal, T., Pande, B., Bhattarai, K., Adhikari, D., and Dahal, A. (2014). *An assessment of export barriers of Nepalese products to India.* Kathmandu: Nepal Rastra Bank. Available at www.nrb.org.np/red/publications/study_reports/Study_Reports—An_Assessment_of_Export_Barriers_of_Nepalese_Products_to_India.pdf. [Accessed 5 September 2015].

Shrestha, P.M. (2015). Realizing potential. *The Kathmandu Post,* 26 January.

Singh, K.R. (2009). *Global dimensions of Indo-Nepal political relations: Post independence.* New Delhi: Gyan Publishing House.

Subramanian, N. (2004). India and Nepal's insurgency. *The Hindu,* 8 September. Available at www.thehindu.com/2004/09/08/stories/2004090802851000.htm. [Accessed 12 August 2015].

Suryanarayana, P.S. (2011). China and India cannot go to war: Lee Kuan Yew. *The Hindu,* 24 January. Available at www.thehindu.com/news/china-and-india-cannot-go-to-war-lee-kuan-yew/article1119062.ece. [Accessed 25 July 2015].

Tandon, P. (2012). Return to investment. *Nepali Times,* 16 November. Available at http://nepalitimes.com/news.php?id=19781#.VcrsNROqqkp. [Accessed 12 August 2015].

Trade and Export Promotion Centre (TEPC) (2014). *A glimpse of Nepal's foreign trade.* Kathmandu: Ministry of Commerce and Supplies, Government of Nepal.

United Nations Environment Programme (UNEP) (No date). *South-South cooperation between Nepal and India on technology transfer for converting waste agricultural biomass into energy.* Nairobi: UNEP. Available at www.unep.org/SOUTH-SOUTH-COOPERATION/case/casefiles.aspx?csno=63. [Accessed 24 July 2015].

United States Agency for International Development (USAID) (2005). *South Asian free trade area opportunities and challenges.* Washington, DC: United States Agency for International Development. Available at http://pdf.usaid.gov/pdf_docs/Pnade563.pdf. [Accessed 5 September 2015].

Yogi, B. (2002). New trade winds. Indo-Nepal trade is becoming more hassle-free, as both sides try to remove bottlenecks, *Nepali Times,* 1 November. Available at http://nepalitimes.com/news.php?id=5247#.VesYZxFViko. [Accessed 5 September 2015].

8 The India–Afghanistan development partnership

Gulshan Sachdeva

Introduction

Over the last 4 decades, Afghanistan has witnessed sociopolitical transformation and diverse projects of nation building, with consequences that have resonated beyond its borders. The Soviet intervention, a failed attempt to impose communism, left more than a million dead and created 5 million Afghan refugees, who chiefly fled to neighbouring countries. Pakistan's push for a conservative Taliban regime in Afghanistan also had broad and disastrous effects, playing a key role in the 9/11 terrorist attacks in the United States, among other events. During the last 13 years, the United Nations has supported the creation of a democratic, market-economy state, with support from a Western alliance led by the United States.

Despite serious difficulties, this latest effort has produced significant, if mixed, results. The country has seen significant gains in education, health, infrastructure, communications, women's empowerment, and economic growth. However, during the last few years the security situation has deteriorated, and narcotics production has increased again (Brookings Institution 2015). In the post-2014 phase of the Afghanistan project, the majority of international forces have already moved out of the country, further complicating these challenges. Such threats to the sustainability of many recent achievements pose renewed questions about the effectiveness of foreign-funded reconstruction efforts. The effectiveness of foreign aid in promoting growth in developing countries has always been controversial (Kanbur 2006). The issue has become more important in situations like Afghanistan's, where aid seeks to build a state in the midst of an ongoing war (OECD 2010; International Crisis Group 2011; World Bank 2011a). Moreover, almost all donors have combined strategic and political considerations with reconstruction efforts, whereas several major bilateral donors have seriously flouted the principles of aid effectiveness.[1]

Within this context, the chapter describes Indian development activities in Afghanistan since 2002. It highlights how increased Indian engagement could help Afghanistan address major economic, political, and security challenges during its 'decade of transformation' (2015–2024).[2] Although political and strategic objectives have informed its Afghan engagement, in the last decade India has concentrated mainly on developmental and trade partnerships. Washington has steered the broader strategic direction of the Afghanistan project during this period, and all others partners have had to adjust their activities accordingly. This scenario, however, will probably change in the coming years. In contrast to the West's withdrawal from Afghan activity, all countries in the region, including India, have begun planning for long-term, enhanced engagement. Although Indian assistance comes within the ambit of South-South cooperation (SSC), this framework may not fully capture all its strategic, diplomatic, and political objectives. This chapter has attempted to capture the simultaneous interplay of all these factors – an approach that may also offer insight into the development cooperation of 'nontraditional' donors.

Current challenges in Afghanistan

In the last few years, most analysts and international reports have highlighted three major challenges for the post-2014 phase: security, political, and economic (UN Security Council 2012; Katzman 2014). Security and political difficulties include transfer of responsibility to the Afghan security forces, presidential and parliamentary elections, and reconciliation with the Taliban. The economic challenges appear equally serious. With declining Western interest, the next decade will likely see significantly fewer resources for development than in the previous one.

Experience suggests that withdrawals of international troops in other parts of the world have reduced civilian aid, with implications for economic growth and fiscal sustainability. Therefore, potential financing gaps in the budget could threaten security and recent developmental progress. According to the World Bank, actual aid to Afghanistan in 2010–2011 was about USD 16 billion, about the size of the nominal gross domestic product (GDP) (World Bank 2011b). Any rapid decline in aid will severely affect growth performance and the national employment scenario. The Asian Development Bank has shown that growth in GDP (excluding opium production) has already declined to 3.3 per cent in 2013 (ADB 2014), far below the 12 per cent growth achieved in 2012 (Bonn Conference 2011; ADB 2014). Despite international commitment for the 'transformation decade of 2015–2014' (ADB 2014), the Afghan government will be forced to deploy its limited resources on maintaining security infrastructure.

A close look at the conferences that shaped the international commitment highlights the centrality of Afghanistan in both regional and global strategies. The 2011 Bonn Conference on partnership in the 'decade of transformation', the 2012 Chicago NATO summit on the road map for an enduring security partnership, and the 2012 Tokyo donor conference establishing a 'mutual accountability framework' all addressed key dimensions of long-term engagement with Afghanistan's future. At the Chicago and Tokyo conferences in 2012, donors agreed to provide USD 14 billion and USD 16 billion, respectively, over the next few years. Moreover, American officials also raised the prospect of a new 'Silk Road Strategy' for Afghanistan, a concept to which we will return later (USDOS 2012).

However, it was the 2011 Istanbul Process conference that most fully articulated Afghanistan's regional significance. The 'Heart of Asia' countries in attendance

(Afghanistan, China, India, Iran, Pakistan, Russia, Saudi Arabia, Turkey, the United Arab Emirates [UAE], and all Central Asian republics) reaffirmed their strong commitment to a 'secure, stable and prosperous Afghanistan in a secure and stable region' (Istanbul Declaration 2011). Among other pertinent matters, these countries agreed to respect the territorial integrity of states, practice nonintervention in the internal affairs of other states, dismantle terrorist sanctuaries and safe havens, disrupt all financial and tactical support for terrorism, and support stability and peace in Afghanistan, as well as to respect Afghanistan's sovereignty, unity, and territorial integrity. This brings us to India's specific commitments and actions in recent years.

India's growing development profile in Afghanistan

Afghanistan's position at the crossroads between different regions cements its importance for India. Although its development activities in Afghanistan have only attracted attention in the last few years, India has been active in the country since the late 1960s through various capacity-building programmes in the fields of health, education, agriculture, industry, irrigation, and power. Except for a brief period during the Taliban regime, historically the countries have always enjoyed very friendly relations (Pant 2010). India therefore has a stake in a stable, independent government in Afghanistan, free from external interference, and it has supported the Afghan government politically and economically since 2001 – relations codified in a formal Strategic Partnership document in 2011 (MEA 2011). India's broad objectives in Afghanistan include orderly security, successful political and economic transition, and ensuring the safety and security of its assets and personnel. Increasing trade, transit, and energy links with Central Asia through Afghanistan supply are added objectives (India Policy Group 2013; IAJWGT 2014).

In the post-Taliban period since 2001, India's economic, political, and strategic linkages with Afghanistan have improved significantly, a result of increasing development assistance, as well as trade and investment cooperation. With a broad understanding that a peaceful and stable Afghanistan is crucial for regional stability, India has played an active role in the reconstruction since 2002. So far it has pledged assistance worth about USD 2 billion, with projects covering the entire country – mainly in the areas of road construction, power transmission lines, hydroelectricity, agriculture, telecommunications, education, health, and capacity building (EOI 2013a; 2013b; 2013c; MEA n.d.; 2011).[3] Every year about 1500 Afghan students come to India on long- or short-term educational fellowships. In addition, a few hundred Afghan officials come to India for different training programmes. In the last few years, cooperation efforts have focused on a large number of small development projects, chiefly implemented by local communities.

Trade, regional cooperation, and connectivity

Because Afghanistan ultimately has to stand on its own feet, trade and connectivity issues will prove more important in the long run than unsustainable, foreign-funded development projects. In this connection, linkages with the Indian economy, a traditional market for Afghan products, will become crucial. Policy-makers in Afghanistan have realised that to offset the negative economic effects of international troop withdrawals, they must concentrate on two issues. First, Afghanistan must attract foreign investment, particularly in sectors such as min-ing, hydrocarbons, infrastructure, telecommunications, agriculture, education, health services, and so forth. According to the World Bank estimates, the Aynak and Hajigak mines alone – potential targets for Chinese and Indian investment – would, if properly developed, create more than 90,000 jobs and approximately USD 500 million in fiscal revenues in the coming years (World Bank 2010). Sec-ond, for long-term sustainability, Afghanistan must also play its traditional role of facilitating trade and commerce through its territories. In both these areas, India and other regional countries could become very significant actors. Both the 2012 'Delhi Investment Summit on Afghanistan' (AISA 2012) and the November 2013 'Doing Business with Afghanistan' meeting organised by the Federation of Indian Chambers of Commerce and Industry (FICCI) emphasised precisely these points (FICCI 2013).

The choice of India to host these summits reflects the scale of existing or announced Indian investments in Afghanistan. A consortium of seven Indian com-panies, led by the state-owned Steel Authority of India (SAIL), have won a USD 10.3 billion deal to mine three iron ore blocks in central Afghanistan. Some Indian companies also plan to bid for copper and gold projects (Bhattacharya 2012). Reports have circulated that India also plans to build a 900-kilometre railway line between Iran's Chabahar Port and Bamiyan Province, where Indian companies have projected large investments (Nelson 2011).

Even from a very narrow base of USD 40 million a year in 2001–2002, India–Afghanistan trade has already grown to about USD 700 million a year in 2013–2014. Afghanistan manages to export about USD 200 million to India each year (Table 8.1). Special trade preferences under the countries' bilateral trade agreement may have positively influenced these figures. Last year, the main import items from Afghanistan were dry figs (USD 62 million), asafetida (USD 51 million), raisins (USD 29 million), almonds, apricots, and pistachios. The chief export items from India were textiles, pharmaceuticals, cereals, and dairy products.

Afghanistan's strategic location will always be important for India, particu-larly in the context of difficult India–Pakistan relations. However, the country's significance transcends this narrow context. Once Afghanistan becomes stable, trade through Pakistan, Afghanistan, and Central Asia has the potential to alter the nature and character of India's continental reach. To date, India has conducted the majority of its trade by sea. Border trade with China halted after the 1962 India-China war; only recently, the Nathu La Pass has supplied a limited opening to renewed Chinese trade (Chaudhury and Saha 2015).

Looking beyond Central Asia, India trades a great deal with other Common-wealth of Independent States (CIS) countries, with Iran, and, of course, with the European continent. In 2012–2013, India's total trade with these countries

Table 8.1 India–Afghanistan trade values, 2001–2002 to 2013–2014 (USD million)

Year	Exports	Imports	Total Trade
2001–2002	24.37	17.52	41.89
2002–2003	60.77	18.46	79.23
2003–2004	145.47	40.51	185.98
2004–2005	165.44	47.01	212.45
2005–2006	142.67	58.42	201.09
2006–2007	182.11	34.37	216.48
2007–2008	249.21	109.97	359.18
2008–2009	394.23	126.24	520.45
2009–2010	463.55	129.19	588.74
2010–2011	422.41	146.03	568.44
2011–2012	510.90	132.50	643.41
2012–2013	472.63	159.55	632.18
2013–2014	474.34	208.77	683.11
2014–2015	422.56	261.91	684.47

Source: GOI (2001–2015)

amounted to around USD 173 billion. Just before the global economic crisis of 2008–2010, India's trade with this region had grown very rapidly, particularly with Afghanistan, Pakistan, and Iran. Simple calculations on the basis of past trends show that India's trade with Europe, CIS plus Iran, Afghanistan, and Pakistan could arrive in the range of about USD 400–500 billion annually within the next few years (GOI 2001–2015; Sachdeva 2010a).

Even if only 20 per cent of this trade took place via roadways, USD 80–100 billion of Indian trade would pass through Afghanistan and Central Asia. With improved India–Pakistan relations, an important portion of Indian trade (particularly from the landlocked northern states, including Jammu and Kashmir) could go through Pakistan as well – meaning that most of the infrastructural projects in the region would become economically viable. These linkages will also transform small and medium-sized industries and agriculture in Central Asia and Afghanistan. A major impediment in realizing this potential lies in the current difficult relations between India and Pakistan. The regional economic dynamics make it clear that both India and Pakistan would pay enormous economic costs for not cooperating in Afghanistan. If Pakistan halts trade routes at its borders, many regional infrastructural projects will never become viable because of low volumes. Direct linkages between Central Asia and India will also give a huge boost to all economies in the region, particularly to Afghanistan.

With Indian continental trade moving through this region, the Pakistani economy will also benefit greatly. Many within Pakistan fear that, with Indian goods moving to Afghanistan and Central Asia, markets for Pakistani products may erode. However, Pakistani trade figures show that even without Indian competition, it cannot export large volumes to Central Asia; in the last few years, such exports have come to less than USD 20 million a year (TDAP 2010–2015). Pakistan has significant exports only to Afghanistan, and a major portion of those should remain unaffected by Indian competition. In fact, with major infrastructural development and movement of goods and services, both India and Pakistan could become important economic players in Central Asia, rather than the insignificant ones they remain at present.

The 'New Silk Road' strategy

Many of these promising outcomes require clear prioritisation of the projects discussed in multilateral meetings (noted earlier). A few studies have indicated that immediate and long-term measures could soften the economic impact of the military withdrawal and create conditions for self-sustained growth (Starr and Farhardi 2012). Afghan and American officials have now repeatedly alluded to the so-called 'New Silk Road' strategy (USDOS 2012; AMFA 2015). The concept of the Silk Road has evolved over centuries, but in the last two decades it has referred to a synthesis of cultures and civilisations, as well as of trade networks and transit and infrastructure corridors. Every major partner in the project – Afghanistan, the Central Asian republics, China, India, Iran, Pakistan, the United States – has its own concept and understanding of the Silk Road, and will continue to pursue its own objectives through specific economic and/or cultural projects. The success of many of these projects will depend on economic viability, as well as prevailing political and security conditions. The Chinese Eurasian Land Bridge concept, linking China and Russia to Europe via Kazakhstan (and more recently the 'One Road One Belt' project), and the International North-South Transport corridor project initiated by India, Iran, and Russia, have already begun implementation (PIB 2014; HKTDC 2015).

Afghanistan's role in the 'New Silk Road' has come up in many academic and policy forums at least since 2005 (CAPF 2012); in the long-term vision of an international trade, transit, and energy network linking Central and South Asian economies, it is always the crucial link (Starr and Kuchins 2010). This useful blueprint has unfortunately run up against regional geopolitics and Western exit strategies from the country; however, it remains the sole viable strategy for Afghanistan to pursue. A scrupulous implementation of the Afghan-Pakistan Transit Trade Agreement (APTTA) would provide a positive step in this direction. Under the agreement, both Afghanistan and Pakistan have agreed to facilitate the movement of goods between and through their respective territories; an extension including Tajikistan is now nearly complete (Sachdeva 2010b; Arshad 2015). However, an expanded APTTA would have only limited interest for other Central Asian countries unless it permits two-way traffic to India. With the inclusion of the Central Asian countries and India, the region will be ready to benefit from the emerging Eurasian Economic Union within a few years.

Despite tensions at the political level, India and Pakistan have also seen some positive developments in trade matters that may have collateral effects on their

Afghan cooperation. Both have agreed on three principles: redressal of trade grievances, mutual recognition, and customs cooperation. Although India had given Pakistan most favoured nation (MFN) status in 1996, Pakistan has refused to reciprocate – but some signs now indicate that it may do so soon. Once that happens, India will bring the South Asian Free Trade Area (SAFTA) 'sensitive list'[4] to just 100, and Pakistan will follow suit within the next 5 years. By 2020, the peak tariff rate will not exceed 5 per cent. Both countries have also agreed to cooperate in investment, banking, electricity and gas trade, railways, and better air connectivity. In addition, they have signed a new liberalised visa regime (PTI 2012; Business Recorder 2015; ICRIER 2015).[5]

Energy projects, security concerns, and regional economic integration

In the last few years, all four countries involved in the Turkmenistan–Afghanistan–Pakistan–India (TAPI) gas pipeline project have already signed most of the agreements required to begin work. These include an Inter-Governmental Agreement (IGA), a Gas Pipeline Framework Agreement (GPFA), and a Gas Sales and Purchase Agreement. The countries have also agreed upon a broad arrangement for transit fees (Sachdeva 2013). In 2014, Veerappa Moily, the Indian minister for petroleum and natural gas, asserted that the four stakeholder nations have fast-tracked the TAPI framework and appointed a transactional advisor for the project, adding that 'gas is expected to reach the border of India by August 2017' (Saikia 2014). The project feasibility study was completed in September 2015 (Kosolapova 2015) and pipeline construction began in December 2015 (Gurt 2015). The Indian public-sector giant Oil and Natural Gas Corporation (ONGC) also plans to bring Russian hydrocarbons to India via Central Asia, Afghanistan, and Pakistan. If implemented, these projects could become 'game changers' in regional geopolitics and economic integration. They also have the potential to ease the 'decade of transformation' for Afghanistan.

Within this broad context, India has continued to support both the Regional Economic Cooperation Conference on Afghanistan (RECCA) and the 'Heart of Asia' (Istanbul Declaration 2011) multilateral processes. In the Istanbul process, India leads the Trade Commerce and Investment Opportunities Confidence Building Measure (TCI-CBM). Uncertainty concerning post-2014 Afghanistan has also added a new dimension to India's relations with Central Asian republics. If the security situation deteriorates in Afghanistan, it will pose common security challenges on all sides. On the other hand, a relatively stable Afghanistan will open tremendous economic opportunities. These factors have considerably increased Central Asia's strategic significance and may have impelled India's announcement of a new twelve-point new 'Connect Central Asia' policy (MEA 2012a). Among other matters, the new policy emphasises stepping up multilateral engagement (through the Shanghai Cooperation Organisation [SCO] membership and a possible trade agreement with the Eurasian Economic Union), reactivating the International North-South Trade Corridor, and strengthening strategic and security cooperation in terms of military training, joint research, counterterrorism cooperation, and close consultations on Afghanistan (Roy 2014; Sachdeva 2015a). At the fifteenth SCO summit in Ufa (Russia) in July 2015, it was decided that both India and Pakistan would soon become formal members of the organisation (Xinhuanet 2015).

Although economic integration both within and between South and Central Asia remains limited, strong economic growth in both regions has pushed policy-makers to support integration strategies (Sachdeva 2010a; Pyatt 2013). As a large, fast-growing economy, India is an attractive market for both regions; regional integration also influences Afghanistan's economic sustainability, because (as noted earlier) it must fulfil its traditional role of facilitating trade and commerce through its territories, a role that took on critical importance between 2006 and 2009. Since then, however, the focus on the military exit (and later on 'negotiated settlement' with the Taliban) pushed the issue of serious regional cooperation into the background. By the time the international community, and particularly the Americans, began addressing the New Silk Road concept, the Chinese, Russian, and Iranian leadership had already become active with their own strategies. Moreover, many observers across the region saw the New Silk Road as a merely political component of a respectable exit strategy for Western forces (Kuchins 2011; Sachdeva 2015a). But as noted earlier, pursuit of regional integration remains Afghanistan's best, if not only, option.

Compared to the modest trade within South and Central Asia, however, continental trade will prove much more important for the South Asian region. As a result, plans for linking South Asia with Europe through Afghanistan and Central Asia have far more value than merely regional or subregional approaches. Different infrastructural plans, such as the South Asian Association for Regional Cooperation (SAARC) multimodel transport linkages, the Asian Development Bank's Central Asia Regional Economic Cooperation (CAREC) action plans, the Northern Distribution Network (NDN), and the International North-South Corridor (INSTC), all constitute pieces of this larger picture. Ultimately, South Asian trade volumes from India and Pakistan will reach Europe through these different schemes (Sachdeva 2010a; Sachdeva 2015a)

Many of these proposals have generated lengthy discussion in recent years, but the success of NDN within a limited time has given new impetus to South Asia–Europe transportation plans (Sprūds and Potjomkina 2013). NDN shows the potential for positive results even when negotiations involve strategically competing nations or other entities – for example, the INSTC and the NDN, or Chabahar and Gwadar ports. Yet all these mechanisms will ultimately facilitate South Asian economic linkages with Europe. Successful implementation of APTTA and TAPI, and formal connections between South Asia and the emerging Eurasian Economic Union (including Belarus, Kazakhstan, and Russia), will further strengthen these connections.

These developments indicate that, in contrast to the decreased role of Western nations after 2014, South and Central Asian countries will gear up for enhanced engagement in Afghanistan. Reasons for this may vary from country to country.

The expected greater role for India presumes that international support to Afghanistan will continue much beyond 2014. Chinese engagement will also increase, both through the SCO and in protecting its USD 3 billion investment in copper mines. The increased Central Asian and Russian engagement will address threats concerning religious extremism and terrorism, drug trafficking, cross-border crime, and flow of refugees (Trenin et al. 2014).

Possibilities of triangular cooperation

With the majority of international forces moving out of Afghanistan, resources for development projects may also decline, particularly after 2016. However, most Western donors have publicly committed to reconstruction efforts in Afghanistan far beyond 2014. Most Western development activities in the coming years will concentrate on training and equipping security forces, infrastructure development, social sectors, and capacity building – the precise areas of focus for India. In these circumstances, India may try to cooperate with other third-country donors on similar projects. Although coordination has not proven easy, even among traditional donors, it may yet produce a win-win situation both for them and for India. Certain areas where India has long shown its strengths – higher education, health, capacity-building training programmes, police and military training, and support for regional cooperation initiatives[6] – could offer opportunities for collaborating with American and European development partners. Similarly, India could work with other countries in strengthening Afghanistan's democratic institutions and decentralised governance.

Future Indian engagement in Afghanistan

Because India has provided significant resources toward the Afghan reconstruction, its experiences there could have a serious impact on the evolving Indian development strategy. The close India–Afghanistan relationship, culminating in the 2011 strategic partnership, suggests a significant fulfilment of many Indian objectives. Many analysts have also indicated that Indian development efforts have proven relatively more effective than those of other nations (see e.g., Hanauer and Chalk 2012). Moreover, many opinion polls document a positive Afghan view of Indian activities in their country – far more than for other countries' interventions.[7] The widespread daily broadcast of Indian films and serials on TV has also contributed to a positive perception of Indian culture.

Like all countries engaged in development efforts, India faces serious concerns about sustainability. Indian policymakers have clearly indicated at every forum that India has no exit strategy in Afghanistan; on the contrary, it seems likely to increase its involvement. At the Tokyo conference in July 2012, Indian External Affairs Minister S. M. Krishna described India's Afghan partnership as neither 'conditions-based or transitory', arguing that the pace and applications of Indian cooperation would rest on 'the preference, comfort level and absorptive capacity of the Afghan government' (MEA 2012b).

In all three crucial areas (political, security, economic), enhanced Indian engagement in Afghanistan could help the country meet these difficult challenges during its 'decade of transformation'. Expanded Indian engagement could easily build on the October 2011 strategic partnership agreement, the first accord of its kind that Afghanistan had signed with any foreign country. Apart from capacity-building support to various departments in the executive, judiciary, and parliamentary branches, the agreement highlights two major points. First, India has agreed 'as mutually determined' to assist in the training, equipping, and capacity-building programmes for Afghan national security forces. Second, it has recognised that regional economic cooperation is vital for the long-term economic prosperity of Afghanistan and the region. In addition, the agreement creates bilateral institutional mechanisms, including annual summit meetings, regular political consultations led by the foreign ministries of both countries, and strategic dialogues on national security led by their national security advisors (MEA 2011). Although many of these processes had already begun, the agreement still provided a concrete institutional basis and clear support for Afghan institutions in the years to come.

Although India has provided limited training to Afghan military officers, this programme could expand significantly in coming years, engaging India more fully in security as well development efforts. India has signed an agreement to pay Russia for supplying arms and equipment to the Afghan security forces, initially sourcing smaller arms such as light artillery and mortars, with a possible later transfer of heavy artillery, tanks, and combat helicopters (Miglani 2014). Recently, India has also provided three Cheetah helicopters to the Afghan security forces.

Although Indian policymakers remain committed to Afghanistan, they will not find it easy to sustain development activities if the security situation deteriorates further. In the last few years, many Indians working in development have lost their lives, and India has not announced any major new development projects. Like many other countries, in the last 2 years India has prioritised completion of previously announced initiatives, with a justifiable focus on small development projects and fellowship programmes. A deteriorating security situation will also hamper involvement from Indian nongovernmental organisations (NGOs) or independent experts in bilateral development activities. As argued elsewhere, enhanced cooperation with the Afghan security forces will prove crucial in securing Indian assets and citizens in Afghanistan (Sachdeva 2015b).

Conclusion

Traditionally, historical, cultural, and civilisation contexts have framed understanding of India–Afghanistan relations. Developments following the Soviet intervention increased Afghanistan's strategic significance for India, but recent decades have seen less analysis of its economic importance. This neglect arose from Afghan instability, as well as difficult India–Pakistan relations. With the new leadership focusing on economic issues in both India and Afghanistan, an opportunity has arisen to transform their bilateral economic ties – which, in turn, may transform the entire regional scenario.

Long and close political relations have informed decades of Indian development aid to Afghanistan. Its scope and sectoral coverage, however, have expanded considerably in the past 13 years. Since 2001, India has committed about USD 2 billion in resources to help (re)build a stable, prosperous, and strategically independent Afghanistan. This development partnership appears to serve many Indian objectives: political (influence in Kabul), economic (preparing a strategy for South-Central Asia economic linkages), diplomatic (acting as an important regional and global player), strategic (a new outlet to Afghanistan and Central Asia, bypassing Pakistan), long-term capacity building (through fellowships and training), and humanitarian (providing relief to vulnerable Afghan citizens). If India realises its proposed investments in the mining sector or completes TAPI or other gas pipeline projects through Afghanistan, enormous consequences for its development strategy may follow.

Additional measures would strengthen the sustainability of Indian engagement in Afghan development. More engagement calls for strengthened ties with the Afghan security forces – a matter not only of strategy, but also of protecting Indian personnel and assets. Longer periods of involvement require India to do thorough homework in project selection, unlike the ad hoc process that characterised early large-scale projects. Similarly, India might direct more efforts to areas where it has a comparative advantage, particularly in capacity building, fellowships, training, and the like. Development projects need further input from Indian NGOs; India's newly established Development Partnership Administration (DPA) in the Ministry of External Affairs has already prepared a list of suitable NGOs that might contribute.[8] The DPA should also expedite their involvement. Indian projects require efforts to make them more visible within Afghanistan, as well as in the discourse of international development; the Indian government should publish full details and success stories on a regular basis. Finally, official clarification of objectives would improve India's ability to evaluate development projects professionally.

Overall, if India can sustain its engagement in the coming years, its development partnership in Afghanistan has the potential to become a broader economic and strategic engagement – one that might transform the regional economies and offer a model for similar initiatives elsewhere.

Notes

1 According to the *Development Partnership Report 2011*, prepared by the Afghanistan Ministry of Finance (2012), 82 per cent of external assistance disbursed between 2002 and 2010 bypassed the national budget process. Development partner agencies directly managed and implemented the programmes and projects, with no direct accountability to the Afghan government.

2 The concept of the 'decade of transformation' first arose at the 2011 International Conference on Afghanistan in Bonn, attended by eighty-five countries and fifteen international organizations. In the wake of US President Obama's announcement that foreign troops would move out of Afghanistan by 2014, all international partners pledged continued support for Afghanistan's development efforts through 2024. 2011–2014 would serve as a transition period, succeeded by the 'transformative' decade between 2015 and 2024 (Bonn Conference 2011; ADB 2014).

3 Some of the major projects built with Indian assistance include construction of the 218-km Zaranj-Delaram road, a power transmission line from Pul-e-Khumri to Kabul, the 42-MW Salma dam power project on the Hari Rud River in Herat province, and the Afghan Parliament building.
4 The list includes 'sensitive' products that are exempted from low SAFTA tariffs. This allows individual member states to protect specific industries. In smaller countries, it also protects government revenues.
5 For regular updates on India-Pakistani trade matters, as well as relevant studies and documents, see the links at IPT (www.indiapakistantrade.org).
6 See, in particular, the chapters by Tuhin and Chaturvedi in this volume.
7 In nationwide surveys conducted by the BBC, ABC News, and the German news agency ARD in 2009 and 2010, 74 per cent and 71 per cent of Afghanis, respectively, had very favourable or favourable opinions about India. The corresponding figures in 2010 for the United States, United Kingdom, Iran, Germany, and Pakistan were 51 per cent, 39 per cent, 50 per cent, 59 per cent, and 15 per cent, respectively (BBC 2010).
8 See also the chapter by Mawdsley and Roychoudhury in this volume.

Works cited

Afghanistan Investment Support Agency (AISA) (2012). *Report on Delhi investment summit on Afghanistan*. Kabul: AISA. Available at http://goo.gl/pxAU0W. [Accessed 22 August 2015].

Afghanistan Ministry of Finance (2012). *Development cooperation report*. Kabul: Ministry of Finance, Government of Afghanistan.

Afghanistan Ministry of Foreign Affairs (AMFA) (2015). *RECCA VI the silk road through Afghanistan*. Kabul: MFA, Government of Afghanistan. Available at http://goo.gl/ZYujmj. [Accessed 15 August 2015].

Arshad M. (2015). Pakistan, Afghanistan, Tajikistan near to finalize trilateral transit agreement. *Customs Today*, 10 April. Available at www.customstoday.com.pk/pakistan-afghanistan-tajikistan-near-to-finalize-trilateral-transit-agreement. [Accessed 15 October 2015].

Asian Development Bank (ADB) (2014). *Asian Development Bank outlook 2014*. Manila: ADB.

Bhattacharya, P. (2012). Indian firms aim to bid for Afghan mines. *The Wall Street Journal*, 26 April. Available at http://goo.gl/dt4YpV. [Accessed 22 August 2015].

Bonn Conference (2011). *Conclusions: Afghanistan and the international community: From transition to the transformation decade*. Bonn: Federal Foreign Office, Government of Germany. Available at http://eeas.europa.eu/afghanistan/docs/2011_11_conclusions_bonn_en.pdf. [Accessed 15 May 2015].

Brookings Institution (2015). *Afghanistan index* [database]. Washington, DC: Brookings Institution. Available at www.brookings.edu/about/programs/foreign-policy/afghanistan-index. [Accessed 15 May 2015].

British Broadcasting Company (BBC) (2010). *ABC News, the BBC and ARD survey conducted by the Afghan Center for Socio-Economic and Opinion Research (ACSOR)*. Kabul: BBC.

Business Recorder (2015). India decides to issue three-year multiple visas to businesspeople. *Business Recorder*, 28 July. Available at www.brecorder.com/business-a-economy/189/1211210/. [Accessed 11 October 2015].

Central Asia Policy Forum (CAPF) (2012). *Discussing the 'New Silk Road Strategy' of Central Asia*. Washington, DC: CAPF, Central Asia Program, George Washington University. Available at http://goo.gl/kcoUE3. [Accessed 10 September 2015].

Chaudhury, A.B.R., and Saha, S. (2015). The Nathu La pass in India-China ties. *The Telegraph*, 30 May. Available at http://goo.gl/xrocwT. [Accessed 15 August 2015].

Embassy of India (EOI) (2013a). *Assistance: India's assistance programme for Afghanistan's reconstruction*. Kabul: EOI. Available at http://eoi.gov.in/kabul/?0356?000.

EOI (2013b). *Development partnership: India's assistance programme for Afghanistan's reconstruction*. Kabul: Embassy of India. Available at http://eoi.gov.in/kabul/?0707?000.

EOI (2013c). *ITEC fellowships*. Kabul: Embassy of India. Available at http://eoi.gov.in/kabul/?0360?000.

Federation of Indian Chambers of Commerce and Industry (FICCI) (2013). *Doing business with Afghanistan, unlocking Afghanistan's economic potential*. New Delhi: FICCI. Available at www.ficci.com/publication-page.asp?spid=20345. [Accessed 29 July 2015].

Government of India (GOI) (2001–2015). *Export import databank*. New Delhi: Ministry of Commence, Government of India. Available at www.commerce.nic.in/eidb/.

Gurt, M. (2015). Turkmenistan to start work on TAPI pipeline in December. *Reuters News Agency*, 16 September. Available at http://goo.gl/uZP4J6. [Accessed 17 September 2015].

Hanauer, L., and Chalk, P. (2012). India's and Pakistan's strategies in Afghanistan: Implications for the United States and the region. *CAPP Occasional Paper*. Centre for Asia Pacific Policy, Rand Corporation, Santa Monica, CA. Available at http://goo.gl/e1dxNo. [Accessed 15 September 2015].

Hong Kong Trade Development Council (HKTDC) (2015). *The belt and road initiative* [webpage]. Hong Kong: HKTDC. Available at http://goo.gl/rennU2. [Accessed 14 October 2015].

India Afghanistan Joint Working Group on Trade, Commerce and Investment (IAJWGT) (2014). Minutes of the first India Afghanistan joint working group on trade, commerce and investment, Kabul, 28 January. Ministry of Commerce, Government of India, New Delhi. Available at http://commerce.nic.in/trade/MINUTES_FIRST_INDIA_AFGHANISTAN_JWG_28Jan2014.pdf.

India Policy Group (2013). Envisioning Afghanistan post-2014: Perspectives and strategies for constructive conflict resolution from the neighbourhood. *India Policy Group Paper*. Friedrich-Ebert-Stiftung, New Delhi. Available at www.fes-asia.org/media/Peace per cent20and per cent20Security/FES_Policy_Paper_India_102013.pdf.

Indian Council for Research on International Economic Relations (ICRIER) (2015). *India-Pakistan trade* [webpage]. New Delhi: ICRIER. Available at http://indiapakistantrade.org/index.html. [Accessed 12 September 2015].

International Crisis Group (2011). Aid and conflict in Afghanistan. *Asia Report*, 210. International Crisis Group, Washington, DC.

Istanbul Declaration (2011). *Declaration of the Istanbul process on regional security and cooperation for a secure and stable Afghanistan*. Available at www.heartofasia-istanbul-process.af/wp-content/uploads/2014/04/2-Nov-Declaration.pdf. [Accessed 22 August 2015].

Kanbur, R. (2006). The economics of international aid. In S. Kolm and J. Ythier (eds.), *The handbook of the economics of giving, altruism and reciprocity*. Amsterdam: North Holland, pp 1559–1585.

Katzman, K. (2014). *Afghanistan: Post-Taliban governance, security and US policy*. Washington, DC: US Congressional Research Service. Available at www.fas.org/sgp/crs/row/RL30588.pdf. [Accessed 1 November 2015].

Kosolapova, E. (2015). TAPI feasibility study completed. *Trend News Agency*, 18 September. Available at http://en.trend.az/business/energy/2434992.html. [Accessed 19 September 2015].

Kuchins, A.C. (2011). Laying the groundwork for Afghanistan's New Silk Road. *Foreign Affairs*, 12. Available at https://goo.gl/AN7pyx. [Accessed 17 October].

MEA (2011). *Text of agreement on strategic partnership between the Republic of India and the Islamic Republic of Afghanistan*, 4 October. Ministry of External Affairs, Government of India, New Delhi. Available at http://goo.gl/VjvM2s. [Accessed 15 August 2015].

MEA (2012a). Keynote address by MOS Shri E. Ahamed at first India-Central Asia Dialogue. Ministry of External Affairs, Government of India, New Delhi. Available at http://goo.gl/gS55fx. [Accessed 29 July 2015].

MEA (2012b). External Affairs Minister's address at the International Conference on Afghanistan, 08 July [speech]. Ministry of External Affairs, Government of India, New Delhi. Available at www.mea.gov.in/Speeches-Statements.htm?dtl/20070/EAMs_Address_at_the_International_Conference_on_Afghanistan.

Migliani, S. (2014). India turns to Russia to help supply arms to Afghan forces. *Reuters*, 30 April. Available at http://in.reuters.com/article/2014/04/30/uk-india-afghanistan-arms-idINKBN0DG19O20140430. [Accessed 2 May 2014].

Ministry of External Affairs (MEA) (no date). *India and Afghanistan: A development partnership*. External Publicity Division, New Delhi: MEA, Government of India. Available at http://mea.gov.in/Uploads/PublicationDocs/176_india-and-afghanistan-a-development-partnership.pdf.

Nelson, D. (2011). India plans world's most dangerous railroad from Afghanistan to Iran. *The Telegraph* (UK), 2 November. Available at http://goo.gl/DlRH58. [Accessed 22 August 2015].

Organisation for Economic Cooperation and Development (OECD) (2010). *Monitoring the principles for good international engagement in fragile states and situations: Islamic Republic of Afghanistan*. Paris: OECD.

Pant, H. (2010). India in Afghanistan: A test case for a rising power, *Contemporary South Asia*, 18(2), 133–153.

Press Information Bureau (PIB) (2014). *India's participation in the development of Chahbahar port in Iran*. New Delhi: PIB, Government of India. Available at http://pib.nic.in/newsite/PrintRelease.aspx?relid=110685. [Accessed 15 October 2015].

Press Trust of India (PTI) (2012). India, Pak sign new liberalized trade agreement. *Hindustan Times*, 8 September. Available at www.hindustantimes.com/world-news/india-pak-sign-new-liberalised-visa-agreement/article1-926441.aspx. [Accessed 29 July 2015].

Pyatt, G. (2013). Regional economic integration in South and Central Asia, 12 March [speech]. Department of State, United States Government, Washington, DC. Available at www.state.gov/p/sca/rls/rmks/2013/205973.htm. [Accessed 17 October 2015].

Roy, M.S (2014). The Shanghai Cooperation organisation: India seeking new role in the Eurasian regional mechanism. *ISDA Monograph Series*, 34. Institute for Defense Studies and Analysis, New Delhi.

Sachdeva, G. (2010a). Regional economic linkages. In N. Joshi (ed.), *Reconnecting India and central Asia: Emerging security and economic dimensions*. Washington DC: Central Asia-Caucasus Institute and Silk Road Studies Program, pp. 115–179.

Sachdeva, G. (2010b). Afghanistan and Pakistan sign trade and transit agreement. *Central Asia Caucasus Analyst*, 12(16), 12–14.

Sachdeva, G. (2013). TAPI: Time for the big push. *The Central Asia Caucasus Analyst*, 13 July. Available at www.cacianalyst.org/publications/analytical-articles/item/12772-tapi-time-for-the-big-push.html.

Sachdeva, G. (2015a). India's objectives in Central Asia. In D.B.H. Denoon (ed.), *China, the United States, and the future of Central Asia: U.S.-China relations,* vol. 1. New York: New York University Press, pp. 262–295.

Sachdeva, G. (2015b). Kabul attack: The odds are stacked against India. *The Hindustan Times,* 18 May. Available at goo.gl/Au0LiA.

Saikia, S. (2014). TAPI project moving ahead: India to get gas by Aug 2017: Moily. *The Hindu,* 14 January. Available at www.thehindubusinessline.com/industry-and-economy/tapi-project-moving-ahead-india-to-get-gas-by-aug-2017-moily/article5577117.ece. [Accessed 29 July 2015].

Sprūds, A., and Potjomkina, D. (eds.) (2013). *Northern distribution network: Redefining partnerships within NATO and beyond.* Riga: Latvian Institute for International Affairs.

Starr, S.F., and Farhardi, A. (eds.) (2012). *Finish the job: Jump-start Afghanistan's economy. A handbook of projects.* Washington, DC: Central Asia-Caucasus Institute and Silk Road Studies Program. Available at www.silkroadstudies.org/resources/pdf/SilkRoadPapers/2012_11_SRP_StarrFarhadi_Afghanistan-Economy.pdf. [Accessed 1 November 2015].

Starr, S.F., and Kuchins, A.C. (2010). The key to success in Afghanistan: A modern silk road strategy. *Silk Road Paper.* Central Asia-Caucasus Institute and Silk Road Studies Program, Washington, DC.

Trade Development Authority of Pakistan (TDAP) (2010–2015). *Export from Pakistan 2010–2015.* Karachi: TDAP. Available at www.tdap.gov.pk/tdap-statistics.php.

Trenin, D., Kulakov, O., Malashenko, A., and Topychkanov, P. (2014). *A Russian strategy for Afghanistan after the coalition troop withdrawal.* Carnegie Moscow Centre, Moscow. Available at http://goo.gl/N2UYzp. [Accessed 18 October 2015].

UN Security Council (2012). The situation in Afghanistan and its implications for international peace and security: Report of the Secretary-General to the Security Council (5 March), No. A/66/728–S/2012/133. United Nations, New York. Available at http://goo.gl/Svnj4L. [Accessed 23 August 2015].

US Department of State (2012). *U.S. support for the New Silk Road.* Washington, DC: United States Government, Department of State. Available at www.state.gov/p/sca/ci/af/newsilkroad/. [Accessed 15 May 2015].

World Bank (2010). *Mining for sustainable growth in Afghanistan* [webpage]. Available at http://goo.gl/GmEgzT. [Accessed 23 August 2015].

World Bank (2011a). *World development report 2011: Conflict, security and development.* Washington, DC: The World Bank Group.

World Bank (2011b). *Transition in Afghanistan: Looking beyond 2014.* Washington, DC: The World Bank Group.

Xinhuanet (2015). Spotlight: Just-concluded BRICS, SCO summits in Ufa highlight China's constructive role. *China News,* 12 July. Available at http://news.xinhuanet.com/english/2015–07/12/c_134404710.htm. [Accessed 19 October 2015].

9 India's evolving blueprint for cooperation with Africa

Ruchita Beri

In recent years, India's engagement with Africa has grown to embrace a variety of areas, spanning political, strategic, trade and investment, and developmental interests. The increasing number of two-way visits by leaders, officials, academics, and businesspeople reflects the vibrancy of the relationship. From an Indian perspective, Africa is not a 'hopeless continent' as suggested by *The Economist* a decade ago (Economist 2000); rather, it has both the potential and conditions to become a 'major growth pole' of the global economy (Kingsley 2012; Sidiropoulous 2014).[1] The latest statistics suggest that Africa's economic output has almost tripled since 2003, and the IMF forecasts that seven of the ten fastest-growing economies in the world over the next 5 years will be African (Economist 2011). The present chapter surveys how India has supported and in some instances steered African growth through its development cooperation and investment, offering some of the most diverse and striking instances of South-South cooperation (SSC).

India's economic and cultural ties with Africa go back to antiquity (Sen 1999); former Prime Minister Manmohan Singh even credited Africa as the inspiration for India's own liberation struggle and for Gandhi's concepts of 'non-violence and peaceful resistance' (Singh [M.] 2011). The shared historical experience of Western exploitation has also proven important; India's anticolonial struggle served as an example for similar political movements in Africa. Furthermore, Indian migration to East and Southern Africa during British colonial rule – initially as plantation workers and later as traders – has left a substantial Indian presence in the region.[2] In the postcolonial period, India has positioned itself as a champion of the interests of developing countries (including African ones), particularly through the Bandung Declaration of 1955,[3] the Group of 77, and the Non-Aligned Movement (NAM) (Itty 2008).

Over the years, India has maintained a consistent worldview in its policy towards African countries, guided by the principles of Afro-Asian solidarity, South-South cooperation, respect for sovereignty, noninterference in the internal affairs of other states, and a desire for peace and friendship (Narang and Staniland 2012). In recent years, New Delhi has often emphasised the vision shared by India and Africa and their mutuality of interests. After convening the first India-Africa Forum summit in 2008, the parties agreed to address the broad areas of cooperation and their shared views on regional and international issues (MEA 2009: 140). India regards the Delhi Declaration a 'blueprint' of this shared vision (Sharma 2009).

This chapter will examine that 'blueprint' by surveying India's South-South cooperation with the African continent. It will address private- and public-sector initiatives successively – trade, development cooperation, and regional coopera- tion. It will detail in particular how India's emergent financial instrument, the line of credit (LOC), has supported African development in agriculture, infrastructure, and construction. Lastly, it reviews India's 'niche' area of human resource devel- opment, highlighting training efforts and institution and capacity building. We conclude by calling for greater attention to project completion, sustainability, and inclusivity.

India–Africa trade and investment

In recent years, India's engagement with African countries has expanded enor- mously, as trade figures demonstrate. The two-way trade between the regions has risen from USD 967 million in 1990–1991 to USD 68 billion in 2013–2014, reflecting a boom in commercial activity. However, Indian firms have also under- taken numerous direct investments in Africa, a trend likely to continue (DOC n.d.). Although media and other observers have highlighted engagement in the energy field (DNA India 2015), Indian investments actually span diverse sectors, such as pharmaceuticals, information technology and telecommunications, and agriculture (NDTV 2014). Moreover, this engagement does not always originate with government institutions; the private sector also plays an important role.

Several complex factors drive this African investment. As India's economy has grown, the demand for energy security has fuelled investments in the hydrocar- bons sector. India depends heavily on crude oil imports to meet its burgeoning domestic demand (Sharma 2009). Although over 70 per cent of India's oil imports come from the Persian Gulf, in the last decade India has expanded its African sources. ONGC Videsh Limited (OVL), an oil and natural gas corporation, has acquired equity assets in Libya, Nigeria, Mozambique, and Sudan, and another firm, Essar, has acquired oil and gas exploration and production assets in Nigeria and Madagascar. Tata Steel, Essar Energy, Coal India Ltd., and Jindal Steel and Power have invested in the coal mines (CMD 2015). Additionally, India's suc- cess in the information and communications technology (ICT) sector has created growing interest in Africa, making it possible for Indian companies such as the Tata Group to make ICT investments in several countries. Similarly, in 2010, the Indian firm Bharti Airtel acquired the USD 10.7 billion African assets of telecom giant Zain (Times of India 2010).

Attracted by direct invitations, the cheap cost of land, and rising food prices, several Indian companies have invested in the African agriculture and water man- agement sectors (Beri 2011). They include Kirloskar Brothers, Mahindra, Karu- turi (agroprocessing), and Kommururi (agrotech) (Surya 2010). Some reports suggest that despite domestic success in food sufficiency, the Indian government may have supported these foreign land leases (Rebello 2013) – a claim categorically rejected by Sharad Pawar, the former Indian agricultural minister, at least in the case of Africa (Dutta 2012). Indian companies also insist that their African land leases form part of business expansion strategies (Surya 2010). Whatever strategic interests the investments might serve, in this instance, the private sector appears to take the lead.

However, initiatives by the Indian government and its elite chambers of commerce and industry also help drive India's African trade and investment. One important instance is the Duty-Free Tariff Preference Scheme for least-developed countries. Under this scheme, India will unilaterally provide preferential market access for exports from all fifty of the least-developed countries, thirty-four of which are in Africa (Rowden 2011). The scheme debuted at the first India-Africa Forum Summit in 2008. At the same time, Indian chambers of commerce – such as the Federation of Indian Chambers of Commerce and Industry (FICCI) and the Confederation of Indian Industry (CII) – have prioritised trading with African countries. The CII has hosted annual India–Africa project partnership conclaves since 2005, and the FICCI has hosted a number of India–Africa business summits. African leaders, high-level officials, and business executives regularly participate in these conferences (Bajpai 2014). The increasing numbers of both business delegations travelling to Africa and commercial conclaves on both continents suggest that Indian business has become an important stakeholder in Africa's development.

In short, although media and other observers have tended to emphasise investment in a few sectors, the actual breadth of Indian engagement shows otherwise; moreover, it receives tacit governmental support. This may or may not reflect a unified government policy or strategy; as we shall see in the next section, official development cooperation shows an equally notable range of sectors, targets, and avenues.

India's development cooperation with Africa

India has often reiterated that its unique engagement with Africa rests on mutual benefit principles. It contributes to Africa's development objectives through a consultative process in which partner countries set the priorities (Tharoor 2011). This may account for the diversity of India–Africa development cooperation, ranging across agriculture, small and medium enterprises, science and technology, health, education, culture, infrastructure, energy, communications, civil society, and governance. Moreover, India's own experience as an aid recipient has often guided its programmes. Salman Khurshid, former Indian External Affairs Minister, noted that although India had received vital industrial and infrastructural aid after independence, education and capacity building had proven just as valuable to its development success (MEA 2013a). Hence India offers the most useful aspects of its own experience as a strategic resource for transforming Africa's economic landscape.

India recognises the regional diversity within the African continent and therefore pursues its engagement at three levels – bilateral, regional, and pan-African.

Since 2010, India has opened dialogue with the eight African Regional Economic Communities (RECs) recognised by the African Union. Two India–REC meetings have taken place in New Delhi, India, to further enhance institutional engagement – the first in November 2010 and the second on 8–9 November 2011. Representatives from six of these organisations participated in the second India–RECS meeting (MEA 2011).[4] In recent years, African countries have accelerated their regional integration, with an emphasis on harmonisation among the RECs. As India's trade and investment in Africa increase, ongoing dialogue with the African RECs takes on critical importance.

At the pan-African level, India has also hosted one of two India-Africa Forum Summits in New Delhi in 2008; the second summit took place in Addis Ababa in 2011. In the past, the summit was not open to all African countries, but relied on the African Union's 'Banjul formula' that limited the number of countries interacting with external powers (African Union 2006). However, the Indian strategic community has raised some questions about the efficacy of this structure (ICWA 2014); as a result, India has invited all African countries to attend a third India-Africa Forum Summit, sending a strong message that every country in the region matters (Press Trust of India 2015).

Other Indian steps toward broader, yet regionally specific, engagement include the India Export and Import (Exim) Bank's 'Focus Africa' policy (initiated in 2002) to deepen trade ties with African countries (Mawdsley and McCann 2011). To enhance its West African cooperation, the Indian government launched the Techno-Economic Approach for the India-Africa Movement (TEAM) in partnership with eight countries in the region: Burkina Faso, Chad, Côte d'Ivoire, Equatorial Guinea, Ghana, Guinea Bissau, Mali, and Senegal. The TEAM 9 initiative envisages transfer of critical technologies from India to the region (Sinha 2010).

Africa faces challenges in ICT integration; low computer literacy and insufficient information technology (IT) infrastructure create a digital divide between the few African countries linked to the Internet and the majority lacking connectivity (Hope Project 2014). India also seeks to enhance inter- and intra-African connections, drawing on its own ICT strengths in particular. One prime example is the Pan African e-Network (PAeN) initiative, where India has partnered directly with the African Union. PAeN seeks to share India's expertise in ICT, education, and health services, and it connects much of Africa through a fibre optics and satellite network. It builds African capacity through e-learning and tele-education, online and tele-medical consultations, and official communications, overcoming barriers to learning and promoting public health across the continent (Pambazuka News 2009). This initiative, officially launched in 2009, has received much praise as a model for South-South cooperation (MEA 2013b).

Although these efforts reflect broad regional and pan-African partnerships, India has also built bilateral cooperation ties through more specific means. In recent years, the government has taken a three-pronged approach – disbursing assistance through lines of credit, providing support for African institutional development, and training African professionals.

Lines of credit: enhancing African capacities

Lines of credit (LOC) provide one of India's key instruments of South-South cooperation. India's Exim Bank acts as the 'apex institution', disbursing LOC on concessional terms to developing countries in Africa, Asia, and Latin America. The Exim Bank defines a line of credit as a form of tied aid, extended to overseas financial institutions, regional development banks, sovereign governments, and other entities overseas, to enable buyers in those countries to import goods and services from India on deferred credit terms (DEA 2010; Sinha 2010). In 2003–2004, the government of India launched the India Development and Economic Assistance Scheme (IDEAS), aiming to share India's development experience through capacity building, skills transfers, trade, and infrastructure development. LOC would serve as the financing, routed through the Exim Bank. Moreover, the terms of access require that, 'as a rule', 75 per cent of the goods and services for the projects come from India (DEA 2010).

African countries have benefitted substantially from IDEAS, receiving around 59 per cent of the Exim Bank's LOC. The bank identifies 142 LOC (amounting to USD 6.9 billion) as currently operational in Africa, extended to thirty-six countries and eight institutions across the continent (Exim Bank 2015). These lines of credit have targeted development support in various sectors in the African countries, reflecting but also extending the sectors of Indian private investment.

Agriculture

With 60 per cent of the world's uncultivated arable land, the African continent has enormous potential for agricultural production (Obasanjo 2012). It remains a vital sector in African economies, providing employment for 57 per cent of the labour force and serving as the main income source for the rural population (Kanu, Salami and Numasawa 2014). Despite this centrality, it has seen low productivity rates; many African countries have therefore committed recently to improving their agricultural output. Initiatives such as the Comprehensive Africa Agriculture Development Programme (CAADP), launched in 2004, and the African Union's 2014 Year of Agricultural Transformation and Food Security in Africa (African Union 2014), indicate the high priority given to the sector.

No wonder, then, that agricultural cooperation has become a key area of partnership between Africa and India. Many analysts have noted that Africa might learn from India's 'Green Revolution' model and its success in increasing outputs (Frankel 2015). A variety of factors appear to have contributed to this success, including (among other means) high-yield seed varieties, pesticides, and expanded infrastructure access – irrigation, machinery, transportation, and storage facilities. India's development assistance programme to Africa attempts, in a small way, to address its gaps in these areas. For example, India has extended a USD 27 million LOC to Senegal for irrigation support in rice-producing areas. Exim Bank claims that this has produced a two-fold increase in the area under irrigation and substantial production growth: northern Senegal now meets half of its rice demand locally. Similarly, an Exim Bank LOC to Mali for agromachinery has led to a 30 per cent increase in agricultural production (Briceno-Garmendia and Foster 2009).

As all these examples suggest, Indian agricultural cooperation reflects its own experience in improving yields by removing bottlenecks and applying targeted, appropriate technologies. In this sense, it supplies a form of knowledge transfer intimately connected to capacity building, an issue to which we will return later.

Infrastructure

According to the World Bank, Africa spends USD 45 billion per annum on infrastructure when it actually requires something closer to USD 93 billion (Briceno-Garmendia and Foster 2009). With a population expected to double by 2050 and swift economic growth, Africa has both a high demand for improved infrastructure (Pflanz 2013) and deep deficits. Bottlenecks may occur due to poor rail and road connectivity and insufficient power systems. With the growing demand for Indian financial assistance in this area, Exim Bank, in collaboration with the African Development Bank (AfDB), has created a project development company in Africa to identify and develop infrastructure projects (IANS 2015). While acknowledging African development needs as an important goal, the Exim Bank has also stressed that the PDC will prioritise projects with a 'strategic relevance' for India (IANS 2015).

This is an important development. In the past, such LOCs have targeted rural electrification and surface connectivity, issues engaging both local development and (to a limited extent) India's strategic interests. Recipients of Indian LOC for power-related and electrification needs have included Burkina Faso, Democratic Republic of the Congo, Equatorial Guinea, Ethiopia, Ghana, Liberia, Mali, Mozambique, Niger, Senegal, and Sudan (Exim Bank 2011; 2015). India has financed railway rehabilitation or extension projects in Angola, Benin, Ethiopia (Box 9.1), Ghana, Mali, and Senegal, and supplied buses to the Central African Republic, Côte d'Ivoire, Ghana, Niger, and Senegal (Exim Bank 2014). Among the countries listed, (unified) Sudan and Mozambique have attracted large investments from Indian companies.

Mozambique, however, provides an example of India providing a 'strategically relevant' LOC. Having identified a mounting need for solar panels in the country, in 2011 India provided a USD 13 million line of credit to set up a solar photovoltaic manufacturing plant in Mozambique – a plant that will considerably reduce its solar equipment imports (Parnell 2013). This action reflects Mozambique's increasing strategic importance to Indian energy investors, whose African projects in turn help meet growing domestic demand in India. A number of Indian companies (such as Coal India, Essar Energy, Tata Steel, and Jindal Steel & Power) have invested in developing Mozambique's coal assets; similarly, Indian national oil companies, such as ONGC Videsh, Ltd. and Oil India, have invested in its natural gas sector. Assistance in these fields spans the continent – and helps infrastructure to do the same, ultimately protecting India's strategic interests, as well as creating goodwill and promoting growth.

Box 9.1 Ethiopia: a case study in Indian cooperation

Ethiopia is one of India's largest development partners, receiving over a billion dollars in LOCs to support critical power and infrastructure needs. In 2006, India provided its first LOC, worth USD 65 million, for a power transmission and distribution project (Exim Bank 2015). Ethiopia's ambassador to India, Gennet Zewide, estimated that this programme would benefit around 100,000 households across the country (Zewide 2015).

A second LOC in 2008 extended USD 640 million for development of Ethiopian sugar factories. Much of this went toward erecting a new sugar factory at Tendaho (Afar Region), and the rest for rehabilitating existing sugar factories in Finchia and Wonji (Oromia Region, completed by Indian contractors). This project proved significant for Ethiopia on several levels. First, it met a goal of self-sufficiency in sugar production; the upgrades meant that Ethiopia ceased to be a net importer (Business Standard 2014). Moreover, it has implications for enhanced renewable energy capacity. Ethiopia's three sugar factories at Finchia, Wonji, and Metehera generate 62 megawatts (MW) of electricity, half going to the sugar plants themselves and the rest sent to the national electric grid (Woldegebriel 2014). These figures will increase significantly once the Tendaho plant starts production.* Tendaho will also contribute to Ethiopia's climate-resilient green economy plan, which aims for a net carbon output of zero by 2025 (Woldegebriel 2014): future use of sugar-process ethanol in cars, stoves, and generators will help reduce the country's carbon footprint.

In 2011, at the second India-Africa Forum Summit, India pledged a USD 300 million LOC to the Ethiopian government for a railway link to improve regional connectivity and boost economic growth (Exim Bank 2015). The rail link will connect the Ethiopian city of Asalta to the port city of Tadjourah in neighbouring Djibouti. It forms part of the Ethiopian government's larger railway expansion project to improve connectivity with its neighbours and their ports. The project remains in the initial phase, awaiting completion of the railway contract before beginning construction.**

*A long legal battle between the two Indian vendors involved in the Tendaho project appears to have delayed its start (Berhane 2014).
**The Ethiopian Railway Corporation may be partially responsible for this delay (Molinari and Gunzinger 2015).

Information technology

Only half a million Africans have access to the Internet, indicating a pressing need to narrow the 'digital divide'. Africa possesses only a limited pool of expertise in this area. In the past, India has provided assistance to countries such as Mauritius and South Africa to develop their software hubs; in 2003, it also set up the

Ghana India Kofi Annan Centre for Excellence in ICT in Accra, Ghana, providing both technology and training – a much-appreciated intervention (Singh [V.] 2011). Since 2004, India has provided LOC to Côte d'Ivoire, Democratic Republic of the Congo, Mozambique, and Senegal for development of technology parks and relevant training (Exim Bank 2011).

All these forms of Indian engagement have had, with some exceptions, positive receptions in Africa, especially given that many of the projects have originated with partner-country requests (Kanth 2011). However, as chapters elsewhere in this volume also demonstrate, India sees its core strengths as residing in capacity building and training, and it has devised Africa-specific offerings in these areas as well.

Indian support for institution building

Even more than direct investment or sectoral intervention, India has made capacity building and human resource development the template for its engagement with Africa. India's strategy would support the African countries' efforts in creating a new generation of educators, entrepreneurs, and technologists (Chand 2011). India offers enormous opportunities to African countries planning to develop their technical and higher education systems. Many experts view educational institutions in advanced countries, such as the United States, the United Kingdom, and Australia, as 'extremely expensive' (Singh [V.] 2011; MEA 2013b). In comparison, Indian institutions provide value for money, supplying quality education with far fewer resources. Moreover, Indian educational curricula may be more 'appropriate' for African countries in comparison to their developed-world counterparts (Jacobs 2012). A number of new institutions demonstrate the range and potential of India's strategy.

At the first India-Africa Forum Summit in 2008, India agreed to create nineteen training institutes across the continent, modelled on their Indian counterparts and established with their assistance (see e.g., Garg 2011). These institutions include the India-Africa Institute of Foreign Trade (IAIFT) in Uganda, the India-Africa Diamond Institute in Botswana, the India-Africa Institute of Education, Planning and Administration (IAIEPA) in Burundi, and the Pan-Africa Stock Exchange in Egypt. The Indian Institute for Foreign Trade (IIFT), Educational Consultants India, Ltd. (EdCIL), and the Indian Diamond Institute (IDA) will also help set up these institutes (Thomas 2011). Although several have faced site and administrative obstacles (as we shall discuss later), all have reached the implementation phase.

The remaining institutes India pledged to create in 2008 included vocational training centres in ten African countries (Burundi, Burkina Faso, Egypt, Ethiopia, Gabon, Libya, Mozambique, Rwanda, The Gambia, and Zimbabwe), set up by India's National Small Industries Corporation (NSIC). The NSIC inaugurated the first of these in Addis Ababa, Ethiopia, on 13 November 2013. The 2008 New Delhi pledge also includes human settlement institutes in five African countries (Democratic Republic of the Congo, Kenya, Mauritania, Togo, and Zambia).

India's Ministry of Housing and Urban Poverty Alleviation, along with the Building Materials and Technology Promotion Council (BMTPC), will take the lead for this project.

The 2008 summit, however, proved merely the beginning of the Indian commitment. During the second India-Africa Forum Summit, held in Addis Ababa in 2011, India announced that it would set up over eighty additional capacity-building institutions (Prime Minister's Office 2011). These institutions will encompass areas ranging from agriculture, rural development, and food processing to information technology, vocational training, English language centres, and entrepreneurship development. Moreover, they will be set up in consultation with countries at the pan-African, regional, and bilateral levels. The India-Africa Food Processing Cluster and an India-Africa Integrated Textiles Cluster, announced at the last summit, aim to enhance industrial capacity; others will boost Africa's agrarian sector, including an India-Africa Centre for Medium Range Weather Forecasting and an India-Africa Institute for Rural Development. India has also unveiled plans to set up an India-Africa Virtual University.

In summary, India has vastly extended the range and depth of its institution building with African partners, and although some efforts target country-specific needs, others may allow greater regional integration through cooperatively built capacities.

Training

Recognising the priority of human resource development in Africa, India offers training programmes and scholarships to African individuals under the umbrella of the Indian Technical Economic Cooperation (ITEC) Programme.[5] This programme provides courses at multiple institutions across the country, in areas such as financial services, telecommunication, English, management, rural development, and environmental science, among others. Since the first India-Africa Forum Summit, India has offered training slots to Africans every year. In 2013–2014, 40 per cent of ITECs training slots went to Africans (IDCR 2015). ITEC also offers training courses according to demand from African countries, covering fields such as agriculture, health, road transport, police training, and other topics (see e.g., Two Circles 2012). At the same time, it has offered more than 22,000 scholarships to African students for 3 year periods of study (Prime Minister's Office 2011). The Indian Council of Cultural Relations administers the scholarships, which principally support graduate studies in India.

Other Indian scholarship programmes have a sectoral focus, such as the India-Africa Agricultural Scholarships that target the increasing demand for curricula in agricultural science. Similarly, the CV Raman Fellowships focus on enhancing the African skills in the field of science and technology; the Federation of Indian Chambers of Commerce and Industry administers them on behalf of the government's Department of Science and Technology. African researchers have expressed appreciation for the way this fellowship scheme brings together the Indian and African scientific communities (FICCI 2012). These fellowships also provide

African researchers an opportunity to access modern technologies and facilities not available in their own countries (IANS 2011). Clearly, these initiatives aim to enhance the skills of Africans and develop in-depth professional qualifications; they provide the centrepiece of India's current engagement with Africa.

Future prospects

India has launched an ambitious development assistance programme in Africa, driven by the aim of sharing its own development experience. These efforts have focused on building partnerships, whether in investment, sectoral aid, or more human-centred assistance. In the case of the new India–Africa institutions, India has worked with the African Union to decide the areas/sectors of intervention, the types of institutions, and the regions and countries that would host them. Their agreements have stipulated that the host countries would provide the land, building, budgetary provision for recurring costs, and governance structures for administration and operations. The Indian implementing agency, on its side, would establish the institution and run it for a period of 3 years, providing appropriate training to enable the host country to take over the institution thereafter. Moreover, each new institution has required two layers of agreements, one between the African Union Commission and the government of India, and a second between the Indian implementing agency and the host country, with the African Union's concurrence.

However, a number of procedural delays have slowed the programme's progress. The consultative process has proven time consuming, requiring frequent visits on both sides. The drawn-out elections for the African Union commissioner also delayed consultations, particularly for the second India Africa Forum Summit institutions. At the same time, the partner countries have often had difficulties in finalising sites for their proposed institutions (Bangar 2013). As a result, most of the institutes proposed at the last India-Africa Forum Summit remain far from implementation; it will take some years to assess their progress and contributions.

Financial issues have also affected Indian cooperation assistance to Africa. During the first India-Africa Forum Summit, India announced that the funding of the new institutions would come through the Aid to Africa budget of the Ministry of External Affairs (Prime Minister's Office 2008). The ministry's current budget allocations, however, seem far from adequate for the task (Piccio 2013). These funds must not only set up around 100 India–Africa institutions across the continent, but also cater to some additional commitments. For example, in 2011–2012, the Indian government supplied Dornier Aircraft vessels to the Seychelles, with funding sourced from the Aid to Africa budget allocations. Moreover, in some already launched projects, such as the Pan-Africa e-Network aimed at all fifty-four African countries, the partners wish to extend the Indian financial and expert support beyond the period of agreement. Most of the African countries do not, in fact, have the capacities to provide running costs of these projects. This undoubtedly opens the question of their financial viability, and also tests Indian capability to provide resources, both human and financial, for an indefinite period.

The Indian government has reiterated that its development assistance programme differs from Africa's engagement with other external partners (Jain 2013). India's model rests on the buzzwords of human resource development and capacity building. More importantly, it reflects the needs and requirements of the African countries, shaped through regular dialogue between the Indian government and the African Union, its key partner institution. One sees this most clearly in the multilateral India-Africa Forum Summits, the venue where India has announced most of its broad development assistance initiatives (IANS 2013). Like other external powers, India to some extent furthers its own interests by developing this cooperation framework with African countries. Although no explicit policy suggests coordination between Indian private-sector African investment in Africa and official cooperation, some cases suggest otherwise. We have already mentioned Mozambique, which hosts around 25 per cent of India's total African investments (MEA 2015) and is also the third largest recipient of Indian LOCs (MEA 2014).

Thus India relies on a hybrid of governmental and corporate avenues, providing a wide range of development opportunities for the continent. But in hinging its engagement on strengthening African capacities and skills, India's partnership should not simply bring the ruling elites on board, but also the concerns and interests of Africans as a whole. The late prime minister of Ethiopia, Meles Zenawi, praised India's national ethos and its solidarity, its refusal 'to impose itself on Africa or lecture to it . . . [its] respect for Africa and its own independent choices . . . unique in the annals of development cooperation' (Zenawi 2011). India and Africa need to ensure the future fulfilment of this belief. The success of India's development cooperation will ultimately rest on a firm partnership between the African and Indian peoples, as well as their respective governments.

Notes

1 A March 2011 World Bank report stated that 'Africa could be on the brink of an economic take off, much like China was 30 years ago, and India 20 years ago' (World Bank 2011).
2 South Africa alone has an approximately 1-million-strong Indian community; other African countries with a sizeable Indian population include Kenya, Uganda, Mauritius, and Nigeria.
3 In April 1955, representatives from twenty-nine Asian and African nations gathered in Bandung, Indonesia, to discuss their role in the Cold War, peace, economic development, and decolonisation. At the close of the conference, attendees signed a communiqué that embraced the UN Declaration of Human Rights and the principles of political self-determination, mutual respect for sovereignty, nonaggression, noninterference in internal affairs, and equality (drawing from the coexistence principles China and India negotiated in 1954). The conference also set goals for mutual economic and cultural cooperation and human rights promotion (Office of the Historian, n.d.).
4 These included the Common Market for Eastern and Southern Africa (COMESA), the East African Community (EAC), the Economic Community of Central African States

(ECCAS), the Inter-Governmental Authority on Development (IGAD), the Southern African Development Community (SADC), and the Economic Community of West African States (ECOWAS).
5 For more detailed discussion of Indian ITEC, see the chapter by Tuhin in this volume.

Works cited

African Union (2006). Decisions and declarations. *Assembly of the African Union, Seventh Ordinary Session*, 1–2 July, Banjul, The Gambia Available at www.africa- union.org/root/au/Conferences/Past/2006/july/summit/doc/Decisions_and_Declarations/Assembly-AU-Dec.pdf.
African Union (2014). The year of agricultural transformation and food security in Africa. *AU Echo*, 1(1). Available at ea.au.int/en/sites/default/files/01%20AUC%20Echo%20March%2025%202014%20APPROVED%202_0.pdf.
Bajpai, K. (ed.) (2014). *India's grand strategy: History, theory, cases.* London: Routledge.
Bangar, R. (2013). *India-Africa: A partnership for the 21st century: Address at ORF*. New Delhi: Observer Research Foundation. Available at http://orfonline.org/cms/export/orfonline/documents/addre.pdf.
Berhane, F. (2014). Ethiopia: Tendaho sugar to be inaugurated, Indians blamed for delay. *Horn Affairs*, 14 May. Available at http://hornaffairs.com/en/2014/05/28/ethiopia-tendaho-sugar-inaugurated-india-blamed/.
Beri, R. (2011). Evolving India-Africa relations: continuity and change. *South African Institute of International Affairs Occasional Paper*, 76. SAIIA, Midrand, ZA.
Briceno-Garmendia, C., and Foster, V. (2009). Africa's infrastructure: A time for transformation. *Africa Development Forum*, The World Bank Group, Washington, DC. Available at http://documents.worldbank.org/curated/en/2009/01/11487313/africas-infrastructure-time-transformation.
Burnstein, S.M. (2001). State formation in ancient Northeast Africa and the Indian Ocean trade. *Conference Proceedings from Interactions: Regional Studies, Global Processes, and Historical Analysis*, 28 February–3 March. Library of Congress, Washington, DC. Available at http://webdoc.sub.gwdg.de/ebook/p/2005/history_cooperative/www.historycooperative.org/proceedings/interactions/burstein.html.
Business Standard (2014). Indian lines of credit help Ethiopia build sugar and power sectors. *Business Standard*, 10 March. Available at www.business-standard.com/article/news-ians/indian-lines-of-credit-help-ethiopia-build-sugar-and-power-sectors-114031000636_1.html.
Center for Media and Democracy (CMD) (2015). *Indian company investments in overseas coal mines* [webpage]. Available at www.sourcewatch.org/index.php/Indian_company_investments_in_overseas_coal_mines.
Chand, M. (2011). A two-way street: India brands its Africa diplomacy. *Pambazuka News*, 9 May. Available at www.pambazuka.net/images/Emerging%20Powers%20newsletter%20May%202011/Issue%209%20May%202011.pdf.
Department of Commerce (DOC) (no date). *Export-import bank databank tradstat* [database]. New Delhi: Government of India. Available at http://commerce.nic.in/eidb.
Department of Economic Affairs (DEA) (2010). Terms and Conditions and Procedure to be adopted in respect of Government of India (GOI) Supported Exim Bank Lines of Credit (LOCs). F.No.21/6/2008-CIE-II, 23 July. Ministry of Finance, Government of India, New Delhi. Available at www.eximbankindia.in/sites/default/files/C.pdf.

DNA India (2015). India, Mozambique to deepen economic engagement in energy sector, indicates PM Modi. *DNA India*, 5 August. Available at www.dnaindia.com/money/report-india-mozambique-to-deepen-economic-engagement-in-energy-sector-indicates-pm-modi-2111352.

Dutta, R. (2012). India has no plans to buy farmland abroad: Agriculture min. *Reuters*, 3 May. Available at http://in.reuters.com/article/2012/03/05/india-farm-land-buy-idINDEE82408M20120305.

Economist (2000). Hopeless Africa. *The Economist*, 11 May. Available at www.economist.com/node/333429.

Economist (2011). Africa's impressive growth. *The Economist*, 6 January. Available at www.economist.com/blogs/dailychart/2011/01/daily_chart.

Export-Import Bank of India (Exim Bank) (2011). *Indian lines of credit: An instrument to enhance India-Africa partnership* [webpage]. New Delhi: DEA, Government of India. Available at www.indiainbusiness.nic.in/trade/presentation_loc/exim.pdf.

Exim Bank (2014). Operative lines of credit, 10 January. New Delhi: DEA, Government of India. Available at www.eximbankindia.in/sites/all/themes/exim/files/locstat.pdf.

Exim Bank (2015). Operative lines of credit. 12 June. New Delhi: DEA, Government of India. Available at www.ExImbankindia.in/lines-of-credit.

Federation of Indian Chambers of Commerce and Industry (FICCI) (2012). *Testimonials of past fellows* [webpage]. New Delhi: FICCI. Available at www.indoafrica-cvrf.in/quotes.aspx.

Frankel, F.R. (2015). *India's green revolution: Economic gains and political costs.* New Jersey: Princeton University Press.

Garg, S. (2011). India to establish foreign trade institute in Uganda. *Business Standard*, 21 June. Available at www.business-standard.com/article/economy-policy/india-to-establish-foreign-trade-institute-in-uganda-111062100079_1.html.

Hope Project (2014). *Challenges and developments of ICT in Africa* [blog]. Available at http://webcache.googleusercontent.com/search?q=cache:y5X7B5V9J-QJ:www.hope-project.org/africa/challenges-and-developments-of-ict-in-africa/&hl=en&strip=0&vwsrc=0.

Indo Asian News Service (IANS) (2011). Indian research fellowship a big hit in Africa. *Yahoo News*, 18 May. Available at https://in.news.yahoo.com/indian-research-fellowship-big-hit-africa-054009243.html.

IANS (2013). India Africa adopt plan of action for enhanced cooperation. *First Post*, 7 September. Available at www.firstpost.com/fwire/india-africa-adopt-plan-of-action-for-enhanced-cooperation-1091543.html.

IANS (2015). African construction boom boon for Indian firms. *Business Standard*, 22 March. Available at www.business-standard.com/article/news-ians/african-construction-boom-boon-for-indian-firms-115032200419_1.html.

Indian Council of World Affairs (ICWA) (2014). *Report on Seventh India-Africa Academic Conference 'India's Partnership with Southern Africa'*, 3–4 February. Centre for Research in Rural and Industrial Development, Chandigarh, India. Available at www.icwa.in/pdfs/Reportoncrrid2014.pdf.

Indian Development Cooperation Research (IDCR) (2015). *50 years of Indian technical and economic cooperation.* New Delhi: Centre for Policy Research.

Itty, A. (2008). From Bandung to NAM: Non-alignment and Indian foreign policy: 1947–65. *Commonwealth and Comparative Politics*, 46(2): 195–219.

Jacobs, S. (2012). India-Africa trade: A unique relationship [webpage]. *Global: The International Briefing*, October. Available at www.global-briefing.org/2012/10/india-africa-trade-a-unique-relationship/.

Jain, P. (2013). Beyond China and Africa: a focus on India. *Democracy in Africa,* 25 June. Available at http://democracyinafrica.org/beyond-china-and-africa-a-focus-on-india/.

Kanth, K.R. (2011). Exim Bank to issue $5-bn fresh line of credit to Africa. *Business Standard,* 13 October. Available at www.business-standard.com/article/finance/exim-bank-to-issue-5-bn-fresh-line-of-credit-to-africa-111101300063_1.html.

Kanu, B.S., Salami, A.O., and Numasawa, K. (2014). *Inclusive growth: An imperative for African agriculture.* Tunis-Belvedere, Tunisia: African Development Bank. Available at www.afdb.org/fileadmin/uploads/afdb/Documents/Publications/Inclusive_Growth_-_An_imperative_for_African_Agriculture.pdf.

Kingsley, I. (2012). African economies capture world attention. *Africa Renewal,* 8: 16. Available at www.un.org/africarenewal/magazine/august-2012/african-economies-capture-world-attention.

Mawdsley, E., and McCann, G. (eds.) (2011). *India and Africa: Changing geographies of power and development.* Oxford: Famahu.

Ministry of External Affairs (MEA) (2009). *Annual report 2009–2010.* New Delhi: Policy Planning and Research Division, Ministry of External Affairs. Available at http://mealib.nic.in/?pdf2537?000.

MEA (2011). *Second India-RECs meeting.* New Delhi: MEA, Government of India. Available at http://mea.gov.in/press-releases.htm?dtl/7316/Second+IndiaRECs+Meetingp.

MEA (2013a). *Address by External Affairs Minister at the meeting with African heads of missions.* New Delhi: MEA, Government of India. Available at http://mea.gov.in/Speeches-Statements.htm?dtl/21838/.

MEA (2013b). *Pan African E network project (PAENP).* New Delhi: MEA, Government of India. Available at www.mea.gov.in/Portal/ForeignRelation/Pan_African_e_docx_for_xp.pdf.

MEA (2014). Visit of Minister of Foreign Affairs and International Cooperation of Mozambique to India, 23–29 November, New Delhi, Government of India. Available at http://mea.gov.in/press-releases.htm?dtl/24310/Visit+of+Minister+of+Foreign+Affairs+and+International+Cooperation+of+Mozambique+to+India++November+2329+2014.

MEA (2015). Transcript of media briefing by Secretary (West) on the State visit of President of Mozambique to India, 5 August. Government of India, New Delhi. Available at http://mea.gov.in/media-briefings.htm?dtl/25653/Transcript_of_Media_Briefing_by_Secretary_West_on_the_State_visit_of_President_of_Mozambique_to_India_August_05_2015.

Molinari, M., and Gunzinger, N. (2015). Ethiopia turns big plans into reality. *International Railway Journal,* 3 June. Available at www.railjournal.com/index.php/africa/ethiopia-turns-big-plans-into-reality.html?channel=538.

Narang, V., and Staniland, P. (2012). Institutions and world views in Indian foreign security policy. *India Review,* 11(2): 76–94.

NDTV (2014). India aims to boost investment in Africa. *NDTV,* 19 October. Available at www.ndtv.com/india-news/india-aims-to-boost-investment-in-africa-681193.

Obasanjo, O. (2012). How Africa could feed the world. *CNN,* 6 November. Available at http://globalpublicsquare.blogs.cnn.com/2012/11/06/how-africa-could-feed-the-world/.

Office of the Historian (No date). Milestones: 1953–1960. Bandung Conference (Asian-African Conference), 1955. United States Department of State, Washington, DC. Available at https://history.state.gov/milestones/1953–1960/bandung-conf.

Pambazuka News (2009). Africa: Pan African e-Network: A model of 'South-South cooperation'. *Pambazuka News,* (429) 24 April. Available at www.pambazuka.net/en/category.
php/internet/55920.

Parnell, J. (2013). Mozambique opens first PV production facility. *PV Tech,* 29 November. Available at www.pv-tech.org/news/mozambique_opens_first_pv_production_
facility.

Pflanz, M. (2013). Africa's population to double to 2.4 billion by 2050. *The Telegraph,*
12 September. Available at www.telegraph.co.uk/news/worldnews/africaandindianocean/
10305000/Africas-population-to-double-to-2.4-billion-by-2050.html.

Piccio, L. (2013). India's foreign aid program catches up with its global ambitions. *Devex,*
10 May. Available at www.devex.com/news/india-s-foreign-aid-program-catches-
up-with-its-global-ambitions-80919.

Press Trust of India (2015). Biggest diplomatic event: India-Africa summit from October 26.
The Times of India, 25 March. Available at http://timesofindia.indiatimes.com/india/
Biggest-diplomatic-event-India-Africa-summit-from-October-26/articleshow/
46691914.cms.

Prime Minister's Office (2008). PM addresses the first India-Africa Summit, 8 April. PMO,
Government of India, New Delhi. Available at http://pib.nic.in/newsite/erelease.
aspx?relid=37177.

Prime Minister's Office (2011). Address by the Prime Minister Dr. Manmohan Singh at the
Plenary Session of the 2nd Africa-India Forum Summit Addis Ababa, Ethiopia. 24 May.
PMO, Government of India, New Delhi. Available at http://pib.nic.in/newsite/PrintRelease.
aspx?relid=72281.

Rebello, S. (2013). India buys land 9 times Delhi's size abroad. *Hindustan Times,* 20 October. Available at www.hindustantimes.com/mumbai/india-buys-land-9-times-delhi-s-
size-abroad/article1-1137264.aspx.

Rowden, R. (2011). India's role in the new global farmland grab. *GRAIN Bulletin Board,*
19 August. Available at www.grain.org/bulletin_board/entries/4342-india-s-role-in-
the-new-global-farmland-grab.

Sen, S.N. (1999). *Ancient Indian history and civilization.* New Delhi: New Age International.

Sharma, A. (2009). India and Africa: Sharing a robust partnership. In R. Beri and U.K.
Sinha (eds.), *Africa and energy security: Global issues, local responses.* New Delhi:
Academic Foundation, p. 23.

Sidiropoulous, E. (2014). Lions and tigers: Africa and India. In R. Beri (ed.), *India and
Africa: Enhancing mutual engagement.* New Delhi: IDSA and Pentagon Press, p.77.

Singh, M. (2011). Address by the Prime Minister Dr. Manmohan Singh at the Plenary Ses-
sion of the 2nd Africa-India Forum Summit Addis Ababa, Ethiopia. Prime Minister's
Office, Government of India, New Delhi. Available at http://pib.nic.in/newsite/
PrintRelease.aspx?relid=72281.

Singh, V. (2011). India steps forward as Africa seeks new academic aid. *New York Times,*
13 February. Available at www.nytimes.com/2011/02/14/world/asia/14iht-educSide14.
html?_r=0.

Sinha, P.K. (2010). Indian development cooperation with Africa. In F. Cheru and C. Obi
(eds.), *The rise of China and India in Africa: Challenges, opportunities and critical
interventions.* London: Zed Books, pp. 77–93.

Surya, M.V.R. (2010). Indian companies buy land abroad for agricultural products. *Economic Times,* 1 February. Available at http://articles.economictimes.indiatimes.
com/2010-01-02/news/27600492_1_land-purchase-food-prices-indian-companies.

Tharoor, S. (2011). Address by Minister of State Dr. Shashi Tharoor at the CII-EXIM Bank Conclave on India-Africa Project Partnership, New Delhi, 15 March 2010. In A.S. Bhasin (ed.), *India's foreign policy relations: 2010 Documents*. New Delhi: Geetika Publishers. Available at www.mea.gov.in/Images/pdf/Indias_Foreign_Relations_2010.pdf.

Thomas, M. (2011). IDI to go global by setting up diamond institute in Botswana. *The Times of India*, 5 January. Available at http://timesofindia.indiatimes.com/city/surat/IDI-to-go-global-by-setting-up-diamond-institute-in-Botswana/articleshow/7225062.cms.

Times of India (2010). Bharti completes acquisition of Zain's Africa biz for $10.7bn, *The Times of India*, 8 June. Available at http://timesofindia.indiatimes.com/business/india-business/Bharti-completes-acquisition-of-Zains-Africa-biz-for-10–7bn/articleshow/6023848.cms.

Two Circles (2012). African countries invite Indian investment agriculture. *Two Circles*, 21 June. Available at http://twocircles.net/2012jun21/african_countries_invite_indian_investment_agriculture.html#.VZ007ROqqkp.

Woldegebriel, E.G. (2014). In search for power, Ethiopia turns to growing sugar. *All Africa,* 27 August. Available at http://allafrica.com/stories/201408271426.html.

World Bank (2011). *Africa's future and the World Bank's support to it*. Washington, DC: The World Bank Group. Available at http://siteresources.worldbank.org/INTAFRICA/Resources/AFR_Regional_Strategy_3–2–11.pdf.

Zenawi, M. (2011). *India matters more than ever* [webpage]. INDIAFRICA, Public Diplomacy Division, MEA, GOI. Available at www.indiafrica.in/FViewsMelesZenawi.html.

Zewide, G. (2015). India Ethiopia cooperation. *Africa Trends,* 4(2). Available at http://idsa.in/africatrends.html.

10 Chinese perspectives on India's development cooperation

Xiaoyun Li and Taidong Zhou

Introduction

An impressive record of rapid economic growth and poverty reduction has enabled India, like China, to become one of the largest South-South cooperation (SSC) providers. India has tripled its development assistance expenditure since the turn of the century. Its footprint not only cuts across its immediate neighbours, such as Nepal, Bhutan, and Afghanistan, but also extends to other regions, including Africa, Central Asia, Latin America, and the Pacific. India has also become an active participant in various multilateral and regional platforms, such as the World Trade Organization (WTO), IBSA (India, Brazil, South Africa) Dialogue Forum, and BRICS (Brazil, Russia, India, China, South Africa). Its broad-based cooperation with other developing countries takes various forms, such as knowledge sharing, loans and credits, debt cancellation, and investment and trade. Such cooperation earns India goodwill and soft-power leverage while facilitating its growing trade investment links with development partners. India also offers developing partners an alternative to traditional forms of aid from Western donors. Together with China and other Southern partners, India's development cooperation arguably has the potential to 'restructure the traditional patterns of the international division of labour, systems of wealth production and trade flows' (Jobelius 2007).

However, although recent studies have thoroughly analysed China's development cooperation (Martyn 2008; Woods 2008; Brautigam 2011; De Haan 2011; Reilly 2012), knowledge of India's role as an SSC provider remains limited. The preponderance of research to date on the so-called 'emerging donors' has either consisted of single-country studies or else blended distinct countries (such as India and China) under the North's perspective. Furthermore, few exchanges have occurred to date between developing countries on their strategies and approaches to development cooperation. This chapter, therefore, intends to fill the gap by comparing India and China – the two fastest-growing economies and largest SSC providers – in terms of their aid principles, strategies, and modalities. Although a lack of reliable data makes a fully systematic comparison difficult, the paper aims for a more nuanced understanding of the similarities and differences between the two countries. This should not only increase our understanding of different approaches among 'emerging donors' (e.g., whether an 'Asian approach to development cooperation'[1], an 'Indian model', or a 'Chinese model' actually exists), but may also facilitate new dialogues between China and India under the SSC framework.

The next section provides a brief analysis of current studies on India's development cooperation. The succeeding section examines similarities and differences between India and China in terms of key principles, strategies, and policies, as well as aid modalities. We then draw on China's experience and evaluate possible challenges and prospects for expansion of Indian aid. The chapter concludes with a discussion on how China and India might join forces with a shift of focus from aid effectiveness to development effectiveness.

The literature on India's development cooperation

Despite India's long-term commitment and increasing activism in South-South development cooperation, few studies existed in this area before the turn of the century. However, with India's rapid increase in assistance volumes, its diversification of tools, and its expansion to more countries and regions, substantial scholarly interest has arisen concerning its approaches and impacts. We identified three strands of analyses in the literature. The first largely focuses on India's evolution from recipient to donor – its recent changes and diversification in assistance volumes, forms, and geographic allocations, as well as its strategies and motives. These analyses, often conducted from a historical and political economic perspective, argue that foreign policy and economic goals have driven changes in Indian aid strategy, including its changing regional and global role, access to markets, and the need to secure natural resources (Agrawal 2007; Jobelius 2007; Chanana 2010; Chaturvedi 2012; Fuchs and Vadlamannati 2012).

The second stream compares Indian development cooperation policy with that of another country, either in general contours or in activity within a specific region. For example, Jerve and Hilde (2009) investigated the aid policies of India and South Korea by exploring their aid expansions, rationales, and motivations, along with the implications for 'traditional' donors. Several studies have also examined parallels between Indian and Chinese development activities in South Asian countries (such as Sri Lanka, Nepal, and Bangladesh), positing a 'tug-of-war' between the two countries for geopolitical and foreign policy influence in the region (Jetly 2010).

The third analysis stream focuses on the so-called 'emerging donors'. Here, the literature examines India together with China and other non-DAC donors, highlighting their impacts on existing aid architecture in general and the development fortunes of Africa in particular (McCormick 2008; Naidu 2010). In this stream, the literature appears divided on India's role as a rising SSC provider; some analysts recognise valuable Indian contributions towards Africa's development, whereas other emerging views characterise it as a 'new scramble' for Africa (Kilambi 2013; Mittal 2013). The negativists argue that although India, China, and other 'emerging donors' have provided additional external financial resources, this does not automatically lead to economic development and poverty reduction. One major problem, as they point out, is that Indian and Chinese aid policies often conflict with aid harmonisation efforts by traditional Western donors; this can overburden recipient governments and increase the transaction costs (Kragelund 2008). Critics also argue that the additional and unconditional supply of finance may damage good governance standards and endanger debt sustainability (Woods 2008).

On the other hand, the more balanced views consider that India and China have not only generated a major increase in external financial flows, but have also introduced a credible alternative for aid-receiving countries, one capable of creating positive and wider impacts (Woods 2008). However, although the literature has applied a range of epithets to Chinese aid in Africa, ranging from 'development partner' to 'resource grabber' and 'new colonizer' (Alden 2007), the few studies on India's African aid have tended to milder critiques, although we note that as India's aid has expanded and grown more similar to China's, it has attracted similar epithets (Sahni 2007; Nelson 2009); for example, India-assisted projects in Ethiopia and Kenya have drawn the 'coloniser' label (Kilambi 2013; Mittal 2013).

This brief review of the literature highlights its focus on geopolitical and/or political economy perspectives, emphasising India's aims of becoming a global power and gaining access to markets and natural resources. As with the literature on China, most Western scholarship rests on a Realpolitik approach, and often disregards (or has shown little interest in understanding) the historical origins, cultural evolution, and character of India's international development cooperation, which is based on its own growth trajectory. Meanwhile, although much writing on Indian SSC references the 'China factor' (Naidu 2010; Mancheri 2011), the 'India factor' rarely enters into the discussion of Chinese assistance. Until now, few Chinese scholars have shown awareness of (or written about) Indian's aid policies. Recent papers have almost exclusively concentrated on basics, such as the evolution, scale, principles, and modalities of Indian SSC (Huang and Qi 2012; Tang 2013; Tang and Li 2013), without addressing similarities and differences between the two countries or how they might cooperate or inform each other's efforts.

Understanding India's development cooperation from China's perspective

Let us consider some of those similarities and differences. Like China, India has a long history of receiving aid from traditional Western donors, and was once the largest recipient country. Both countries' outflow assistance dates back to the early 1950s, when they provided aid to neighbouring countries. Although the modality, scope, and volume of aid changed frequently with different political and economic situations in China (Li et al. 2014), India has shown more consistent and linear trends, despite some institutional changes (Chaturvedi 2012). Before China and India opened up their economies, political ideologies and foreign policy goals chiefly determined the direction of outflows. For both countries, foreign assistance reflected solidarity with relatively poor states and active support for the Non-Aligned Movement (NAM).

Since the 1980s for China and the 1990s for India, SSC patterns have changed, becoming less politicised and more pragmatic, with a greater emphasis on mutual economic benefits. With the new century's swift economic growth and enhanced overall strength, both have rapidly expanded their development cooperation scale and diversified its content and methods. This section will look at Indian principles, strategies, policies, and modalities through an extended comparison with China.

Key principles

For both India and China, the foreign policies of the 1950s and 1960s created path dependencies and ideologies that continue to shape SSC policymaking and discourses today. Chinese Premier Zhou Enlai reiterated the 'Five Principles of Peaceful Coexistence' in 1953 during an Indian delegation visit. The five principles included respect for sovereignty and territorial integrity, mutual nonaggression, mutual noninterference in domestic affairs, equality and mutual benefit, and [sic] peaceful coexistence (MFA-PRC n.d.). India and China both played key roles in the 1955 Bandung conference that launched South-South cooperation and advocated Afro-Asian economic and cultural cooperation around 'mutual interest and respect for national sovereignty'. Both countries have also worked at the forefront of the NAM and the Group of 77. These histories have affected both countries' approaches to development cooperation, as well as their broader foreign policy; over the past 6 decades, both have frequently emphasised their historical links with developing countries, along with key guiding principles – 'mutual benefit', 'respecting sovereignty', 'equal partnership', and 'no strings attached'.

Drawing from these principles, India and China have signalled that they would oppose political interference in their own affairs by outsiders and would not interfere in the affairs of countries they assisted. However, both maintain that political independence may only arise from economic independence. They see an obligation to promote economic development in the Third World (and thus establish a new and just economic order), while developing their own economies. SSC therefore represents neither charity nor pure altruism; instead, it rests on 'win-win' relationships from which both development partners may legitimately benefit. Adhering to the sovereignty and noninterference principles, India and China have consistently stressed experience sharing without political conditions and have avoided prescribing recipient actions. Both countries see development cooperation as a partnership of equals, calling themselves 'development partners' or 'SSC providers' rather than the implicitly hierarchical 'donors'.

In summary, we can see that India and China share common development principles and discourses that differ from those of traditional Western donors, which tend to emphasise good governance, human rights, and empowerment.

Aid scale, allocation, and administration

However, Indian and Chinese forms of SSC differ greatly in scale, geographic focus, and institutional settings. Overall quantification proves difficult due to lack of clear definitions, not to mention the wide range of tools involved and opacity in reporting, but India's development cooperation volume appears to be much smaller than China's. Whereas China disbursed about USD 5 billion to SSC programs in 2012 (SCIO 2014), India spent around USD 1.3 billion (Piccio 2013). In part due to this relatively smaller budget scale, India's development cooperation has less regional diversification. Whereas China provides aid to about 121 countries in Africa, Asia, East Europe, Latin America, and the South Pacific, with relatively even regional distribution (see SCIO 2014)[2], India has invested most of its development assistance in its regional neighbours – Bhutan, Nepal, and Afghanistan (Chaturvedi 2012). Although India has had African partners since the 1960s, the scale of its cooperation has historically remained very small and seldom taken the form of grants. This suggests that geographical proximity determines most of India's outflows, although this may change as India seeks broader political influence and economic interests.

Both India and China offer development cooperation in the forms of financial and technical aid, as well as emergency humanitarian aid. The main financial aid instruments in both countries include grants, concessional loans or lines of credit (LOCs), contributions to international and regional organisations, and debt relief. Whereas China uses grants to fund social welfare projects – such as hospitals, schools, and low-cost housing – in all its partner countries, India mainly uses them to support health, education, and infrastructure, chiefly in neighbouring South Asian countries. Concessional loans or LOCs, provided through China and India's respective Export-Import Banks, occupy a relatively larger share of outgoing assistance for both. Although no official data are available for India's LOCs, scholars have suggested that they comprise 80 per cent of India's development assistance (Chaturvedi 2012); in China, concessional loans accounted for 55.7 per cent from 2010 to 2012 (SCIO 2014). This contrasts sharply with the Organisation for Economic Co-operation and Development's (OECD) Development Assistance Committee (DAC) countries, where grants accounted for about 82 per cent for 2010 and 2011 (Tang and Li 2013). Unlike India, China also provides interest-free loans (about 8.1 per cent of total assistance from 2010 to 2012) and other financial arrangements, such as preferential buyer's credit, China-Africa development funds, and African small and medium-sized enterprise (SME) development loans. We should also particularly stress that both countries have witnessed a rapid increase in debt cancellation and higher contributions to multilateral agencies in recent years, indicating a policy shift in a less self-interested direction. Both countries have also actively taken part in emergency relief operations in foreign countries and have played stronger roles in international emergency relief (Chaturvedi in this volume; Meier and Murthy 2011; UNDP 2015).

SSC administration and institutional arrangements vary significantly between the countries. Where China has placed development cooperation primarily under its Ministry of Commerce (MOFCOM), Indian cooperation is largely managed by the Ministry of External Affairs (MEA 2013), reflecting the close ties between aid and broader foreign policy strategy (Sharan, Campbell and Rubin 2013). Indian management of programmes has little centralisation or coherence; the multiple players involved, such as the MEA, the ministries of finance and commerce, and the Indian Export-Import Bank, lack sustained contact, coordination, or shared strategies and goals. To address this, in 2012 India established a Development Partnership Agency (DPA) under the MEA to coordinate and streamline all aspects of development assistance. The DPA's three divisions will cover appraisal of projects and lines of credit, capacity building, disaster relief, and Indian Technical and Economic Corporation (ITEC) programmes, as well as project implementation. One should note, however, that the MEA and DPA remain severely constrained by lack of staff resources (Mullen 2013).

Although China's aid programmes also involve several ministries and have no independent agency oversight, MOFCOM's Department of Foreign Assistance has taken the lead in their coordination and management. First, the department holds responsibility for nearly 90 per cent of China's aid budget. Its functions include foreign aid policy formulation, regulations, overall planning and annual plans, review and approval of various kinds of aid projects, and the whole process and management of project delivery (SCIO 2011). Second, MOFCOM has created several ministerial-level mechanisms to coordinate the different aid components. For example, in drafting foreign aid programmes and foreign aid funds plans for each country, MOFCOM regularly communicates with ministries of foreign affairs and finance and China's Export-Import Bank. In 2008, MOFCOM established an interagency coordination mechanism among the ministries of commerce, foreign affairs, and finance. Last but not least, SSC management reflects the broader process of Chinese public administration reform; thus, although MOFCOM's Department of Foreign Assistance formulates and monitors aid projects, three of its subinstitutions implement different components of aid programmes. These arrangements allow the Department of Foreign Assistance to focus more on formulating foreign aid policies and regulations, and give it greater independence in monitoring and evaluating project outcomes.

Development cooperation strategies and policies: 'soft' versus 'hard' infrastructure

Officially, both India and China consider development cooperation a useful tool for consolidating bilateral relations, promoting economic and trade cooperation, and contributing to economic and social growth in developing countries (MEA 2008; SCIO 2011). However, unlike the DAC members, neither India nor China has an overarching development cooperation policy or clearly stated goals. India and China also do not share the DAC definition of development cooperation. Instead, both countries adopt a broad definition of development and consider trade and foreign direct investments, along with aid, legitimate elements of it. Apart from a relatively large number of grant-based projects originated by China, both countries provide much of their assistance bilaterally through loans or credits, as discussed earlier, with limited or nonexistent budget and programme support.

India and China also use 'tied aid' in most of their development cooperation programmes, providing assistance in kind or requiring purchase of goods and services from their own countries. Both countries view tied aid as not only justified by the 'mutual benefit' principle, but also as favourable for the recipients, because the purchased products and services are cheaper and better adapted to the needs of developing countries. Adhering strictly to the 'sovereignty' and 'demand-driven' principles when identifying needs and implementing programs, India and China largely deal with central authorities in recipient nations, rarely consulting with local stakeholders. In addition, neither country typically provides aid to or through nongovernmental organisations (NGOs), although both have consulted with national civil society organisations about possible involvement with cooperation efforts (Mawdsley and Roychoudhury in this volume; Li 2015).

These similarities aside, India and China have chosen different paths in promoting social and economic development in other countries. India's SSC has consistently focused on capacity building and human resources. Even today, as India tends towards more 'hard infrastructure' projects, technical cooperation still accounts for the bulk of its foreign assistance. For example, in 2012–2013, India's technical cooperation spending reached USD 589 million, representing 58 per cent of the country's foreign aid budget (Piccio 2013). India considers lack of skills a major impediment to realising developmental goals, and knowledge sharing as 'a requirement for economic growth and independent policy-making' in developing countries (Mathai 2013). The focus on training also derives from India's own experience, when Indian engineers from the Indian Institute of Technology (IIT) provided technical support in the postindependence period (Chaturvedi 2012).

Over the years, India has therefore launched a series of capacity-building programmes, including the flagship Indian Technical and Economic Corporation (ITEC), the Special Commonwealth Assistance for Africa Programme (SCAAP), and most recently, the Pan-African e-Network. The Pan-African e-Network aims to create a massive continental network through satellites and fibre optics, linking the fifty-three African countries through telemedicine, education, and governance. India believes that this network will foster skills and human resources critical for sustainable development, and thus make contributions to the quantity and quality of African economic growth. At the India-Africa Forum Summits in 2008 and 2011, India also announced the allocation of USD 700 million to establish about 100 new training institutions in different African countries. India's assistance to Africa thus plays to its competitive strengths in areas such as information and telecommunication, education, and health services. African countries have in turn recognised Indian contributions: India remains the sole Asian member in the African Union's Capacity Building Foundation.

One should note, meanwhile, that India has begun to introduce democratic and human-rights concerns in many of its capacity-building programmes. Although these remain a small component, India has recently organised support for other developing countries in organising elections, strengthening judicial independence, supporting freedom of press, and protecting human rights (Wagner 2009). India has also expanded such activities in conjunction with the international community. For example, India joined the United Nations (UN) Democracy Fund in 2005, and is now the second-largest donor after the United States (MEA 2013). In such assistance programmes, India emphasises its distinct model of development – a 'pluralistic' model suited to Africa's multiple 'ethnic, linguistic, religious and tribal divisions' (Jacobs 2012). This differs greatly from China's definition of assistance, and suggests that Indian and traditional Western donor programs may converge on this point.

In contrast, China began its foreign aid by providing goods and materials, and later expanded into complete project aid, technical cooperation, human resource development, medical teams, emergency humanitarian aid, volunteer programs, and debt relief. Although detailed figures on areas of investment are not available, China has unquestionably put substantial aid resources into infrastructure (Tang and Li 2013). Reports reveal that as of 2013, China had established more than 1000 large-scale economic infrastructure projects in Africa alone. This trend will continue, as shown by Premier Li Keqiang's announcement during his African visit in May 2014 of further support for roads, railways, telecommunications, and electricity (Xinhua 2014). Economic infrastructure has become a key aspect of China's aid – not only because China has a comparative advantage in this area, but also because it views infrastructure as a primary bottleneck for poverty reduction and development in recipient countries. As a common Chinese saying has it, 'If you want to get rich, build roads first'.

Therefore, although India and China adhere to similar principles, they have diverged from each other in aid strategies based on their comparative advantages and development experiences. India's approach, similar to that of traditional Western donors, is more 'software'-oriented, emphasising skill development and a people-centric strategy; its advantages include a good-quality, affordable higher-education sector and advanced IT (Mawdsely and McCann 2011). By contrast, China has focused on 'hardware infrastructure' that aims for direct and visible benefits to the host country. These different strategies and approaches have also led to varied assessments from the international community. In general, China's tangible assistance complements traditional donor efforts and helps fill the financial gap in infrastructure development. However, some have argued that Chinese aid does not produce local benefits in job creation, education, or health improvement, and that it may damage local environments (Woods 2008).

India's 'soft infrastructure' approach garners considerable recognition and influence in Africa at limited cost, but also prevents close scrutiny or strong criticisms from the Western countries. Capacity-building programmes anchor this 'soft power' strategy; they not only pass on knowledge and skills, development ideas, and models and values, but also nurture friendly attitudes towards India, presumably reflected in policies and bilateral relationships. Although ITEC has remained small-scale in monetary terms, it has borne fruit over several decades, with many bureaucrats and politicians from developing countries receiving their training in India. Technical assistance and capacity building are sustainable approaches for empowering other developing countries.

Both countries, however, have seen recent changes in aid delivery strategies. China has realised that the emphasis on infrastructure may limit the impacts of its aid, and has increased allocations to its human resource programme. For example, economic infrastructure projects declined to 44.8 per cent of the total for the 3-year period from 2010 to 2012, down from 61 per cent before the end of 2009 (SCIO 2014). During that same period, China held 1951 training sessions for officials and technical personnel, as well as on-the-job academic education programmes in China, training a total of 49,148 people from developing countries. Within those 3 years, the number of people trained in China has jumped from 8109 in 2010 to 17,072 in 2012, with an average increase of 55 per cent (SCIO 2014). Most recently, China has launched the 'African Talent Initiative' and 'China-Africa Agricultural Sunshine Plan' to provide scholarships to 18,000 African students and train 30,000 technicians (SCIO 2014). Nevertheless, China's human resource aid programmes still receive less funding than its infrastructure assistance. Although the number of people trained in China has significantly exceeded that of India, in our experience, the effectiveness and impacts of the Chinese programs seem less fully realised.

By contrast, India has also shifted its traditional long-term and soft-power approach, seeking more direct benefits. As Chanana (2010: 5) points out, India now apparently believed that its traditional aid does not garner the immediate geostrategic influence that China often enjoys. India has made rapid gains in infrastructure and large-scale projects, China's traditional strength, and although Indian investments do not yet compete in scale, their quantity and significance are both on the rise (Bijoy 2010; Chaturvedi 2012). India uses lines of credit to finance projects involving Indian companies. For example, at the second India-Africa Forum Summit (in Addis Ababa 2011), India announced the construction of a railway line between Ethiopia and Djibouti with an investment of USD 300 million (McLymont 2011). Indian firms have also engaged heavily in African energy production.[3]

Both countries, then, appear to draw lessons from their past experiences and from each other. Both still give assistance based on priorities identified by recipient governments; but where in the past their aid sectors have diverged or complemented one another, India and China have moved toward convergence in their blend of 'soft' and 'hard infrastructure' approaches (Table 10.1).

Table 10.1 Comparison of Indian and Chinese development cooperation

Categories	India	China
Fundamental Principles	Mutual benefit, attaching no political conditions, respect for sovereignty and noninterference	Mutual benefit, attaching no political conditions, respect for sovereignty and noninterference
Amount of Aid (2012)	About USD 1.3 billion	About USD 5 billion
Percentage of GNI	0.13 per cent (2012)	0.07 per cent over the period of 2010–2012 (authors' calculation)
Forms of Aid	Grants, lines of credit	Grants, concessional loans, interest-free loans
Modality	Projects, technical assistance, scholarships, debt cancellation, humanitarian assistance	Projects, technical assistance, scholarships, debt cancellation, humanitarian assistance, medical teams abroad, volunteers
Key Responsible Entities	Ministry of External Affairs, Ministry of Commerce and Industry, Export-Import Bank, and Indian Council for Cultural Relations	Ministry of Commerce, Ministry of Foreign Affairs. Ministry of Finance, Export-Import Bank, Ministry of Agriculture, and Ministry of Education
Geographic Allocations	Immediate South Asia neighbourhood and Africa	Asia, Africa, Latin America, and the Pacific
Sectoral Focus	Agriculture, information and communications technology, infrastructure and transport	Infrastructure, productive sectors, health, education, prestige projects
Coordination Among Donors	Limited with traditional donors and unlikely to join OECD-DAC, but active coordination with some developing countries	Limited with traditional donors and unlikely to join OECD-DAC

Sources: MEA (2012), SCIO (2014)

Challenges and future prospects

As its development cooperation expands in scale and breadth, India will probably encounter challenges at several levels, much as China has. The primary one will be aid program effectiveness. Despite creating the DPA to oversee administration, India still faces institutional constraints in staff shortages and high turnover. Lack of consultation with local stakeholders and limited investment in monitoring and evaluation will become increasing and prominent disadvantages. Currently, governments of partner countries identify development cooperation priorities. Although this may ensure greater policy autonomy, the resulting projects may not benefit local populations. This in turn jeopardises the sustainability and visibility of cooperation projects, as well as development effectiveness. Additionally, developing a standardised and high-quality monitoring and evaluation system presents a major hurdle for improving SSC quality. Although India may draw upon the Western-donor system for monitoring aid effectiveness, the complexity and high cost entailed will likely prevent its full adoption.

India's second challenge lies in justifying its foreign expenditure to its own citizens, given the daunting development tasks it faces at home. In China, the Internet and social media often witness sharp criticisms of the government for its large-scale assistance abroad, in light of its domestic challenges – poverty reduction, environmental protection, and inadequate social security systems. To address such concerns, China has published two white papers on its foreign aid, articulating and justifying its programmes to the public (and the international audience) (SCIO 2011; SCIO 2014). By contrast, India has yet to make such moves; perhaps surprisingly, research indicates that the elites and 'middle classes' show broad support for India's growing profile in international development, with little public discussion on how this relates to domestic poverty (Mawdsley 2011).

Yet one should note that India's poor population exceeds that of all African countries combined. The current lack of debate or public awareness in India (also in China, to a lesser degree) may partly arise from lack of publicity around aid programmes and the limited involvement of civil society organisations. As their aid profiles rise and attract growing international scrutiny, India and China will likely face stronger public opinion pressure in delivering foreign assistance. The problem calls for a wider dialogue between aid officials, civil society organisations, think tanks, and the private sector. This will not only broaden the aid constituency, but also enhance policymaking and development practices.

Third, with the rise of global actors from the South, coordination with traditional Western donors – and shaping a new agenda for development cooperation – will test the wisdom of Indian and Chinese leaders alike. India's development cooperation, like China's, has been primarily bilateral. Unlike South Korea, India will probably not join the OECD 'Club'. Western donors have tried hard to engage both India and China in policy dialogues. So far, India has integrated to a lesser extent with OECD-led initiatives, although it has recently shown some interest in partnering with Western countries. For example, India worked with Australia, Japan, and the United States to coordinate disaster assistance after the Indian Ocean tsunami of 2004. It has also joined the Nepal Development Forum, the Afghanistan Reconstruction Trust Fund, and the multidonor fund for Iraq (Price 2011), and cooperated with the United Kingdom's Department for International Development (DFID) in treating malaria and HIV/AIDS (Mitchell 2011).

Although these initiatives might seem proof of its openness to Western donor experience, and its willingness to go beyond the 'mutual benefit' principle into longer-term social and environmental development, India has not developed a clear strategy for coordinating with Western donors on aid delivery. On the whole, India prefers working with other developing countries, such as South Africa and Brazil through IBSA, or through multilateral bodies such the UN Development Cooperation Forum, rather than traditional Western donors or OECD-DAC. Trade-offs will certainly appear as India moves forward. Its distance from established donor rules and institutions could expose it to the Western community criticisms currently directed at China (outlined earlier in the section on China's perspective). However, joining the Western policy bodies would also bring costs; this could irritate relations with traditional allies in various international fora, such as the Group of 77 (Paulo and Helmut 2010).

Conclusion

In this chapter, we have sought to provide a more nuanced understanding of Indian development cooperation through the comparative lens of Chinese aid. Despite Indian tendencies to maintain 'boundaries' with China (Mawdsley 2011), we have shown that India and China do share many similarities, primarily in the fundamental principles of SSC delivery. By following precepts of mutual benefit, noninterference, and respect for sovereignty, India and China diverge from traditional 'donor–recipient' relationships and ensure that the recipient countries retain real policy ownership. India and China also adopt a broad definition of development that intertwines aid with trade, investment, and technology transfer, thus offering an alternative to the OECD's aid definition.

Nevertheless, we have shown that India and China have diverged from each other in past areas of focus, drawing on their own development experiences and comparative strengths. Although China spends most of its money in filling in the 'hard infrastructure gap' by building transportation and power facilities, India addresses the 'capacity gap', making full use of its advantages in education, service, and the IT sector. These different focuses have brought different results: India's SSC has garnered goodwill and avoided international criticisms or scrutiny, whereas China's aid has gained it access to more markets, but also drawn conflicting responses. Both countries have accordingly adjusted their development cooperation strategies, with India extending more loans for building local infrastructure and China increasing investment in human resource development.

India and China both emphasise South-South cooperation in development assistance, but to date have largely confined this to their bilateral partnerships; they have had little dialogue or coordination with each other. Although they have approached challenges in divergent ways, in some areas they share a clear scope and a desire for better mutual coordination. The two countries have worked together to advance similar positions in global trade and climate change negotiations. They participate actively in many of the same multilateral and regional fora, such as Group of 20, BRICS, Shanghai Cooperation Organisation (SCO), South Asian Association for Regional Cooperation (SAARC), and Association of Southeast Asian Nations (ASEAN). We consider BRICS in particular a promising platform for coordinating cooperation policy, the better to reduce high transaction costs in aid delivery, along with the 'trust deficit' between India and China (Sen 2012). BRICS has institutionalised SSC as an important dimension of international development cooperation strategy. Politically, it creates spaces for autonomous discussion independent of OECD countries, and economically, it can promote dialogue on trade, financing, and development assistance. It can also facilitate exchange of expertise and technological know-how. The 2014 establishment of a BRICS bank, as well as the Asia Infrastructure Investment Bank (AIIB), should increase interactions among the different member countries, and may lead to some common approaches and joint development initiatives. India and China might also initiate BRICS and AIIB funds to promote health, education, and agriculture in developing countries.

In South Asia, China and India could organise joint projects in infrastructure and capacity building to increase mutual trust and improve aid effectiveness. The two countries might also assist with initiatives such as the Bangladesh-China-India-Myanmar (BCIM) economic corridor and the new 'Maritime Silk Road' (an oceanic trade route linking China and Europe via Southeast Asia, India, and Africa). Such projects not only fit both countries' economic interests, but also promote regional integration. When Chinese Premier Li Keqiang visited India in May 2013, he said that the countries had agreed to 'support each other in enhancing friendly relations with their common neighbours for mutual benefit, and win-win results' (Sibal 2013). After all, the South Asian infrastructure projects (such as ports, airports, and power projects) that China and India have supported not only complement development efforts by the World Bank and other organisations, but may also directly benefit the two countries, as well as their partners.[4] Similarly, within the framework of the New Partnerships for African Development (NEPAD), China and India could support African industrialisation through knowledge sharing, capacity -building, and infrastructure development. These multilateral and regional fora provide an opportunity for India, China, and other key rising powers – those sharing their status as developing countries and growing SSC providers – to develop alternative modalities for development cooperation.

Notes

1 Discussions on Asian approaches to development cooperation or models for aid include the Chr. Michelsen Institute (CMI) seminar on 'Asian Models for Aid: Is there a Non-Western Approach to Development Assistance?' in Oslo, December 2006; this addressed similarities and differences among China, India, South Korea, and Japan and their implications for Western donors (Jerve 2007). The Asia Foundation, in cooperation with the Korea Development Institute, has also facilitated discussions on this topic; see e.g., Mulakala, et al (2012).

2 According to China's Foreign Aid White Paper (SCIO 2014), over the period of 2010–2012, China's aid mainly flowed to Africa (51.8 per cent) and Asia (30.5 per cent), but also covered countries in Latin America and the Caribbean (8.4 per cent), Oceania (4.2 per cent), and Europe (1.7 per cent).

3 For example, India's leading national overseas oil company, NOGC Videsh (OVL), bought a 25 per cent stake in Sudan's main oil consortium in 2005. Indian companies have also bought stakes in other major oil-producing African countries, such as Cote d'Ivoire, Equatorial Guinea, Ghana, Nigeria, and Senegal (Dadwal 2011).

4 For example, Indian companies already use the Chinese-built port of Hambantota in Sri Lanka to tranship automobiles to East Africa.

Works cited

Agrawal, S. (2007). *Emerging donors in international development assistance: The India case*. Ottawa: International Development Research Centre. Available at www.idrc.ca/ EN/Documents/Case-of-India.pdf.

Alden, C. (2007). *China in Africa*. London: Zed Books.

Bijoy, C.R. (2010). India: Transiting to a global donor. *The Reality of Aid Network Special Report*, 6. Ibon Foundation, Philippines. Available at www.realityofaid.org/wp-content/ uploads/2013/02/ROA-SSDC-Special-Report6.pdf.

Brautigam, D. (2011). *The dragon's gift: The real story of China in Africa*. Oxford: Oxford University Press.

Chanana, D. (2010). India's transition to global power: Limitations and prospects. *ARI*, 123. Real Institutio Elcano, Madrid. Available at www.realinstitutoelcano.org/wps/wcm/ connect/cdde8a804350e71cafc1ef9b8a04b37a/ARI123–2010_Chanana_India_Transition_ Global_Donor_Limitation_Prosopects.pdf?MOD=AJPERES&CACHEID=cdde8a8043 50e71cafc1ef9b8a04b37a.

Chaturvedi, S. (2012). India's development partnership: Key policy shifts and institutional evolution. *Cambridge Review of International Affairs*, 25(4): 557–577. Available at DOI:10.1080/09557571.2012.744639.

Dadwal, S.R. (2011). India and Africa: Towards a sustainable energy partnership. *SAIIA Occasional Paper*, 75. South African Institute of International Affairs, Midrand, ZA.

De Haan, A. (2011). Will China change international development as we know it? *Journal of International Development*, 23(7): 881–908.

Fuchs, A., and Vadlamannati, K.C. (2012). The needy donor: An empirical analysis of India's aid motives. *World Development*, 44(4): 110–128. Available at www.sciencedirect. com/science/article/pii/S0305750X12003063.

Huang, M., and Qi, X. (2012). Comments on the performance and trend of foreign aid from India. *International Economic Cooperation*, 1: 63–68.

Jacobs, S. (2012). India-Africa trade: A unique relationship [webpage]. *Global, the International Briefing*. Available at www.global-briefing.org/2012/10/india-africa-trade-a-unique-relationship/.

Jerve, A.M. (2007). Asian models for aid: Is there a non-Western approach to development assistance? *CMI Report*, 12. Chr. Michelsen Institute, Bergen, Norway. Available at www.cmi.no/publications/file/2767-asian-models-for-aid.pdf.

Jerve, A.M., and Hilde, S. (2009). Self-interest and global responsibility: Aid policies of South Korea and India in the making. *CMI Report*, 9. Chr. Michelsen Institute, Bergen, Norway. Available at www.cmi.no/publications/publication/?3372=self-interest-and-global-responsibility.

Jetly, R. (2010). India and China: Emerging dynamics and regional security perspectives. *ISAS Working Paper*, 114. Institute of South Asian Studies, Zurich.

Jobelius, M. (2007). New powers for global change? Challenges for the international development cooperation: The case of India. *FES Briefing Paper*, 5. Freidrich Ebert Stiftung, Berlin. Available at http://library.fes.de/pdf-files/iez/global/04718.pdf.

Kilambi, S. (2013). India emerges as leader in 21st century 'scramble for Africa'. *San Francisco Bay View*, 20 March. Available at http://sfbayview.com/2013/03/india-emerges-as-leader-in-21st-century-scramble-for-africa/.

Kragelund, P. (2008). The return of non-DAC donors to Africa: New prospects for African development? *Development Policy Review*, 26(5): 555–584.

Li, A. (2015). The role of China's NGOs in foreign aid and international development. *CIDRN Policy Recommendations*, 5. China International Development Research Network, Beijing.

Li, X., Banik, D., Lixia, T., and Jin, W. (2014). Difference or indifference: China's development assistance unpacked. *IDS Bulletin*, 45(4): 22–35. Available at DOI:10.1111/1759-5436.12090.

Mancheri, N.A. (2011). Resources, development cooperation and the China factor: Emerging issues in India's engagement with Africa. *International Politics*, 4(7): 69–90.

Mathai, R. (2013). India's perspective on South-South cooperation. *Keynote Address at Conference of Southern Providers-South-South Cooperation: Issues and Emerging Challenges*, 15 April, New Delhi. Available at www.mea.gov.in/Speeches-Statements.htm?dtl/21549/Keynote+address+by+Foreign+Secretary+at+Conference+of+Southern+Providers+SouthSouth+Cooperation++Issues+and+Emerging+Challenges.

Martyn, D. (2008). How China delivers development assistance in Africa. *A Centre for Chinese Studies Research Report*, University of Stellenbosch, Beijing.

Mawdsley, E. (2011). The emerging powers and the changing landscape of foreign aid and development cooperation: Public perceptions of development cooperation. *Summary Paper 2: India*. University of Cambridge, Cambridge, UK. Available at www.geog.cam.ac.uk/research/projects/foreignaidperceptions/summaries/india.pdf.

Mawdsley, E., and McCann, G. (eds.) (2011). *India and Africa: Changing geographies of power and development*. Oxford: Pambazuka Press.

McCormick, D. (2008). China and India as Africa's new donors: The impact of aid on development. *Review of African Political Economy*, 35(115), 73–92.

McLymont, R. (2011). India moves in. *The Network Journal*, July. Available at www.tnj.com/departments/africa-focus/india-moves.

Meier, C., and Murthy, C.S.R. (2011). India's growing involvement in humanitarian assistance. *GPPi Working Paper*, 13. Global Public Policy Institute, Berlin. Available at www.gppi.net/fileadmin/user_upload/media/pub/2011/meier-murthy_2011_india-growing-involvement-humanitarian-assistance_gppi.pdf.

Ministry of External Affairs (MEA) (2008). *Annual report 2008–2009*. New Delhi: MEA, Government of India.

MEA (2012). *Annual report 2012–2013*. New Delhi: MEA, Government of India.

MEA (2013). *Annual report 2013–2014*. New Delhi: MEA, Government of India.

Ministry of Foreign Affairs, The Peoples' Republic of China (MFA-PRC) (no date). *China's initiation of the five principles of peaceful co-existence*. Beijing: MFA, PRC,. Available at www.fmprc.gov.cn/mfa_eng/ziliao_665539/3602_665543/3604_665547/t18053.shtml. [Accessed 23 August 2015].

Mitchell, A. (2011). Emerging powers [speech]. Chatham House, Royal Institute of International Affairs, London. Available at www.dfid.gov.uk/Media-Room/Speeches-and-articles/2011/Emerging-powers/. [Accessed 12 May 2011].

Mittal, A. (2013). Indian land grabs in Ethiopia show dark side of south-south cooperation. *The Guardian*, 25 February. Available at www.theguardian.com/global-development/poverty-matters/2013/feb/25/indian-land-grabs-ethiopia.

Mulakala, A., Reed, E., Lee, K., and Kim, Y.J. (eds.) (2012). *Emerging Asian approaches to development cooperation*. Seoul: Korean Development Institute and The Asia Foundation. Available at http://asiafoundation.org/resources/pdfs/EmergingAsianApproachestoDevelopmentCooperationConferencePapers.pdf.

Mullen, R.D. (2013). Holding back on soft power. *The Indian Express*, 4 March. Available at http://archive.indianexpress.com/news/holding-back-on-soft-power/1082532/2.

Naidu, S. (2010). India's Africa relations: in the shadow of China? In F. Cheru and C. Obi (eds.), *The rise of China and India in Africa*. Uppsala, Sweden: Zed Books, pp. 34–49.

Nelson, D. (2009). India joins 'neo-colonial' rush for Africa's land and labour. *The Daily Telegraph*, 28 June. Available at www.telegraph.co.uk/news/worldnews/asia/india/5673437/India-joins-neocolonial-rush-for-Africas-land-and-labour.html.

Paulo, S., and Helmut, R. (2010). Eastern donors and western soft law: Towards a DAC donor peer review of China and India? *Development Policy Review*, 28(5): 535–552.

Piccio, L. (2013). India's foreign aid program catches up with its global ambitions. *Devex*, 10 May. Available at www.devex.com/news/indias-foreign-aid-program-catches-up-with-its-global-ambitions-80919.

Price, G. (2011). For the global good, India's developing international role. *A Chatham House Report*. Royal Institute of International Affairs, London.

Reilly, J. (2012). A norm-taker or a norm-maker? Chinese aid in Southeast Asia. *Journal of Contemporary China*, 21(73): 71–91.

Sahni, C. (2007). India's foreign policy: key drivers'. *South African Journal of International Affairs*, 14(2): 21–35.

SCIO (State Council Information Office) (2011). *China's foreign aid, 2011*. Beijing: Foreign Languages Press Co. Ltd.

SCIO (2014). China's foreign aid, 2014. The State Council, People's Republic of China. Available at http://english.gov.cn/archive/white_paper/2014/08/23/content_281474982986592.htm.

Sen, T. (2012). The trust deficit in India-China relations. In S.T. Devare, S. Swaran and M. Reena (eds.), *Emerging China: prospects of partnership in Asia*. London: Routledge.

Sharan, V., Campbell, I., and Rubin, D. (2013). India's development cooperation: charting new approaches in a changing world. *ORF Special Report,* 2. Observer Research Foundation, New Delhi.

Sibal, K. (2013). India must demand clarity on the LAC and redress the balance in a complex relationship with China. *Mail Online India*, 27 May. Available at www.dailymail.co.uk/indiahome/indianews/article-2331732/India-demand-clarity-LAC-redress-balance-complex-relationship-China.html.

Tang, L. (2013). India's foreign aid and its management. *International Economic Cooperation*, 9.

Tang, L., and Li, X. (2013). India's international development aid: An analytical review. *South Asian Studies Quarterly*, 3: 7–12.

United Nations Development Programme (UNDP) (2015). *China's humanitarian aid*. Issue Brief, 9. UNDP, New York. Available at www.cn.undp.org/content/china/en/home/library/south-south-cooperation/issue-brief – china-s-humanitarian-aid.html.

Wagner, C. (2009). Promotion of democracy and foreign policy in India. *SWF Research Paper,* 13. German Institute for International and Security Affairs (SWF), Berlin.

Woods, N. (2008). Whose aid? Whose influence? China, emerging donors and the silent revolution in development assistance. *International Affairs*, 84(6): 1205–1221.

Xinhua (2014). Premier's Africa visit to help accelerate co-op. *China Daily,* 12 May. Available at www.chinadaily.com.cn/world/2014livisitafrica/2014–05/12/content_17499462.htm.

11 Australian and Indian development cooperation

Some similarities, more contrasts

Stephen Howes and Jonathan Pryke

As emerging economies become richer, their aid budgets will likely continue to grow. Recent analyses of aid from nonmembers of the Organisation for Economic Development and Co-operation (OECD)[1] have helped clarify its distinctive features.[2] However, although commentators often note the differences between OECD and non-OECD aid, few have undertaken comparative case studies. This chapter compares Indian and Australian aid through an analysis of volumes, recipients, modalities, and objectives. It draws on available statistics for both countries and recent research into new and traditional aid donors. Overall, we argue, the differences between these two aid programmes are more striking than the similarities.

Aid volumes

Australia follows the OECD definitions in determining what constitutes aid; India does not. We cannot be sure that we are comparing apples and apples. But the OECD definition is itself quite flexible, and we find that in practice the two countries use broadly the same definition. For example, neither country includes export credits in their aid budgets; see the section of this chapter on aid modalities for further discussion of this.

Figure 11.1 shows aid from India and Australia since the turn of the millennium, in both cases setting at one the initial value of aid from each country, in its own currency, and adjusting for inflation. Australian aid increased by 70 per cent from 1999–2000 to 2014–2015, whereas Indian aid more than doubled, increasing 260 per cent by 2014–2015. The increase in Australian aid is almost identical to the increase in OECD aid (72 per cent by 2013), also shown in Figure 11.1.[3]

Whereas the increase in Indian aid appears to have accelerated, the increase of Australian aid came to a halt a couple of years ago. The earlier bipartisan commitment to increase Australian aid to 0.5 per cent of gross national income (GNI) lost support on both sides over the last few years; the newly elected government replaced it with a commitment simply to hold aid constant in real terms. The increase in Indian aid has proved erratic over the last decade, but since 2011–2012 it seems to have re-established an upwards trajectory.

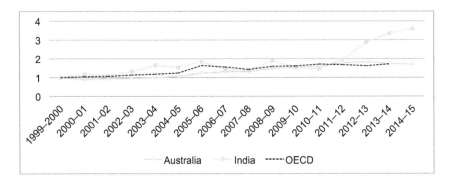

Figure 11.1 Australian and Indian aid in local currency, 1999–2000 to 2014–2015

Note: Budget documents for each country (Australian DFAT 1999–2014; Indian Ministry of Finance 1999–2014), with additional calculations by the authors.[4]

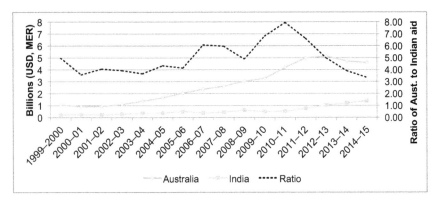

Figure 11.2 Australian and Indian aid in USD at constant prices, 1999–2000 to 2014–2015

Note: As per notes to Figure 11.1, with exchange rates from Ozforex (2015).

Figure 11.2 expresses aid volumes in current US dollars (USD); it shows that Australia began the millennium with an aid programme just over five times as large as the Indian aid programme, and ended in 2014–2015 with a programme just over three times as large. (The dashed line, plotted on the right-hand axis, shows the ratio of Australian to Indian aid.) The reduction in the gap between the two programmes is less than what one might expect given the data in Figure 11.1, because over this period the Australian dollar appreciated against the US dollar whereas the Indian rupee lost value.

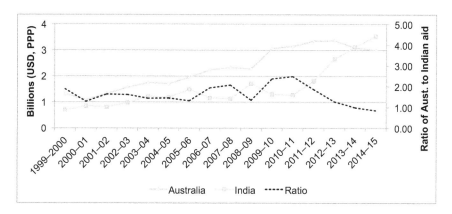

Figure 11.3 Australian and Indian aid in USD for PPP, 1999–2000 to 2014–2015

Note: As per Figure 11.1, with exchange rates from World Bank (2014) and 2013–2014 and 2014–2015 PPP fixed at the 2012–2013 rate (for Australia AUD 1.53/USD 1, for India INR 0.39/USD 1).

A comparison based on market exchange rates may mislead us, because the purchasing power of one US dollar is greater in India than in Australia. Most Indian aid expenditure goes to Indian goods and services (Mullen 2013); despite progress in untying, the same probably holds for Australian aid – and where it does not, expenditures would still occur at Australian prices. Figure 11.3 shows the volume of aid from both countries in USD, using purchasing power parities (PPP) rather than market exchange rates. This gives a very different picture. Over the entire period, the Indian aid programme has gone from being half the size of the Australian aid program to slightly larger in 2013–2014, and has clearly surpassed it in 2014–2015.

This is remarkable. Australia sits outside the first tier of ODA donors (the largest five, by a considerable margin, being the United States, Great Britain, Germany, Japan, and France), but occupies the second tier of OECD donors (along with Sweden, Norway, the Netherlands, and Canada). That Indian aid roughly equals Australia's when measured by purchasing power attests to the growth of non-OECD aid in general.

Figure 11.4 shows each country's aid as a proportion of GNI. India's aid-to-GNI ratio has remained remarkably constant at around the 0.05 per cent mark for the past decade. Australia's aid/GNI ratio increased from 0.25 per cent to 0.35 per cent over the same period.

Figure 11.5 shows each country's international development expenditure as a proportion of total government spending. Almost 1.4 cents in every Australian dollar spent goes to aid, up from 1 cent a decade ago. In India, 0.4 paise in every rupee goes to aid.[5] However, the gap has begun to close. At the turn of the millennium, aid ranked just under five times as highly in the Australian budget as it did in the Indian budget; the current ratio is closer to 3.5 to 1.

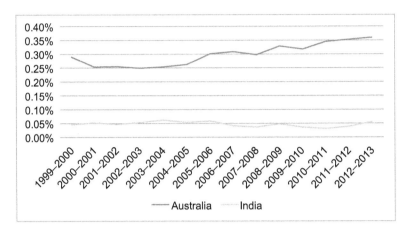

Figure 11.4 Australian and Indian aid as a proportion of GNI, 1999–2013

Notes: Aid volumes as per notes to Figure 11.1. Gross national income from World Bank (2014) and measured by the calendar year (e.g. 1999–2000 uses 1999 GNI figures).

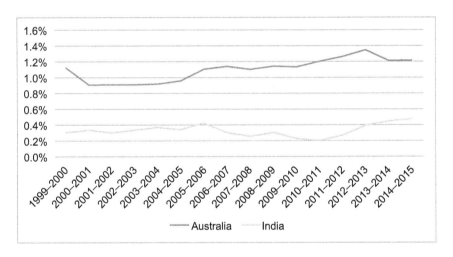

Figure 11.5 Government aid as a proportion of total government expenditure in Australia and India, 1999–2013

Notes: Aid volumes as per notes to Figure 11.1. Total expenditure figures from Australian and Indian budget documents (Australian Treasury, 1999–2014; Indian Ministry of Finance, 1999–2014).

Aid recipients

Both countries target their aid to their immediate neighbourhoods – in India, aid goes largely to South Asia; for Australia, East Asia and the Pacific.

We analyse aid to the ten largest recipient nations and regions from both countries, using 2014–2015 budget estimates for India, and 2013–2014 revised budget estimates for Australia. As Figure 11.6a shows, Bhutan alone receives 63 per cent of India's 'total' aid (i.e., the total aid to the ten largest recipients). Strategic concerns underpin the preference shown to Bhutan – not only an immediate neighbour situated between India and China, but also a major provider of India's hydroelectricity; much of India's aid finances the construction of hydroelectric plants. Other South Asian recipients get another 25 per cent of the total, with Afghanistan the second largest after Bhutan (with 8 per cent). Africa receives only 4 per cent of India's aid.

Australia does not focus so much aid on any single country; indeed, India's concentration on Bhutan may well be unique among all donor–recipient aid relationships. Nonetheless, 78 per cent of Australian top-ten recipient aid goes to countries in East Asia and the Pacific (Figure 11.6b).

In both countries, the increased volume of aid has changed its distribution. In 1999–2000, 90 per cent of India's aid went to South Asian nations[6] (Figure 11.7a). By 2014–2015, that region still received 88 per cent, but Bhutan's share of the total had fallen from 74 per cent to 61 per cent. Afghanistan has also proven a big winner in India's aid expansion: it has gone from being outside the top nine in 1999–2000 to an 8 per cent share of top-ten aid in 2014–2015.

In 1980–1981, Papua New Guinea accounted for 64 per cent of Australia's top-ten recipient aid, giving it a status similar to Bhutan's in the Indian aid programme today (Figure 11.7b). In 1999–2000, Papua New Guinea's share had fallen to 35 per cent, and in 2013–2014, 22 per cent. The focus of Australia's aid on the Asia Pacific region remains, although the region's share in top-ten recipient aid fell from 90 per cent in 1999–2000 to 78 per cent in 2013–2014. The big winners from the Australian scale-up were Indonesia, Afghanistan, and sub-Saharan Africa.

Australia and India give their aid to countries with quite different profiles. For a start, Australia's recipients have a much lower per capita income; India gives aid to both richer and poorer countries. The weighted average per capita 2012 income of an Australian aid recipient was USD 2800, where the weights represent relative shares in Australia's top-ten aid budget. We will call this the average recipient income; it comes to one-thirteenth of Australia's own per capita income of USD 35,600. Indonesia is the richest recipient of Australian aid, with an income just one-seventh of Australia's. There is, in other words, a massive distance in living standards between Australia and its recipients, as Figure 11.8a shows.

The average recipient of Indian aid has an income of USD 4800. India's own per capita income in 2012 was USD 3400. In other words, India gives aid to countries that are, on average, 40 per cent richer! However, if we remove Bhutan – richer than India and its largest recipient – from the calculations, India's average aid recipient does become poorer than India's average citizen. Nonetheless, among top-nine recipients, Sri Lanka, the Maldives, and Eurasia also have higher per capita incomes than India itself (Figure 11.8b).[7]

The progressive or redistributive character of aid has traditionally served to justify it as an international equivalent (if only a pale shadow) of domestic progressive taxation. Inequality aversion underpins this argument – an additional dollar is worth more in the hands of a poor than a rich person. Economists, with

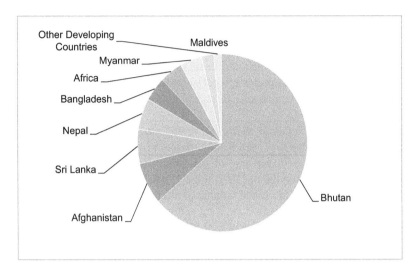

Figure 11.6a Top ten Indian aid recipient nations and regions, 2014–2015
Source: Indian Ministry of Finance (2014) and Australian DFAT (2014b)

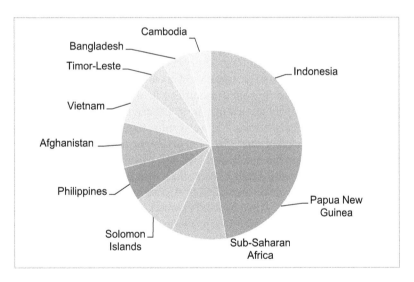

Figure 11.6b Top ten Australian aid recipient nations and regions, 2013–2014
Source: Indian Ministry of Finance (2014) and Australian DFAT (2014b)

their penchant for quantification, define an inequality aversion parameter, eta
(or η). In the economic literature, a moderate value for eta is 1 and a higher value
would be 2. Quantification helps us see just how powerful this humanitarian argument for aid can be – or not – depending on the distance between the donor and
its recipients. Okun's 'leaky bucket' thought experiment (Okun 1975) asks us to

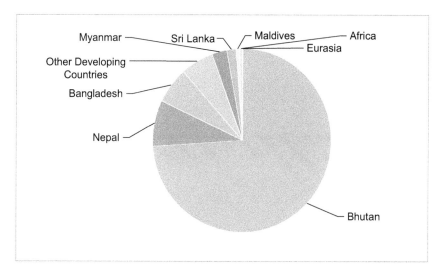

Figure 11.7a Top nine Indian aid recipient nations and regions, 1999–2000
Source: Indian Ministry of Finance (2014) and Australian DFAT (2014b)

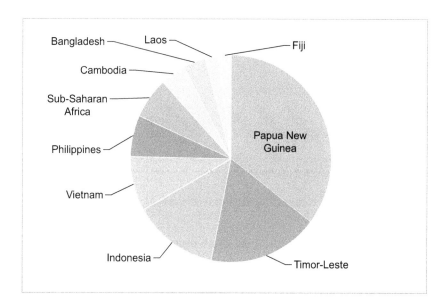

Figure 11.7b Top ten Australian aid recipient nations and regions, 1999–2000
Source: Indian Ministry of Finance (2014) and Australian DFAT (2014b)

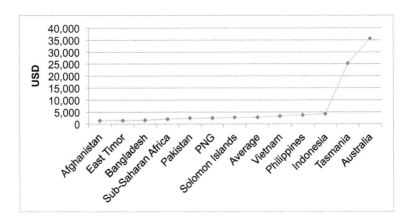

Figure 11.8a Australian per capita GDP compared to top ten Australian aid recipients, 2012

Source and notes: World Bank (2014), with additional calculations by the authors.[8]

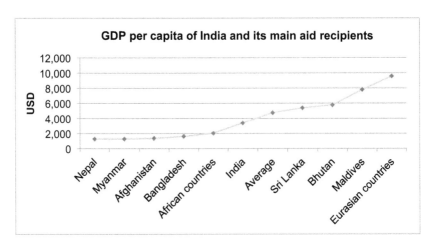

Figure 11.8b Indian per capita GDP compared to its main aid recipients, 2012

think about a one-dollar transfer from a rich person to a poor person, and to say how much of that one dollar we could see wasted and still support the transfer. (In our context, 'waste' could arise from the administrative costs of managing aid, aid projects that do not work, or adverse economy-wide effects of aid. It could also come from the deadweight losses involved in raising taxes to finance the aid programme.)[9]

If we think of aid from Australia as a transfer from the average Australian to the average citizen of the average recipient country, then, as Figure 11.9a shows, Australian aid is 'justified' even with wastage of 92 per cent (if $\eta = 1$) or 99 per cent (if $\eta = 2$). Indeed, in Australia's case the bars nearly all exceed 90 per cent, and often stand at 100. India provides a stark contrast (Figure 11.9b). Aid from India to the average recipient cannot be justified as a progressive transfer, because its average recipient is better off than the average Indian. The bars for aid from India stand as often below 50 per cent as above it, and become negative for countries with a higher per capita income than India itself.

This does not imply that Indian aid lacks justification; aid has many rationales beyond the humanitarian ones. But it does suggest that Indian aid carries a higher justificatory burden or opportunity cost. Australian aid can have high wastage and remain justified from a humanitarian perspective; not so with Indian aid.

Australia is not only much richer than its aid recipients; it also has much better governance. Figure 11.10a shows how Australia and its top ten aid recipients rank in 'Government Effectiveness', from the *Worldwide Governance Indicators*

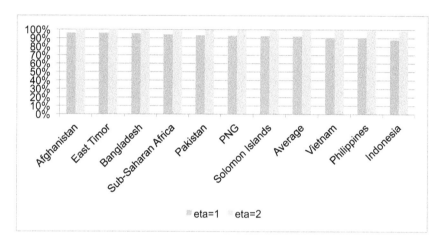

Figure 11.9a Australia and its aid recipients: levels of permitted waste, 1999–2014

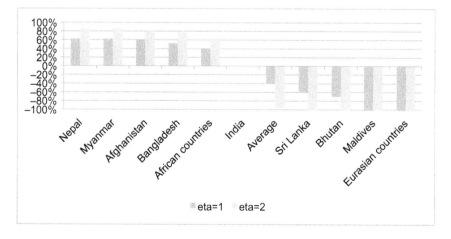

Figure 11.9b India and its aid recipients: levels of permitted waste, 1999–2014

(World Bank 2013). Australia has one of the most effective governments in the world (in the top 6 per cent), whereas its average top-ten recipient ranks in the bottom third. Even the Philippines, the highest-ranking recipient on the chart, has only a 58 per cent rating.

Again, India provides a sharp contrast. India itself has a median government effectiveness rating. Bhutan, Maldives, and Eurasia all have higher rankings, with Bhutan pulling the ranking of the average recipient above that of India itself (Figure 11.10b).

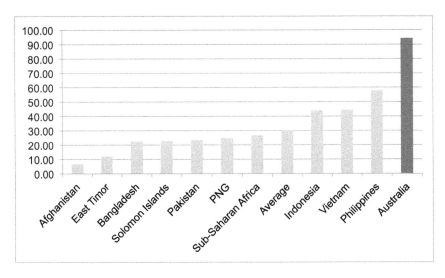

Figure 11.10a Australia's government effectiveness percentile rating, compared to major aid recipients, 2012

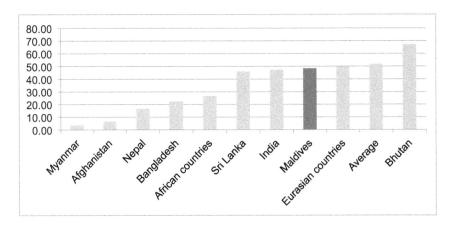

Figure 11.10b India's government effectiveness rating percentile rating compared to major aid recipients, 2012

Aid modalities

Before 2012, India's aid administration came under its Ministry of External Affairs (for technical assistance and bilateral grants) and the Ministry of Finance (for multilateral organisations).[10] In January 2012, the Indian government created the Development Partnership Administration (DPA), housed within the Ministry of External Affairs (MEA). The administration has brought the control of India's development assistance streams under the one roof. (The Export-Import [Exim] Bank still provides concessional export credits, but these do not count as aid; see the next subsection.) According to the DPA website, the centralisation of development assistance aims for efficiency and effectiveness throughout the life of aid projects, with the 'close cooperation and facilitation of the partner countries' (Indian MEA 2014). Although housed within the MEA, the DPA has a clearly established and separate organisational structure and reports directly to its own secretary – one of four in the ministry, responsible for the DPA, as well as investment, trade promotion, and multilateral relations.

Australia, by contrast, no longer has a specialised agency responsible for all of its aid activities. Until 2013, such an agency had existed, in one form or another, for close to 40 years. The Australian Agency for International Development (AusAID), an executive government agency responsible for managing the overseas aid programme, reported directly to the minister of foreign affairs. When the coalition took control of the federal government in 2013, it announced that the aid portfolio would merge with the Department of Foreign Affairs and Trade (DFAT) (ABC 2013).

Many of the AusAID aid specialists remain in service, despite the end of the agency. The 2011–2012 AusAID budget provided for a staff of just over 1500. Several hundred redundancies have since occurred, but the latest estimates suggest that the Australian aid programme's administration still counts in excess of 1000 staff (Towell 2014). India's DPA cannot boast the same pool of centralised, experienced talent; Mullen noted its 'notorious' understaffing (Mullen 2014:10). The rapid expansion of India's aid programme suggests that such personnel constraints may have worsened.

Many other signs demonstrate Australia's more articulated and formal approach to the aid programme. It has an official objective, although this changes from time to time, and a website with a vast (although still incomplete and often out-of-date) reservoir of information. An Office of Development Effectiveness acts as an internal evaluator of aid projects; many of its reviews are published, and a separate document on the aid budget appears at budget times. The entire aid programme comes under periodic review, and official government strategies (such as aid white papers) appear every 5 years or so. All of these evaluation processes set it apart from the Indian aid programme, although as Sinha (2011) notes, India's lines of credit through its Exim Bank demonstrate considerable transparency.

The Indian aid programme appears more demand driven, although this is harder to prove. The DPA website states that 'India's development partnership is based on the needs identified by the partner countries' and that the ministry tries to accommodate as many of its received requests as 'technically and financially possible' (Indian MEA 2014). By contrast, the Australian programme may consider partner country requests, but has no policy for prioritising them; instead, Australian government officials and their consultants often take responsibility for project design.

According to the OECD, loans may count as part of official development assistance, provided that they include a significant concessional element. All multilateral banks, as well as a few of the largest bilateral donors (particularly France, Germany, and Japan), provide concessional loans to developing nations. Over time, grants have become relatively more and loans relatively less important forms of aid. According to the World Bank (2008), grants constituted 60 per cent of OECD bilateral aid in 1975 and 90 per cent in 2005.

Australia has traditionally steered clear of loans in its aid programme, with the large support to Indonesia after the 2004 Asian tsunami being a prominent exception. India, on the other hand, has long relied on concessional loans as an important part of its development assistance. As Figure 11.11 shows, the volume of loans in India's total aid fluctuates, but the share tends to hover around 30 per cent.

We should note that these loans represent those directly provided by the Indian government. They do not include the lines of credit distributed by India's Exim Bank. As discussed by Saxena in this volume, the Exim Bank's concessional loans have expanded rapidly, allowing developing countries to import Indian goods and services and to finance infrastructure, productive activities, and capacity building. In 2003, the Indian government set up a programme to reimburse the Exim Bank for introducing a concessional funding window. According to Saxena's figures, the amount provided varies from year to year,

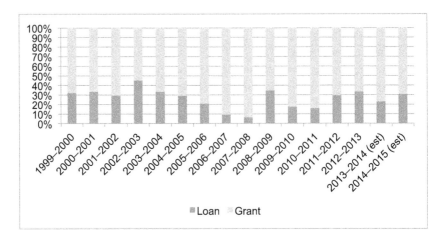

Figure 11.11 Indian development assistance by loans and grants, 1999–2015

Source: Indian Ministry of Finance (1999–2014)

but over the last 5 years it has averaged a total equal to about 90 per cent of the aid budget. However, India has never regarded such funding – neither the total nor the budgetary cost of the concessional financing – as aid, on the grounds that the lines of credit primarily serve as 'an instrument for promoting international trade' (Sinha 2011: 1).

Figure 11.12, based on data released by AusAID (now DFAT) shows how, or through whom, Australia spends each aid dollar – demonstrating the changes that Howes (2011) termed Australia's 'aid revolution'. Traditionally, private contractors supplied the dominant mode of spending Australian aid – as high as 40 per cent in 2005–2006, by far the largest share. However, a strong shift away from contractors has since taken place – driven, as Howes (2011) argues, by a perception that overreliance on contractors undermines aid effectiveness and influence. Multilaterals have proven the biggest beneficiaries (the World Bank, the largest single beneficiary, received AUD 764 million in 2011–2012). Nongovernmental organisations (NGOs), universities, and partner governments have all benefited as well.

Australia has not tended to support the multilateral system in terms of core funding. Among OECD donors, Australia ranks twenty-sixth out of twenty-seven as of 2010 (OECD 2012: 64) in the share of aid passed to multilaterals without earmarking. Australia has long felt that the multilateral system does not focus sufficiently on its region of interest, East Asia and the Pacific, and has maintained earmarking to ensure that emphasis.

Comparable data are not available for India. However, the country relies heavily on technical assistance and loans tied to the use of Indian goods and services. One therefore might reasonably assume that Indian companies (through loans and tied aid) and the Indian public sector (in the case of technical assistance) serve as the major modes of delivery for Indian aid.

Indian policy requires that most of its aid be spent on Indian goods and services (Mullen 2013). By contrast, Australia has gradually untied its aid. Since 2006, private contractors from all over the world may bid on Australian aid contracts. The heavy reliance on multilateral aid also acts as a form of untying; Australian firms and NGOs receive no special privileges in relation to that aid. Even today, however, Australian aid retains some tied elements. With only a few exceptions, its programmes only provide scholarships to Australian universities. The Australian public sector controls about 20 per cent of the aid programme, and Australian NGOs receive about 50 per cent of total NGO funding (Wulfsohn and Howes 2013). We have not ascertained what proportion of total private-contractor aid delivery comes through Australian firms, but it appears to be a significant one. International Development Contractors Australia, a representative body for private-sector development agencies engaged with the Australian aid programme, lists twenty-two members, with eighteen Australia-based contractors. Australian firms have a comparative advantage, given extensive experience with both the region and the aid programme. We might also note that the aid programme is quite active in sectors of interest to Australian firms – such as agriculture and, increasingly, mining.

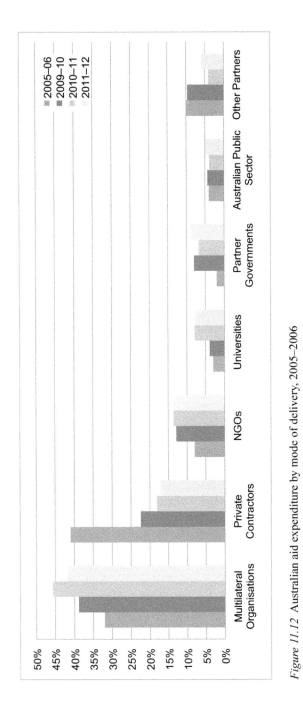

Figure 11.12 Australian aid expenditure by mode of delivery, 2005–2006

Source: Panpruet and Pryke (2013)

Aid justifications and objectives

Although it is never easy to tell why a country gives aid, the fact that both India and Australia focus on their immediate neighbourhood suggests the importance of strategic considerations for both countries. Australia's focus on much poorer countries also shows the importance of humanitarian motivations. For India, by contrast, 'solidarity' offers an important motivation for aid to other poor countries like itself (Chaturvedi 2012). Unlike India, Australia articulates an official objective for the aid programme. The wording changes from time to time, sometimes alongside changes in government; the new government's version stresses '[promoting] Australia's national interests by contributing to international economic growth and poverty reduction' (Australian DFAT 2014b). Although this supports the role of both strategic and humanitarian objectives in the aid programme, it suggests that the former currently have more weight.

For Australia, we can also draw on a recent survey of aid programme stakeholders (Howes and Pryke 2013). The 356 respondents to this survey included NGO and contractor senior executives and staff, as well as multilateral, governmental, and partner government staff. Respondents were asked to attach weights, adding up to 100, to three different goals: poverty reduction, strategic concerns, and commercial interests. On average, and across all stakeholder groups, respondents gave the goals of poverty reduction and strategic interests roughly the same weight of 40 per cent, and commercial interests a lesser weight, about 20 per cent (Figure 11.13).

This lesser weight for commercial aims reflects Australia's decrease in tied aid and the fact that it has few, if any, projects with the narrowly defined goal of promoting particular Australian firms. Evidence of this decline in importance over time includes the 1996 cessation of a soft-loan aid programme in support of

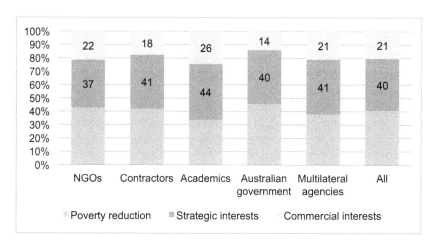

Figure 11.13 The relative importance of Australian aid objectives: responses from the 2013 Australian aid stakeholder survey

Australian firms and the (partial) untying of Australian aid in 2006. The newly elected government often speaks about aid as support for Australia's 'economic diplomacy' (for example, Bishop 2013). It remains to be seen whether this will lead to an increased weight for commercial interests in the future.

Mullen (2013) states that when India's development assistance began in the 1960s, its objectives rested on the 'commonality of anti-colonial struggle and solidarity among developing countries' (Mullen 2013: 7). As India's aid programme has evolved beyond its traditional base in technical assistance, Mullen notes that its objectives have also evolved, and now include:

1   Securing natural resources to feed the needs of India's growing economy
2   Securing markets for Indian goods and services, particularly through the use of credit
3   Supporting India's larger geostrategic objectives in its neighbourhood and beyond

Empirical analysis of India's aid programme between the years 2008–2010 shows that 'commercial and political interests dominate India's aid allocation' (Fuchs and Vadlamannati 2013a). In Australia, by contrast, national interest and humanitarian objectives dominate.

Common development wisdom holds that aid must transform as well as assist. Andrew Natsios, a former United States Agency for International Development (USAID) administrator, argues this explicitly, writing that all aid projects 'should be subordinate to the larger institution-building task' (Natsios 2010: 4). This view has many adherents in Australia. Alexander Downer, the Australian minister for foreign affairs from 1996 to 2007, argued that one must first assure that basic governmental institutions work properly in order to achieve 'sure and sustainable' social progress leading to 'better living standards' (Downer 1998). Current Prime Minister Tony Abbott has concurred, emphasising that government aid should aim to 'improv[e] other countries' governance and strengthen their economies' (Abbott 2013). In 2012–2013, Australia gave roughly 18 per cent of its aid (AUD 881 million) under the heading of governance. Technical assistance accounts for most of the total, with a focus on central agencies and the law and justice sector.

India, by contrast, shows little interest in trying to 'fix' governance, build institutions, or transform countries. It does provide considerable technical assistance and training, but with the emphasis on the word 'technical'. As Mullen notes, Indian aid remains firmly committed to 'non-interference in a country's political affairs and a focus on economic causes of underdevelopment' (Mullen 2013: 5).

Conclusion

Indian and Australian aid share some similarities. Both countries now give more aid than ever, in programmes of roughly the same size (when measured using purchasing power parities), and both give largely to countries in their region. Beyond this, however, the two programmes offer a study in contrasts. Indian aid has increased rapidly where Australian aid remains flat. Australia embodies the traditional aid paradigm: a rich country assisting countries much poorer and worse governed than itself, with improving governance as a key objective. It has an elaborate aid architecture, and is proactive in shaping aid projects. India, on the other hand, gives to countries that resemble it – that is, also poor and relatively poorly governed. It relies more on the recipient to design and propose projects, and shows much less concern with improving governance.

It is difficult to assess which approach works better. The Australian aid program has attractive features: it is less tied, more transparent, and more open to evaluation. And Australia can afford to give aid much more than India can: Figure 11.9 shows the opportunity cost of Indian aid is far higher than that of Australian aid. But the practical orientation of Indian aid has its merits: throughout its history, Western aid has often faced many justifiable accusations of hubris (see e.g., Easterly 2007; Munk 2013). And India's proximity to its recipients, not only geographically but developmentally, might allow it to tailor its aid better than a traditional OECD donor would.[11]

We should also bear the temporal dimension in mind. Twenty years ago, Australia had more forms of tied aid, provided loans as well as grants, had less focus on governance, and largely gave to a single recipient. This accords with Kragelund's observation that emerging donor aid 'strongly resembles' the aid activities that OECD donors provided 20 to 30 years ago (Kragelund 2011: 587).

What does the future hold? Will non-OECD donors 'catch up' to the OECD Development Assistance Committee (DAC) over the coming decade? Certainly, some signs of convergence have arisen. India's aid architecture has become more elaborate; Australia's, less so. As suggested earlier, commercial objectives may receive more weight in Australia's aid program (and in OECD aid generally) in the coming years. But given the deep differences between the countries' programmes, we should not overemphasise these elements of convergence. Australia's focus on governance, its reliance on quite a different and diverse set of partners (in particular, multilaterals and NGOs), its distance in terms of income and governance from its recipients – all will likely remain, for the foreseeable future, points of contrast with Indian aid.

These (probably persistent) contrasts underpin the distinct positions that Australia and India occupy in the international development field. They help explain, for example, why India has no interest in joining the OECD-DAC. Why should it join a club whose endeavours differ so strongly from its own path? Attempts to find common ground will probably prove more successful in particular bilateral instances, where shared objectives can provide a basis for cooperation. Afghanistan comes to mind as a potential example.

It appears almost inevitable that the share of non-OECD donors in total aid will continue to rise. As this comparative study suggests, that rise will dramatically shift the very nature of global aid.

Notes

1 Non-OECD donors are often called nontraditional or emerging donors. Both labels are problematic because non-OECD donors have in fact been around for a long time; hence our usage of the more prosaic but also more accurate 'non-OECD' tag. Even the word 'donor' can be problematic (some view it as a traditional term that should be reserved for OECD members), but we take it simply as a descriptive label for a country that provides foreign assistance. The word 'aid' is also problematic. Non-OECD donors and even some OECD donors do not like the word and prefer to refer to their assistance as 'development cooperation', or, for non-OECD donors, 'South-South engagement'. We bow to this preference in our title, but in the text use 'aid' as a convenient shorthand.

2 See, for example, Brautigam (2009; 2011) on China, Chanana (2009) and Mullen (2013; 2014) on India, and Burges (2014) on Brazil. For general surveys, see Greenhill et al (2013) and The Asia Foundation (2014).

3 For relevant figures (11.1 and following) the DFAT documents contain Australian aid totals in constant prices; Indian aid totals have been calculated from 'Statement 11: Grants and Loans to Foreign Governments' and the 'Technical & Economic Cooperation with Other Countries and Advances to Foreign Governments' component of the Ministry of External Affairs expenditure budget. The Indian deflator is calculated from Reserve Bank of India (2014). For Australia, we have assumed that 2014–2015 inflation equals that of 2013–2014. Total ODA derives from the OECD QWIDS database (OECD 2014), measured by the calendar year, in constant USD. For India, the years 1999–2000 to 2008–2009 show revised estimates; 2009–2010 to 2012–2013 show actual volumes, and 2013–2014 to 2014–2015 represent budget estimates. For Australia, 1999–2000 to 2012–2013 show actual volumes; 2013–2014 are budget estimates revised in January 2014, and 2014–2015 are the authors' projections, based on the assumption of no real growth in Australian aid.

4 The DFAT documents contain Australian aid totals in constant prices; Indian aid totals have been calculated from 'Statement 11: Grants and Loans to Foreign Governments' and the 'Technical & Economic Cooperation with Other Countries and Advances to Foreign Governments' component of the Ministry of External Affairs expenditure budget. The Indian deflator is calculated from Reserve Bank of India (2014). For Australia, we have assumed that 2014–2015 inflation equals that of 201–-2014. Total ODA derives from the OECD QWIDS database (OECD 2014), measured by the calendar year, in constant USD. For India, the years 1999–2000 to 2008–2009 show revised estimates; 2009–2010 to 2012–2013 show actual volumes, and 2013–2014 to 2014–2015 represent budget estimates. For Australia, 1999–2000 to 2012–2013 show actual volumes; 2013–2014 are budget estimates revised in January 2014, and 2014–2015 are the authors' projections, based on the assumption of no real growth in Australian aid.

5 The paise equals 1/100 of the rupee in India, Nepal, and Pakistan.

6 At the time, India only recorded the top nine recipient countries and regions.

7 For Figure 11.8a and 11.8b, incomes are measured in USD using current PPP. The averages use weights yielded by the relative shares of the top ten Australian aid recipients in 2012–2013, and the top nine Indian aid recipients from 2010–11 to 2012–13, respectively. (The top nine for India exclude 'Other Developing Countries'.)

8 Incomes are measured in USD using current PPP. The averages use weights yielded by the relative shares of the top ten Australian aid recipients in 2012–2013, and the top nine Indian aid recipients from 2010–2011 to 2012–2013, respectively. (The top nine for India exclude 'Other Developing Countries.')

9 The formula used to obtain the results here is $1 - (C_1/C_2)^n$.

10 See Chaturvedi (2012) for a detailed discussion of types of aid and institutional arrangements.

11 India makes this claim itself with respect to its aid programme, arguing that it 'possess[es] skills of manpower and technology more appropriate to the geographical and ecological conditions and the stage of technological development of several developing countries'. (See Fuchs and Vadlamannati (2013b), who attribute this claim to 'the webpages of several [Indian] embassies'.)

Works cited

Abbott, T. (2013). Address to the 2013 Sir Edward 'Weary' Dunlop Lecture at Asialink's Chairman Dinner, University of Melbourne. Office of the Prime Minister, Australian Government, Canberra.

The Asia Foundation (2014). *The changing aid landscape in East Asia: the rise of non-DAC providers*. Manilla: The Asia Foundation. Available at http://asiafoundation.org/publications/pdf/1362.

Australian Broadcasting Corporation (ABC) (2013). Australian government criticised over AusAID merger. *ABC,* 19 September. Australian Broadcasting Corporation, Canberra. Available at www.abc.net.au/news/2013–09–19/an-ausaid-merger-reaction/4966976.

Australian Department of Foreign Affairs and Trade (Australian DFAT). (1999–2014). *Official development assistance (ODA) budget*. Canberra: Department of Foreign Affairs and Trade, Australian Government. Available at http://aid.dfat.gov.au/budgets/Pages/default.aspx.

Australian DFAT. (2014b). *Portfolio additional estimates statements 2013–14*. Canberra: Department of Foreign Affairs and Trade, Australian Government. Available at www.dfat.gov.au/dept/budget/2013–2014_paes/2013–14_DFAT_PAES.pdf.

Australian Treasury. (1999–2014). *Budget paper no. 1*. Canberra: Australian Government. Available at http://budget.gov.au/past_budgets.htm.

Bishop, J. (2013). Address to ACFID Chairs and CEOs Dinner [speech]. Ministry of Foreign Affairs, Australian Government, Canberra. Available at www.foreignminister.gov.au/speeches/Pages/2013/jb_sp_131030.aspx?ministerid=4.

Brautigam, D. (2009). *The dragon's gift: the real story of China in Africa.* Oxford: Oxford University Press.

Brautigam, D. (2011). Aid 'with Chinese characteristics': Chinese foreign aid and development finance meet the OECD-DAC aid regime. *Journal of International Development,* 23: 752–764.

Burges, S. (2014). Brazil's international development cooperation: Old and new motivations. *Development Policy Review,* 23(3): 1–44.

Chanana, D.I. (2009). India as an emerging donor. *Economic and Political Weekly,* 44(12): 11–14. Available at http://papers.ssrn.com/sol3/papers.cfm?abstract_id=1410508.

Chaturvedi, S. (2012). India and development cooperation: Expressing southern solidarity. In S. Chaturvedi, T. Fues and E. Sidiropoulos (eds.), *Development cooperation and emerging powers: new partners or old patterns?* London: Zed Books, pp. 169–189.

Downer, A. (1998). Opening address. Speech to open the Centre for Democratic Institutions conference: Accountability and corruption in Melanesia: Evaluating the roles of the ombudsmen and leadership code. Ministry of Foreign Affairs, Australian Government, Canberra. Available at www.cdi.anu.edu.au/CDIwebsite_1998–2004/speeches/speeches_downloads/melanesiaDownerNov98.rtf

Easterly, W. (2007). *The White Man's burden: Why the West's efforts to aid the rest have done so much ill and so little good.* London: Penguin Books.

Fuchs, A., and Vadlamannati, K.C. (2013a). The needy donor: An empirical analysis of India's aid motives. *World Development,* 44: 110–128.

Fuchs, A., and Vadlamannati, K.C. (2013b). Why does India provide development aid to other developing countries? *Popular Social Science.* Available at www.popularsocialscience. com/2013/06/24/why-does-india-provide-development-aid-to-other-developing-countries/.

Greenhill, R., Prizzon, A., and Rogerson, A. (2013). The age of choice: Developing countries in the new aid landscape. Overseas Development Institute, London. Available at www.odi.org/publications/7163-age-choice-developing-countries-new-aid-landscape.

Howes, S. (2011). The quiet revolution in Australian aid: A blog for Tim Costello and Aid Watch. *The Development Policy Blog,* 12 August. Development Policy Centre, ANU, Canberra. Available at http://devpolicy.org/the-quiet-revolution-in-australian-aid-a-blog-for-tim-costello-and-aid-watch20110812/.

Howes, S., and Pryke, J. (2013). *Benchmarking Australian aid – Results from the 2013 Australian aid stakeholder survey.* Canberra: The Development Policy Centre, ANU. Available at https://devpolicy.crawford.anu.edu.au/australian-aid-stakeholder-survey.

Indian Ministry of External Affairs (Indian MEA) (2014). *Development partnership administration.* New Delhi: Ministry of External Affairs, Government of India. Available at http://mea.gov.in/development-partnership-administration.htm.

Indian Ministry of Finance (1999–2014). *Union budget.* New Delhi: Ministry of Finance, Government of India. Available at http://indiabudget.nic.in/.

Kragelund, P. (2011). Back to the BASICs? The rejuvenation of non-traditional donors' development cooperation with Africa. *Development and Change,* 42(2):585–607.

Mullen, R.D. (2013). India's development assistance: Will it change the global development finance paradigm? *Paper prepared for the Workshop on Innovation in Governance of Development Finance: Causes, Consequences & the Role of Law Conference.* Institute for International Law and Justice, New York University, New York. Available at www. iilj.org/newsandevents/documents/mullen.pdf.

Mullen, R.D. (2014). The state of Indian development cooperation. *IDCR Report,* Spring. Centre for Policy Research, New Delhi. Available at http://cprindia.org/Spring_2014_IDCR_Report_the_State_of_Indian_Development_Cooperation.pdf.

Munk, N. (2013). *The idealist: Jeffrey Sachs and the quest to end poverty.* New York: Doubleday.

Natsios, A. (2010). The clash of counter-bureaucracy and development. *Centre for Global Development Essay.* Centre for Global Development, Washington, DC. Available at www.cgdev.org/files/1424271_file_Natsios_Counterbureaucracy.pdf.

Organisation for Economic Co-operation and Development (OECD) (2012). *Multilateral aid report.* Paris: OECD Development Assistance Committee. Available at www.oecd. org/development/aid-architecture/DCD_DAC(2012)33_FINAL.pdf.

OECD (2014). *Query Wizard for International Development (QWIDS)* [database]. Paris: Organisation for Economic Co-operation and Development. Available at http://stats. oecd.org/qwids/.

Okun, A.M. (1975). *Equality and efficiency: the big tradeoff.* Washington, DC: Brookings Institution Press.

Ozforex (2015). Yearly average rates. *Ozforex Foreign Exchange Services* [database]. Available at www.ozforex.com.au/forex-tools/historical-rate-tools/yearly-average-rates.

Panpruet, P., and Pryke, J. (2013). The continuing revolution in Australian aid. *The Development Policy Blog*, 10 August. Development Policy Centre, ANU, Canberra. Available at http://devpolicy.org/the-continuing-revolution-in-australian-aid-20131008/.

Reserve Bank of India (2014). *Handbook of statistics on Indian economy.* New Delhi: Reserve Bank of India. Available at www.rbi.org.in/scripts/AnnualPublications.

aspx?head=Handbook per cent20of per cent20Statistics per cent20on per cent20Indian per cent20Economy.

Sinha, P. (2011). *A non-DAC donor case study: India's lines of credit programme*. Birmingham University. Available at www.birmingham.ac.uk/Documents/college-social-sciences/government-society/idd/research/aid-data/non-dac-donor-case-study.pdf.

Towell, N. (2014). DFAT puts the brakes on staff cuts. *The Canberra Times*, 15 September. Available at www.canberratimes.com.au/national/public-service/dfat-puts-the-brakes-on-staff-cuts-20140915–10h6e9.html.

World Bank (2008). *Aid architecture: an overview of the main trends in official development assistance*. Washington DC: The World Bank Group. Available at http://siteresources.worldbank.org/IDA/Resources/Aid_Architecture-May2008.pdf.

World Bank (2013). *Worldwide governance indicators*. Washington, DC: The World Bank Group. Available at http://info.worldbank.org/governance/wgi/index.aspx#home.

World Bank (2014). *World databank* [database]. Washington, DC: The World Bank Group. Available at http://databank.worldbank.org/data/home.aspx.

Wulfsohn, M., and Howes, S. (2013). How reliant are Australian development NGOs on government funding? *Development Policy Blog*, 27 March. The Development Policy Centre, ANU, Canberra. Available at http://devpolicy.org/how-reliant-are-australian-development-ngos-on-government-funding-20140327/.

12 Conclusion

Anthea Mulakala and Sachin Chaturvedi

Since independence in 1947, India's 'one world' philosophy and historical support for anticolonial movements, particularly in Africa, has shaped its foreign policy and defined the broad contours of economic diplomacy and development cooperation. India has preferred synergistic modalities of engagement, in keeping with the fundamental development compact framework and the largely project-oriented 'mission approach'. This philosophy, so distinct from that of 'traditional' Organisation for Economic Co-operation and Development's Development Assistance Committee (OECD-DAC) donors, might suggest a lack of continuity between India's experiences as a donor and as an aid recipient. Few mechanisms seem to demonstrate the lessons gleaned from the latter; India did take part in triangular cooperation with DAC donors in the 1950s and 1960s (as noted by Chaturvedi in Chapter 4), but such projects thereafter disappeared from the scene. As the chapters in this volume show, however, Indian cooperation evolved along a parallel track with its recipient experience and, over time, has shaped a new understanding of donor and recipient as mutual beneficiaries and equal partners.

Accordingly, India centres its development compact on five components: capacity building and skills transfer, technology and technical assistance, development finance (which includes concessional loans and lines of credit), grants, and trade and investment. In the early days, capacity building formed the cornerstone of India's cooperation. As Tuhin describes in Chapter 3, the Indian Technical and Economic Cooperation Programme (ITEC) evolved to meet partner-country needs and requests. ITEC operations have expanded to offer around 10,000 scholarships slots for 179 countries. Tuhin calls for developing countries to work together towards an equitable, inclusive, and balanced world order, claiming ITEC capacity development programmes have enabled Southern countries to negotiate and compete more effectively at the global level. Today, ITEC still anchors the whole of Indian South-South cooperation (SSC).

South Asia continues to receive the bulk of Indian SSC. Pyakuryal, Chaturvedi, and Sachdeva (Chapters 7 and 8) all observe that enhanced security, connectivity, and integration offer the greatest hope for long-term regional stability and prosperity. Pyakuryal and Chaturvedi nudge the South Asian Association for Regional Cooperation (SAARC) towards realising this aim by improving information flow and accessibility to the region's raw materials, utilities, infrastructure, human resources, products, and markets. They also call on the Indian and Nepali political leadership to reduce the 'trust deficit' and build confidence between the two nations. Sachdeva suggests that a successful partnership between India and Afghanistan – one spanning economic, political, strategic, diplomatic, and developmental actions – may leverage similar Indian efforts across the region. India's USD 2 billion package of infrastructure, education, health, and capacity development projects in Afghanistan, coupled with improving India–Pakistan relations, could deliver increases in continental trade for all the countries in the region.

At the same time, Indian cooperation has expanded and diversified over the years, extending its reach beyond its immediate neighbourhood to more distant partners in Africa. As Beri notes (Chapter 9), India–Africa cooperation arose from a shared history of anticolonial struggle. Between 1990 and 2012, trade between India and Africa has risen from USD 967 million to USD 68 billion, with the Indian private sector in the forefront amounting to USD 6.9 billion. Both Beri and Saxena (Chapter 5) illustrate the rise of the line of credit (LOC) as India's new cooperation instrument of choice with African partners, launching Indian companies into the 'business' of development. Africa receives 72 per cent of India's 176 LOCs, currently amounting to USD 6.9 billion. Beri also raises some concerns about the slow implementation and financial viability of initiatives in Africa – points that Saxena, from his experience within India's Department of Economic Affairs, can confirm. Sustainability, she notes, hinges on streamlining cumbersome procedures and ensuring that both partners possess the human and financial capacity to execute projects over the long term.

India's vibrant nongovernmental organisations (NGOs) have also extended their reach beyond national borders. Mawdsley and Roychoudhury (Chapter 6) advocate for deeper Indian NGO engagement in Afghanistan, harnessing NGO domestic experience to support the poorest and most vulnerable Afghani populations. At the same time, they emphasise that Indian NGO activism and influence within national boundaries will deliver a more progressive model of South-South cooperation for the future. As these new channels for development finance and cooperation grow, measurement, transparency, and efficient management of cooperation become more complex, but increasingly critical to success. Saxena rightly points out that Indian LOCs will only deliver their potential as engines of growth and development in Africa if they can emerge from the current mire of opaque procurement, sluggish execution, and insufficient quality control. In his opinion, the private sector could play an enhanced role with removal of the tied component of the aid, thereby letting Indian companies compete on their strengths. Evaluation also remains a gaping hole. Although the Indian Ministry of External Affairs charts the broad foreign policy framework, it does not tinker in details of execution.

Meanwhile, India's Development Partnership Administration (DPA) has yet to fully realise its role as a central repository for all Indian projects. In fact, the DPA needs to go beyond this: it must develop implementation strategies that reflect Southern-led principles, find mechanisms for project evaluation across partner countries, and decentralise management structures. The DPA could delegate the latter to local mission implementing agencies and to India's Exim Bank. As Indian civil society becomes more vocal and influential in development policy, and as transparency and accountability become more intrinsic to SSC, critical viewpoints – constructive or not – will gain public visibility. This underscores the urgency of developing and implementing robust systems for impact evaluation and assessment.

Convergence or divergence

India must also consider how its development cooperation sits within the wider global framework. The OECD-DAC has made efforts to coax India, China, Brazil, and others to join the traditional donor forum. In 2011, the Busan High Level Forum on Aid Effectiveness launched a new vision for development cooperation – one that replaced aid effectiveness with development effectiveness, widened the 'tent' of partners to include providers such as India and China, and proposed a new paradigm for development cooperation that tossed out the North-South dichotomy and introduced an 'equatorless' framework, the Global Partnership for Effective Development Cooperation (GPEDC) (Day 2014). Since 2011, however, the momentum for GPEDC has waned – in part because the newly invited 'outsiders' had had no say in constructing the 'tent'. Additionally, several competing development fora allow the rising powers selective engagement with multilateral cooperation – for example, the United Nations Development Cooperation Forum, G77+, and various post-2015 and Global Sustainable Development Goals–related summits.

It comes as no surprise, then, that China and India have to some extent participated half-heartedly in these fora while at the same time charting their own path, bilaterally and multilaterally. India has already begun to shape its own narrative on development cooperation. The Forum on Indian Development Cooperation (FIDC 2015), launched in January 2013, unites India's development cooperation actors, including the DPA, civil society, and academia. The FIDC has hosted consultations, seminars, and meetings, and has undertaken assessments of specific projects. We see the value of the FIDC paralleled in other countries, such as the China International Development Research Network (CIDRN) (RCID 2015) and the Network of International Development Cooperation (NIDC) in Thailand (NIDC 2015).

India has also led a global effort to articulate a distinctly Southern discourse on development cooperation, defining new rules of the game rather than following old ones. In 2013, India hosted the first Conference of Southern Providers of Development Cooperation (titled 'South-South Cooperation: Issues and Emerging Challenges'), and will convene a second one in 2016. Howes and Pryke echo this divergence from OECD-DAC mechanisms, arguing that those fora offer limited scope for India to find common ground with other providers. Although the BRICS (Brazil, Russia, India, China, and South Africa) have yet to evolve their own platforms for formal discussion of development cooperation issues, they have effectively addressed financial flows through the New Development Bank [BRICS] (NDB BRICS, formerly referred to as the BRICS Development Bank).

Li and Zhou suggest that the BRICS forum offers China and India a platform for easing their 'trust deficit' and promoting dialogue on trade, investment, and development cooperation. These writers also predict rising convergence in Indian and Chinese SSC. China's historical and traditional tracks in infrastructure and India's in capacity building have adjusted course in recent years, with India extending more loans for building local infrastructure and China increasing investment in human resource development.

These measures suggest that Southern providers have moved toward converging approaches, whereas the global North and South appear to have diverged, at least in some respects. The Southern (and Indian) adage of demand-driven development – where partner or recipient country narratives serve as the common element – may prove the key, unifying principle of future North-South convergence. As several authors point out, attempts to find common ground with OECD-DAC donors appear more likely to succeed in country contexts (such as Afghanistan) or in sectors such as disaster assistance.

Twenty-first-century development discourse speaks of a world beyond aid. The newly launched Global Goals for Sustainable Development in 2015 offer a set of priorities reflecting global consensus and converging aims for all nations. The framework accords with India's 'one world' philosophy. At this critical juncture in the development landscape, India has the opportunity to provide leadership in ideas and advocacy on how the shared but differentiated responsibilities of all countries can deliver this vital agenda.

Works cited

Day, B. (2014). *Paradigm shift or aid effectiveness adrift? Previewing the first High Level Meeting of the Global Partnership* [blog]. Canberra: Development Policy Centre. Available at http://devpolicy.org/paradigm-shift-or-aid-effectiveness-adrift-previewing-the-first-high-level-meeting-of-the-global-partnership-20140416/. [Accessed 13 October 2014].

Forum for Indian Development Cooperation (FIDC) (2015). Events 2013–2015. *Research and Information System for Developing Countries* [website]. Available at www.ris.org.in/events/fidc.html. [Accessed 13 October 2015].

Network for International Development Cooperation (NIDC) (2015). *Projects* [webpage]. Available at http://nidc.org/nidc-research-project. [Accessed 13 October 2015].

Research Center for International Development (2015). *China international development research network* [website]. Available at http://rcid.cau.edu.cn/art/2013/12/2/art_7640_229164.html. [Accessed 13 October 2015].

Index

Note: Page numbers with *f, t,* and *b* indicate figures, tables, and boxes respectively.

Abbott, T. 172
academics/think tanks, as critical engagers 85, 86–7
Action Aid India 87
Afghanistan 110–20; challenges in 111–12; energy projects 116–18; future Indian engagement in 118–19; India's development profile in 112; 'New Silk Road' strategy 115–16; trade/connectivity issues in 112–15; triangular cooperation possibilities 118
Afghan-Pakistan Transit Trade Agreement (APTTA) 115
Africa: Afro-Asian solidarity and 125; agricultural production 129–30; Delhi Declaration and 125–6; future assistance for 134–5; India credit lines and 65–7, 66*t,* 129; India's development cooperation with 127–34; India's economic/cultural ties with 125; information technology 131–2; infrastructure 130; institution building, Indian support for 132–3; ITEC Programme in 133–4; trade/investment with India 126–7
African Development Bank 70
African Regional Economic Communities (RECs) 128
African Talent Initiative 149
African Union (AU) 33
Agarwal, M. 14–25
agricultural biomass 105*b*
agricultural production, Africa and 129–30
aid, from India and Australia 1999-2000 to 2014-2015 157, 158*f*
aid, objectives of 15–16; capacity creation as 16; growth as 15, 16; institution building as 16; poverty alleviation as 16; welfare as 16
aid in India's economic development 14–25; bilateral 21–2; capacity building and 23; effectiveness of 17; external factors and 17–21; financial 18–20, 18*t,* 19*t;* growth and 17; importance of 23; international/political dimensions of 21–3; introduction to 14–15; lessons for 23–5; multilateral 22–3; objectives of 15–16; policy design/implementation and 23–4; savings and 17; technological capacity and 20–1
aid justifications/objectives, Australian and Indian 171–2, 171*f*
aid modalities, Australian and Indian 167–9, 168*f,* 170*f*
aid recipients, Australian 160–6; government effectiveness percentile rating, compared to Australia's 166*f;* levels of permitted waste, 1999-2014 165*f;* nations and regions, 1999-2000 163*f;* nations and regions, 2013-2014 162*f;* per capita GDP compared to Australian 164*f*
aid recipients, Indian 160–6; government effectiveness percentile rating, compared to India's 166*f;* levels of permitted waste, 1999-2014 165*f;* nations and regions, 1999-2000 162*f;* nations and regions, 2014-2015 161*f;* per capita GDP compared to Indian 164*f*
aid revolution, Australia's 169
aid volumes in US dollars, Australian and Indian 1999-2000 to 2014-2015 158, 158*f;* as a proportion of gross national income 159, 160*f;* as a proportion of

total government spending 159, 160*f*; using purchasing power parities 159, 159*f*

Argentina: monetarist stabilisation programmes in 4; structuralist stabilisation programmes in 4; Substantive Patent Law Treaty and 55

Asia Cooperation Dialogue (ACD) 39

Asia Infrastructure Investment Bank (AIIB) 153

Australian Agency for International Development (AusAID) 167, 169

Australian aid modality, 2005-2006 170*f*

Australian and Indian aid comparison 157–73; *see also* aid recipients, Australian; aid recipients, Indian; aid volumes in US dollars, Australian and Indian 1999-2000 to 2014-2015; justifications and objectives 171–2, 171*f*; modalities 167–9, 168*f*, 170*f*; overview of 157; recipients 160–6, 161–6*f*; volumes 157–9, 158*f*–160*f*

Ayeyawady-Chao Phraya-Mekong Economic Cooperation Strategy (ACMECS) 39

balance of payments (BOP) crisis 14, 15

Bangladesh: biotechnical research papers 49*f*; economic strengths of 94; health problems in 48–9; withdrawal of IMF support from 5

Bangladesh-China-India-Myanmar (BCIM) initiative 153

Barefoot College 88

Bay of Bengal Initiative for Multi-Sectoral Technical and Economic Cooperation (BIMSTEC) 33

Beri, R. 125–35

Bharti Airtel 126

Bhattarai, K. P. 97

bilateral aid: importance of 19*t*; India's dependence on 21–2

Bilateral Investment Promotion and Protection Agreement (BIPPA) 100

bilateral relations, 4 C's of 106

Biological E 48

Bliss, K. 46

Blouin, C. 46

Bolivia, monetarist stabilisation programmes in 4

Brazil: biotechnical research papers 49*f*; Embrapa in 40; Fiocruz in 40; monetarist stabilisation programmes in 4;

SENAI in 40; South-South health and biotech collaborations 50*f*; structuralist stabilisation programmes in 4; Substantive Patent Law Treaty and 55; technical cooperation in 39–40

Brazil, India, China, and South Africa (BICS): global health initiatives contributions of 47, 48*t*; health-sector challenges 45

Brazil, Russia, India, China, and South Africa (BRICS) 180–1; health-sector challenges 45

Bretton Woods Institution (BWI) 2; heavily indebted poor countries initiatives of 8

Busan High Level Forum on Aid Effectiveness 180

CAADP *see* Comprehensive Africa Agriculture Development Programme (CAADP)

Cabinet Committee on Economic Affairs (CCEA) 65

capacity building; *see also* Indian Technical and Economic Cooperation (ITEC) Programme: aid to India and 23; through ITEC 34–8*b*

capacity creation, as aid objective 16

Central African Republic (CAR) 70

Central Asia Regional Economic Cooperation (CAREC) 117

Central Scientific Instruments Organisation 54

Chanana, D. 149

Chaturvedi, S. 9–10, 45–57, 82, 89, 94–106, 178–81

Chile, monetarist stabilisation programmes in 4

China: biotechnical research papers 49*f*; South-South health and biotech collaborations 50*f*; trade engagement in 7

China, India's development cooperation and 141–53; aid scale, allocation, and administration 145–6; challenges 150–1; future prospects for 151–2; Indian/Chinese comparison 150*t*; introduction to 141–2; key principles 144; literature on 142–3; 'soft' *versus* 'hard' infrastructure 146–9; understanding 143–9

China-Africa Agricultural Sunshine Plan 149

China Agricultural University (CAU) 87
China International Development Research
    Network (CIDRN) 180
civil society organisations (CSOs) 79–90;
    critical engagers as 85–8; government
    partners and 88–9; independent
    activists as 83–5; Indian development
    cooperation and 81–3; overview of 79;
    state relations, changing 80–1
Coal India Ltd. 126
Colombo Plan for Economic Development
    and Cooperation in South and South
    East Asia 30, 31, 39
Comprehensive Africa Agriculture
    Development Programme (CAADP) 129
Comprehensive Economic Partnership
    Agreement (CEPA) 99
Confederation of Indian Industry (CII) 127
Conference of Southern Providers of
    Development Cooperation *see* South-
    South cooperation (SSC)
Council of Scientific and Industrial
    Research 20
credit lines, India's 60–76, 179; *see also*
    lines of credit (LOCs); Africa and 65–7,
    66*t*; detailed project report and 69–70;
    distribution of LOCs 64–5, 64*f*; ex-post
    evaluation and 72; growth of LOC
    portfolio 62–5, 63*f*; IDEAS guidelines
    reform 74–5; IDEAS programme
    61–2, 62*t*; idle-time lag and 71–2;
    introduction to 60; LOC programme
    60–1; monitoring mechanisms and
    72; policy issues of 67–9, 68*t*; project
    delivery and 69; re-energising 67–73;
    sectorial distribution 63–4, 63*t*; selection
    procedures and 70–1; soft projects and
    73–4; supply contracting and 72–3;
    terms and conditions 62*t*
critical engagers 85–8; academics/think
    tanks as 85, 86–7; INGOs as 85, 87–8;
    national organisations/networks as 85,
    86
CSO *see* civil society organisations
    (CSOs)
Cuba, South-South health and biotech
    collaborations 50*f*

DAC *see* Development Assistance
    Committee (DAC)
Dalal, A. 20
demand-driven partnerships, ITEC
    framework of 31–3

Department of Foreign Affairs and Trade
    (DFAT) 167
detailed project report (DPR) 69–70
development assistance: economics theory
    and 2–3; Indian, by loans and grants,
    1999-2015 168*f*; value of India's, to
    South Asia 7*f*
Development Assistance Committee
    (DAC) 2–3, 87, 173, 178
development compact 9–10; components
    of India's 178
development cooperation: civil society
    organisations and 81–3; DAC approach
    to 4–5; divergent approaches to 3–5;
    Indian aid experience and 24–5;
    India's, with Africa 127–34; India's
    commitments to 6*f*
Development Partnership Administration
    (DPA) 8, 33–4, 51, 69, 82, 120, 167,
    179–80
domestic gap model 15
Downer, A. 172
Duty-Free Tariff Preference Scheme 127

Economic Commission for Africa 33
economics theory, development assistance
    and 2–3
Economist, The 125
Educational Consultants India, Ltd.
    (EdCIL) 132
Egypt, South-South health and biotech
    collaborations 50*f*
emerging donors 142
engagement, types of 9
Enlai, Z. 144
Entrepreneurship Development Institute
    (EDI) 30
Essar Energy 126
Ethiopia, Indian cooperation case study
    131*b*
Export-Import (Exim) Bank, India's 61,
    70, 72; 'Focus Africa' policy 128

Federation of Indian Chambers of
    Commerce and Industry (FICCI) 113,
    127
financial aid in India's economic
    development 18–20; First through
    Eleventh Plans, 1951-2011 18*t*;
    importance of 23; multilateral/bilateral
    grants and loans, 1962-2011 19*t*
Foreign Contribution Regulation Act
    (FCRA) 80

foreign gap model 15
Forum on Indian Development
  Cooperation (FIDC) 82, 180
framework approach to development
  cooperation 9

Gandhi, I. 80, 103
Gas Pipeline Framework Agreement
  (GPFA) 116
Gas Sales and Purchase Agreement 116
Genetic Resources Action International
  (GRAIN) 84
Gerschenkron, A. 17
Global Alliance for Vaccines and
  Immunization (Gavi) 47, 48*t*
Global Fund 47, 48*t*
Global Goals for Sustainable
  Development, 2015 181
global health diplomacy (GHD) 46–7
Global Partnership for Effective
  Development Cooperation (GPEDC) 180
government partners, as CSOs 88–9
Green Revolution 22, 30, 31, 129
Group of 15 33
Group of 77 33
growth: aid and 17; as aid objective 15, 16
Gujral, I. K. 98

Hamid, S. 82
Harrod-Domar growth model 15
'Heart of Asia' countries 111–12
heterodox stabilisation policies 4, 11
Hilde, S. 142
Howes, S. 157–73, 169
human resources, providing health 51–3
hydropower opportunities 100–2, 101*t*

IDEAS programme *see* Indian
  Development and Economic Assistance
  Scheme (IDEAS)
independent activists, as CSOs 83–5
India–Afghanistan development
  partnership 110–20; *see also*
  Afghanistan; challenges 111–15; future
  of 118–19; introduction to 110–11;
  'New Silk Road' strategy 115–18; trade
  values 114*t*
India-Africa Diamond Institute 132
India-Africa Forum Summit 33, 65
India-Africa Institute of Education,
  Planning and Administration (IAIEPA)
  132
India-Africa Institute of Foreign Trade
  (IAIFT) 132

India–Africa trade and investment 126–7
India–China–Nepal relationship 95–6
India International Development
  Cooperation Agency (IIDCA) 33
Indian Cooperation Mission (ICM) 52
Indian cooperation policies/practices 24–5
Indian Development and Economic
  Assistance Scheme (IDEAS) 61–2,
  129; phasing of, LOCs 62*t*; reforms in,
  guidelines 74–5; terms of credit 62*t*
Indian Diamond Institute (IDA) 132
Indian engagement in South-South
  health cooperation 50–6; global health
  governance/policy dialogue 55–6;
  institutionalisation 50–1; medicine/
  vaccine availability 53–4; policy
  architecture 50–1; providing human
  resources for 51–3; training and capacity
  building 54–5
India-Nepal Peace and Friendship Treaty
  96
India–Nepal South-South cooperation
  (SSC) 94–106; economic development
  and 102–3, 104–5*b*, 105; evolution
  of 96–7; future for 106; hydropower
  and 100–2, 101*t*; India–China–Nepal
  relationship and 95–6; introduction
  to 94; investment and 100; market
  dependency constraints 97–8; SAARC
  and 94–5; trade barriers 98–9; trade
  facilitation measures 99–102; trade
  volumes 97, 97*t*; trust and political
  leadership, importance of 96–7
Indian Institute for Foreign Trade (IIFT)
  132
Indian Institutes of Management (IIMs) 23
Indian Institutes of Technology (IITs) 20,
  23
Indian Ocean Rim-Association for
  Regional Cooperation (IOR-ARC) 33
Indian Social Action Forum (INSAF) 83,
  84
Indian Technical and Economic Cooperation
  (ITEC) Programme 10, 29–42, 81, 147,
  178; African training programmes/
  scholarships under 133; Brazil
  comparison with 39–40; budget allocated
  for 34*f*; capacity building through
  34–8*b*; components of 32; courses
  covered under 36*t*; demand-driven
  partnerships framework of 31–3; growth
  in participants under 36*f*; introduction
  to 29; Malaysia comparison with 38–9;
  monetary allocations for 35*t*; operations

33–4; partner countries under 37*t*; philosophy/historical context of 30–1; policy architecture and 50; proposals/new practices under 40–1; regional distribution of 37*t*; Thailand comparison with 39; value of, 1990-2015 10*f*

India's development assistance programme: economics theory and 2–3; by loans and grants, 1999-2015 168*f*; objectives of 8; value of, to South Asia 7*f*

India's development cooperation; *see also individual headings*: Africa and 125–35; aid in 14–25; Australian comparison with 157–73; China and 141–53; civil society organisations and 79–90; credit lines and 60–76; India–Afghanistan development partnership 110–20; India–Nepal South-South cooperation (SSC) 94–106; Indian Technical and Economic Cooperation (ITEC) and 29–42; mission approach 1–11; South-South health cooperation 45–57

Indira Gandhi Institute of Child Health (IGICH) 52

Indo-Nepal Trade Treaty 98

Industrial Development Unit of the Commonwealth Secretariat 33

Infrastructure Leasing and Financial Services, Ltd. 70

INGOs *see* international nongovernmental organisations (INGOs)

ingredient approach to development cooperation 9

institution building, as aid objective 16

Instituto de Pesquisa Econômica Aplicada (IPEA) 87

Inter-Governmental Agreement (IGA) 116

International Centre for Diarrhoeal Disease Research 48

International Centre for Genetic Engineering and Biotechnology (ICGEB) 55

International Development Association (IDA) 19, 22–3

International Development Contractors Australia 169

International Development Initiative 61

international nongovernmental organisations (INGOs) 85, 87–8

International North-South Corridor (INSTC) 117

Iran, biotechnical research papers 49*f*

Israel, blended orthodox/heterodox stabilisation policies in 4

ITEC *see* Indian Technical and Economic Cooperation (ITEC) Programme

Jaipur Leg 88

Japan International Cooperation Agency (JICA) 72

Jerve, A. M. 142

Jindal Steel and Power 126

justifications of aid 171–2, 171*f*

Kalpvriksha 84

Karuturi 126

Keqiang, L. 95, 153

Khurshid, S. 127

Kirloskar Brothers 126

Koirala, G. P. 97

Kommururi 126

Krishna, S. M. 118

Krueger, A. 22

Kukuza Project Development Company 70

Kumar, S. 89

Li, X. 141–53

Lim, W. 9

lines of credit (LOCs) 60, 179; *see also* credit lines, India's; African capacities and 129; detailed project report and 69–70; economic classification distribution of 64–5, 64*f*; ex-post evaluation practices 72; growth of 62–5, 63*f*; India's African 65–7, 66*t*; policy constraints of 67–9, 68*t*; re-energising 67–73; regional distribution of 63*t*; soft projects and 73–4; supply 72–3

LOC programme 60–1

LOCs *see* lines of credit (LOCs)

macroeconomic disequilibrium 3

macroeconomic stability 3

Mahindra 126

Malaysia, biotechnical research papers 49*f*

Malaysian Technical Cooperation Programme (MTCP) 38–9

'Maritime Silk Road' 153

Mawdsley, E. 79–90

McNamara, R. 16

medicine/vaccine availability, broadening 53–4

Meier, C. 81

Mekong-Ganga Cooperation (MGC) 33

Mendiratta, S. 89

Mexico: biotechnical research papers 49*f*; blended orthodox/heterodox stabilisation policies in 4

Millennium Development Goals (MDGs) 16
Ministry for Development Cooperation 8
Ministry of External Affairs (MEA) 8, 50,
   60, 81, 167
Ministry of Finance 167
Ministry of Micro, Small and Medium
   Enterprises (MMSME) 98
mission approach, India's 1–11, 178;
   development assistance and 2–3;
   development compact and 8–10, 10*f*;
   divergent approaches to 3–5; features
   of 9; introduction to 1–2; structuralist
   foundations 6–7*f,* 6–8
Modi, N. 106
Mohanty, Saroj Kumar 1–11
Moily, V. 116
Molenaar, B. 46
monetarist approach to macroeconomic
   theory 2, 3–4
Mulakala, A. 178–81
Mullen, R. D. 172
multilateral aid in India 22–3
Murthy, C. 81

National Alliance of People's Movements
   (NAPM) 83, 84
National Institute of Cholera and Enteric
   Diseases 48
national organisations/networks, as critical
   engagers 85, 86
Natsios, A. 172
Nehru, J. 29; South-South cooperation and
   50
Nepal: foreign investment areas for 100;
   hydropower opportunities 100–2, 101*t*;
   trade barriers in 98–9; trade facilitation
   measures 99–102
Nepal–India relationship, evolution of
   96–7; *see also* India–Nepal South-South
   cooperation (SSC); import market
   dependency and 97–8
Nepal Netra Jyoti Sangh (NNJS) 103,
   104–5*b*
Network of International Development
   Cooperation (NIDC) 180
Network of Southern Think Tanks (NeST)
   87
New Partnerships for African Development
   (NEPAD) 153
'New Silk Road' strategy 115–18
Nigeria, biotechnical research papers 49*f*
nongovernmental organisations (NGOs)
   79, 179; as beneficiary of Australia's

aid 169; deteriorating security situation
   and Indian 119; state relations with,
   overview of 80
Northern Distribution Network (NDN)
   117

Oakland Institute 84
objectives of aid 171–2, 171*f*
Office of the External Affairs Minister
   (OEAM) 71
Oil and Natural Gas Corporation (ONGC)
   116
'one world' philosophy, India's 178
Organisation for Economic Co-operation
   and Development (OECD) 61, 87, 88;
   aid definitions 157; aid from, 1999-2000
   to 2014-2015 157, 158*f*
Organisation for Economic Co-operation
   and Development Development
   Assistance Committee (OECD-DAC)
   2–3, 46, 87, 173, 178
orthodox stabilisation policies 4, 11
Oxfam India 87

Pakistan: biotechnical research papers
   49*f;* South-South health and biotech
   collaborations 50*f*
Pan African e-Network (PAeN) initiative
   128, 147
Pan-Africa Stock Exchange 132
Pancheshwor Development Authority 102
Participatory Research Institute in Asia
   (PRIA) 85
Patkar, M. 84
Pawar, S. 127
PEACE 84
Pearcey, M. 46
Peru: monetarist stabilisation programmes
   in 4; structuralist stabilisation
   programmes in 4
Philippines: biotechnical research papers
   49*f;* South-South health and biotech
   collaborations 50*f*
poverty alleviation, as aid objective 16
Pryke, J. 157–73
purchasing power parities (PPP) 159
Pyakuryal, B. 94–106

Regional Economic Cooperation
   Conference on Afghanistan (RECCA)
   116
Right to Information Act 80
Roychoudhury, S. 79–90

SAARC *see* South Asian Association for Regional Cooperation (SAARC)
Sachdeva, G. 110–20
Sanya Declaration 45
savings, aid and 17
Saxena, P. 60–76
Self-Employed Women's Association (SEWA) 88
Sen, S. 80
Shastri, L. B. 29
Singh, J. 61
Singh, M. 65, 125
Sinha, P. 167
soft projects, LOCs and 73–4
South Africa: biotechnical research papers 49*f*; South-South health and biotech collaborations 50*f*
South African Institute on International Affairs (SAIIA) 87
South Asian Association for Regional Cooperation (SAARC) 94–5, 117, 178–9
South Asian Farmers' Committee 84
South Asian Free Trade Area (SAFTA) 116
South Indian Coordination Committee of Farmers' Movements 84
South-South cooperation (SSC) 1, 6; civil society organisations and 79; development compact for 10, 29; health related (*see* South-South health cooperation); India–Nepal (*see* India–Nepal South-South cooperation (SSC)); Network of Southern Think Tanks and 87; Pan African e-Network initiative and 128
South-South health cooperation 45–57; biotechnical research papers 49, 49–50*f*; dynamics of 47–50; global health diplomacy and 46–7; Indian collaboration and 48–9, 49–50*f*; Indian engagement in (*see* Indian engagement in South-South health cooperation); introduction to 45–6; multilateral picture of 47–8, 48*t*; Task Team on 56
Special Commonwealth Assistance for Africa Programme (SCAAP) 30, 147
Sri Lanka, South-South health and biotech collaborations 50*f*
state-CSO relations, changing 80–1
Steel Authority of India (SAIL) 113
structural adjustment 16
structuralist approach to macroeconomic theory 2, 3–4; developing economy

growth and 10–11; emphasis of 7–8; in India 6–7*f*, 6–8
Substantive Patent Law Treaty (SPLT) 55

Tata Group 126
Tata Steel 126
technical assistance 74
Techno-Economic Approach for the India-Africa Movement (TEAM) 128
technological capacity, aid and creation of 20–1
Technology Cooperation Mission programme 20
technology imports, India 14
Thailand: biotechnical research papers 49*f*; South-South health and biotech collaborations 50*f*
Thailand International Cooperation Agency (TICA) 39
think tanks, as critical engagers 85, 86–7
Trade Commerce and Investment Opportunities Confidence Building Measure (TCI-CBM) 116
Trade-Related Aspects of Intellectual Property Rights (TRIP) agreement 55
triangular cooperation, Afghanistan 118
Triple A advantage 74
Tuhin, K. 29–42
Turkmenistan-Afghanistan-Pakistan-India (TAPI) gas pipeline project 116

underemployment equilibrium 3–4
United Nations Children's Fund (UNICEF) 39
United Nations Development Programme (UNDP) 30, 39
United Nations Environmental Programme (UNEP) 105*b*
United Nations Industrial Development Organization (UNIDO) 33
United Nations Population Fund (UNFPA) 39
United Nations Relief Works Agency for Palestine 52
United States, bilateral aid to India by 21–2
United States Agency for International Development (USAID) 172

Venezuela, monetarist stabilisation programmes in 4
Via Campesina 84
Videsh Limited (OVL) 126
'Vision 2020: The Right to Sight' 104*b*

Voluntary Action Network of India (VANI) 85
V. V. Giri National Labour Institute 54

Wada Na Todo Abhiyan (WNTA) 85
Washington consensus 2, 16
welfare, as aid objective 16
White (dairy) Revolution 30
Wits School of Governance (WSG) 87
World Bank 16, 168; basic needs approach 16; International Development Association 19

World Health Organization (WHO) 45
World Intellectual Property Organisation (WIPO) 55
World Trade Organization (WTO) 33

Yanagihara, T. 9
Year of Agricultural Transformation and Food Security in Africa, 2014 129
Yew, L. K. 95

Zain 126
Zhou, T. 141–53

For Product Safety Concerns and Information please contact our EU
representative GPSR@taylorandfrancis.com
Taylor & Francis Verlag GmbH, Kaufingerstraße 24, 80331 München, Germany